GODLY ZEAL AND FURIOUS RAGE
The Witch in Early Modern Europe

G. R. QUAIFE

ST. MARTIN'S PRESS
New York

© 1987 G.R. Quaife
All rights reserved. For information write:
Scholarly & Reference Division,
St.Martin's Press, Inc., 175 Fifth Avenue, New York, NY 10010
First published in the United States of America in 1987
Printed in Great Britain
ISBN 0-312-00475-3

Library of Congress card number: 87-4622

Contents

Introduction

The witch has been the subject of thousands of articles and books. Many of these advance untenable propositions and together are contradictory and confusing. Recent research in a wide range of disciplines now makes it possible to see more accurately the figure that allegedly terrified the inhabitants of Western Europe and the American colonies between 1450 and 1700. The aim of this book is twofold. It seeks to consolidate the multi-disciplinary research into a form which will provide a comprehensive introduction to a complex phenomenon; and, secondly, to advance a specific interpretation of the witch and the craft. Any study of witchcraft presents difficulties. Definitions are usually part of a circular argument and discussion of the nature of witchcraft often assumes that which should be tested. Primary evidence is suspect as much of it is an elitist version of popular confessions extracted through physical and psychological terror. Many interpretations rest on untestable explanatory models drawn from theology and the social sciences. Inconvenient gaps are filled by references to other times and places and the nature of reality against which the evidence for the phenomenon is tested is itself controversial.

For purposes of discussion it is assumed initially that witchcraft is an omnibus term which includes a range of objective phenomena and subjective perceptions. It accepts that a witch in early modern Europe was, or was thought to be, an innocent victim; a deluded or deranged individual; a benevolent or malevolent sorcerer; a member of a deviant, dissenting or minority group; or a servant of the Devil. The witch, whatever the real nature of his or her behaviour, was a person accused of harmful acts using occult means (*malificia*) or of serving the Devil (diabolism) or both.

Beyond this fact there is little agreement among the students of witchcraft. A wide range of interpretations has been advanced and a multitude of different aspects emphasised. An overview of current historiography begins this analysis — a chapter organised around the dichotomy between those that see witches as fantasy, a subjective perception of the believer, and those that accept their objective existence but cannot agree as to their nature or role (Ch. 1).

The image of the witch which had considerable contemporary

1

impact and which consolidated a number of earlier developments was that presented by fanatical German inquisitors in the *Malleus Maleficarum*. The subsequent elaboration, modification and rejection of this image by scholars and propagandists of the sixteenth and seventeenth centuries reflected the changing and varied views of the political, religious and academic establishment (Ch. 2). A major component of the image was magic — high, low and folk. The high magician throughout the Middle Ages provoked establishment responses. These responses were manifest in attitudes, Bulls, statutes and institutions which in time were directed against the lowly witch. The endemic existence of low and folk magic throughout Europe provided a total population of potential witches if the establishment chose to label or libel this key element of popular culture as diabolic and dangerous (Ch. 3). The other major input in developing the concept of the witch and society's reaction to it was Christian heresy. Heresy was gradually redefined in terms of diabolism, devil-worshipping, and subject to increasingly resolute persecution; an intensification of attitudes and actions due in part to the threat of dualism. The power of Satan was exaggerated and constantly emphasised. Magic was defined as heresy and the proponents of both seen as members of a diabolic cult. The features of this cult — the sabbat, the pact and the mark — came to dominate the elite's image of the witch and gradually coloured popular conceptions of the phenomenon (Ch. 4).

A view of witchcraft that until recently had much credence in England rejected the diabolic nature of witches and saw them as members of a pre-Christian fertility cult. Pagan animism certainly dominated the world view of most peasants and there were groups of people labelled as witches who were members of cults. These cults could be fertility, phallic or escapist in nature. The last used drugs, dance, drink or sex as the medium of transfiguration (Ch. 5). In many parts of Europe the witch image was heavily laden with sexual connotations and it was believed that witches made men impotent and women infertile. The sabbat was conceived as an orgy in which the most perverted and deviant forms of sexual activity occurred. Individual witches could have sexual intercourse with the Devil or his minions anywhere, at any time, but most often Satan preferred the comfort of a matrimonial bed. Over four-fifths of alleged witches were women. This in part reflected the prevalent misogyny of the period due to the value system of patriarchal Christianity and the changing demographic

2

profile which revealed an increasing number of unattached females. However, the lowly role and stature of all women was less important than the economic vulnerability of most in the ascription of witch. The level of vulnerability, not gender *per se*, determined the label (Chs. 6–7).

The most significant development that elevated the link between popular magic and academic demonology into a vibrant ideology and a basis of widespread persecution was the acceptance by the political elite that witches did exist and were dangerous. The adoption of witch hunting as a necessary element in the legitimisation of new regimes in a period of political and religious turmoil turned elderly peasant villagers into subversives intent on destroying the godly regime. The adaptations in the law and legal procedures with the expansion of the inquisitorial method and the use of torture to make prosecutions more effective laid the foundation for the major witch hunts and witch panics of the period. (Chs. 8–9).

The unscrupulous used such contemporary concern with witchcraft and played on popular fears and gullibility to achieve personal gain. Corruption was a parasitic growth on the legal system and the false accusation of neighbours a not uncommon weapon in village feuds. Where property, power and status were at stake, defamation, slander and blackmail were readily used. Frauds and hoaxes were foisted on the public for political, personal or religious advantage. Nevertheless, this was a cynical exploitation by the few of a cultural phenomenon accepted by the majority of both peasants and princes (Ch. 10).

Social, economic and demographic changes and accompanying attitudinal mutations created anxieties at the village level. Although natural explanations were accepted for harvest failures, epidemics and mortality in general, individual misfortunes in the face of neighbourly success were often inexplicable. Personal incompetence or godly discipline were difficult explanations to swallow. It was more acceptable and remediable to blame misfortune on the malicious diabolical enmity of a neighbour. Neighbours who were dependent, deviant, defiant, disagreeable and who lacked deference were most likely to be labelled as witches (Chs. 11–12). Some witches and their accusers confessed and genuinely believed that they had participated in a range of fabulous and fantastic activities — flying through the air, changing into animals and fornicating with the Devil. Their perception of reality had been perverted by an inability or refusal to separate

3

dreams from waking consciousness, by the ingestion of hallucinogenic drugs, and more rarely by mental illness (Ch. 13).

The emergence of the witch as a key figure in early modern Europe was due to a confluence of trends — ideological, social, economic, legal and political. In essence the witch rose to prominence, or in many cases was created, by the furious rage of a neighbour anxious to explain his own misfortunes and by the godly zeal of the political establishment fearful for the safety of their regime and of the Christian society they were determined to protect and purify.

1

Fact and Fantasy: An Overview

Some forty interpretations of the essence or aetiology of the witch warrant attention. They divide into those which depict the witch as primarily a fantasy, and those which accept her as an objective fact, although most theses include elements of both. Early modern Europe believed in the fact, the nineteenth century in the fantasy. The late-twentieth century is confused.

Those expositions which affirmed that witchcraft was a delusion disagreed as to the causes of the fantasy. Recent work in nutrition, biochemistry and pharmacology suggested that the craze resulted from the deliberate or unknowing ingestion of drugs by the alleged witches and their accusers. Bernard Barnett noted that 'since the concept of hallucinogenic drugs was not defined, the Devil, not surprisingly, got the blame', and Michael Harner suggested that 'once the use and effects of these natural hallucinogens are understood, the major features of past beliefs and practices suddenly seem quite logical and consistent'. These natural hallucinogens included belladonna, mandrake, henbane and thorn apple. When witches believed they were travelling through the air to meet the Devil at the infamous gathering, the sabbat, they were indeed tripping — but in the modern sense of the term.

Linnda Caporael maintained that the Salem outbreak of 1692 was the result of accidental ergot poisoning. Ergot, a fungus on cereals, is a source of lysergic acid, the base for one of the most powerful of modern synthetic drugs LSD. This base itself was an effective hallucinogen which could explain the odd behaviour of the afflicted accusers and sundry witnesses.[1]

A court physician, Johann Weyer, wrote in 1563 that witches were mentally ill. The French psychiatrists of the last century,

5

Pinel, Esquirol and Charcot, adopted this argument and Sigmund Freud saw great similarities between the demonological theory of possession and his psychoanalytical theory of hysteria. Gregory Zilboorg, in the 1930s turned these ideas into the dogma that dominated histories of psychiatry until recently. He asserted that the mentally sick were labelled witches. The *Malleus Maleficarum*, the great handbook for witch hunters, was a casebook of clinical psychiatry if reference to the Devil was ignored and the word 'patient' substituted for 'witch'. This book described disturbed persons preoccupied with unreasonable ideas, illogical fears, false impressions and feelings of guilt. It recorded cases of people subjected to irresistible impulses who engaged in irrational acts and who suffered losses of appetite, sensation and contact with reality — all symptoms of mental illness. R. M. Hemphill alleged that without the mentally ill 'the witchcraft delusion could hardly have been made credible'. Others attributed the delusion to the mental illness of the witch hunter or of society in general, to mass hysteria — a term which is now considered meaningless. Sandra Shulman found the answer in dreams. People believed their own fantastic confessions on the dominant evidence of their nightmares.[2]

To other scholars, witchcraft was a vast hoax perpetrated on society by one or other of the key interest groups. Marvin Harris blamed the establishment. He proclaimed that:

> the witch mania . . . shifted responsibility for the crisis of late medieval society from both Church and State to imaginary demons in human form. Pre-occupied with the fantastic activities of these demons, the distraught, alienated, pauperized masses blamed the rampant Devil instead of the corrupt clergy and rapacious nobility. Not only were the Church and State exonerated, but they were made indispensable. The clergy and nobility emerged as the great protectors of mankind.

This neo-Marxist interpretation reworked the anti-clerical, liberal rationalist view of the late-nineteenth and early-twentieth century associated with Burr, Lea and Hansen. A more recent protagonist of this older position was Rossell Hope Robbins who asserted categorically that 'witchcraft . . . was invented, introduced and imposed by the Inquisition'; that the Inquisition, having crushed existing heresies, 'set about to invent a new heresy, one with so

broad a base that the supply of victims would never dry up.'[3]
Some saw the witch as a fantasy figure created by sexually frustrated monks. W. R. Trethowan emphasised that 'the most ardent persecutors of witches were those sworn to celibacy and whose sexuality, for this reason, was bound to seek vicarious expression'. Robert D. Anderson contended that the 'suppression and repression of normal sexual impulses' was the major factor leading to the delusion and that perverse sexuality was 'the main theme of witchcraft'. The *Malleus Maleficarum* was filled with castration anxieties and the authors, two German Dominicans, placed great emphasis on both genital deprivation and impotence. On the former they pondered:

> And what then is to be thought of those witches who in this way sometimes collect male organs, as many as twenty or thirty members together, and put them in a bird's nest or shut them up in a box, where they move themselves like living members and eat oats and corn, as has been seen by many as is a matter of common report.

On the latter, impotence, it gave clear advice to the worried male: 'when a member is in no way stirred and can never perform the action of coition this is a sign of frigidity of nature, but when it is stirred and yet cannot become erect, it is a sign of witchcraft.' Witchcraft as a sex-crazed fantasy of celibate monks has received strong support in recent times from one wing of the feminist movement.[4]

Others credit the delusion to the clergy, not as celibates but as academics. The masses had traditionally accepted natural, magical and religious explanations of the world around them. The revival of Aristotelian thought, canonised in scholasticism, destroyed one of these sources of knowledge. Events now could only have a rational or supernatural cause. There was no place for magic. Therefore peasant maleficient magic, if not natural, must be supernatural. As God was not the cause it had to be the Devil. Academic blinkers elevated the Devil to new heights. Diabolism explained deviant behaviour and a crusade against it became an academic obsession.[5]

To some historians children were responsible for the delusion. John Demos noted that victims were old and accusers young, that the conflict was generational and often took place *within* the family or kin group. Where this did not happen Demos explained it as the result of the projection of aggressive impulses onto socially marginal women by young girls whose real hostility was towards their mothers — mothers too powerful to threaten directly. The favourable community response to such accusations revealed a deep-seated antagonism within young women towards their mothers.[6]

Norman Cohn saw the delusion, as a complex reflection of the darker and basic emotions of mankind reacting against the austerity of Christianity, a collective fantasy that became part of the individual psyche. In an excursion into psycho-history he argued:

> It is . . . unconscious resentment against Christianity as too strict a religion, against Christ as too stern a task master. Psychologically it is altogether plausible that such an unconscious hatred would find an outlet in an obsession with the overwhelming power of Christ's great antagonist, Satan, and especially in fantasies of erotic debauches with him. It is not at all surprising that the tension between conscious beliefs and ideals on the one hand and unconscious desires and resentments on the other should lead some frustrated or neurotic women to imagine that they had given themselves body and soul to the Devil. Nor is it surprising that these tensions operating in a whole stratum of society should end by conjuring up an imaginary outgroup as a symbol of apostasy and licentiousness — which is practically what witches became.

Cohn concluded that witches were 'victims of an unconscious revolt against a religion which, consciously, was still accepted without question'. In other words, society created a mythical group who allegedly did terrible things which excited its subconscious and basic instincts and which it then had to punish in conformity with its conscious rules and requirements. The witch–scapegoat served the dual purpose of satisfying at least in part the deep stirrings of natural man and the necessary reinforcement of the values of an ordered, austere society.[7]

To other scholars witches really existed. To a few they belonged to an organised cult, but there was little agreement as to the nature of the cult. The dominant sixteenth-century view experienced a renaissance in the 1920s with Montague Summers. He wrote:

> I have endeavoured to show the witch as she really was an

evil liver; a social pest and parasite; the devotee of a loath
[some] and obscene creed; an adept at poisoning, blackmail,
and other creeping crimes; a member of a powerful secret
organization inimical to Church and State; a blasphemer in
word and deed; swaying the villagers by terror and superstition . . . a bawd, an abortionist; . . . a minister to vice and
inconceivable corruption: battening upon the filth and foulest
passions of the age.

Witches worshipped the Devil and carried out his instructions. To
W. B. Crow this vile sect was not limited to a Christian context.
Witchcraft was the manifestation of evil itself: 'The origin of
witchcraft is not connected with any particular religion . . . It is a
rebellion against all religion, against nature, against God.'
Tenenbaum held that the greatest impulse towards witchcraft was
perversion and that the witch was evil personified. Jeffrey Russell
reformulated this 'ultimate evil' interpretation to show that witchcraft was an organised anti-Christian cult — the most extreme of
Christian heresies. He contended that:

> The most important point . . . is that the phenomenon of
> witchcraft had sprung out of the medieval heresy trials. The
> formal renunciation of God, the longing for the triumph of
> Satan . . . all these characteristics of classical witchcraft had
> their origins, not in sorcery but in medieval heresy.

The essential element in witchcraft was defiance of church and
society on behalf of the power of evil. Russell concluded that
'European witchcraft is best viewed as a religious cult of the Devil
built on the foundations of low magic and folk traditions but
formed and defined by the Christian society within which it
operated'.[8]

The most popular interpretation of witchcraft in England
during the middle half of the twentieth century was that of
Margaret Murray. Murray argued that people labelled in late-
medieval times as witches were adherents of an old fertility cult.
Beneath the Christian veneer the community held beliefs and prac-
tised rituals which could be traced back to pre-Christian times, to
the ancient religion of the hunting and pastoral peoples of Western
Europe. She traced the worship of the Horned God from its
Palaeolithic origins through its entanglement with the two-faced
Janus or Dianus. Murray originally observed of medieval England

that 'though the rulers professed Christianity the great mass of the people followed the old gods'. In a later work she suggested that the English monarchs were themselves leaders of the Dianic Cult who suffered actual or surrogate sacrifice — a renewal ritual, according to Sir James Frazer, common in primitive religions. The Reformation finally brought Christianity to England and 'the Old Religion was gradually relegated to the lowest classes of the community and to those who lived in remote parts'.[9] The French religious sociologist, Jean Delumeau, agreed. It was not until the fifteenth century that the urban areas of Western Europe awakened to the Christian message. However, the rural countryside and therefore the majority of Europeans had to await the successful evangelism of the Reformation and Counter Reformation — a process delayed in the more isolated regions of Europe until the eighteenth century. To Muchembled the witch hunt was a product of the general assault on popular culture by this revitalised and ethically oriented Christianity. Before this assault rural France was hardly Christian. Peasants displayed a primitive animist mentality which Christians called satanism. It was really tenacious residual paganism.

Carlo Ginzburg uncovered an agrarian cult in north-eastern Italy. Those born with cauls, the *benandanti*, went into trances at prescribed times during which their souls battled with evil witches to guarantee fertility. The *benandanti* had healing powers, could recognise witches and counter their evil spells. This cult operated unmolested within Christendom until the Inquisitors remodelled it according to their own perceptions into a diabolic witch cult — the very reverse of the truth.

Folklorists have explored local witch beliefs and these differed in emphasis over time and place. Swiss witches concentrated on the climate, south German on sex, the French on diabolic possession, the English on familiars (pet cats and dogs) and those of Friuli and Navarre on bewitching children. Witches may have been simply a group of local misfits given wider importance and ideological consistency by the stereotype in the mind of the witch hunter but nevertheless unable to escape the underlying obsessions and fantasies of their environment.[10]

Elliot Rose depicted witchcraft as a Dionysian dancing cult, others as a drug or sex cult aimed at achieving ecstatic religious experience. For Mircea Eliade the sex cult was not primarily interested in lustful gratification: 'it was the magico–religious forces of prohibited sexual practices that tempted one to become a

10

witch'. Sexual orgies recovered 'a lost beatific perfection'. These orgiastic practices achieved 'a return to an archaic phase of culture — the dreamlike time of the fabulous beginnings'. Witches were a special people who retained some of the original other-consciousness which had been lost during the millenia of European civilisation — a civilisation which overdeveloped the rational and logical aspects of the individual. Witches retained alone within rational Western Christendom knowledge of the deeper spiritual mysteries experienced by the shamans of old, and preserved and developed within the religions of India.[11]

The aetiology of witchcraft presented an even greater range of conflicting interpretations. To some, witchcraft performed the necessary function of enforcing order and suppressing dissent. To others it relieved tension and was an escape mechanism for the deprived. Jules Michelet saw it as a secret religion of the feudal serfs, a vehicle through which they escaped the pressures and frustrations of the world and the religion of their noble and clerical masters. Ladurie recently updated this approach. He claimed that witchcraft was the religion of the rural masses alienated from the urban culture of the French establishment. It was a religion that aimed at the creation of another world existing within that of the establishment — 'a world turned upside down' — and not at social rebellion. It aimed at psychic succour not radical revolution.[12]

Pennethorne Hughes considered witchcraft to be the first feminist movement of modern times — a view taken up by many feminist writers. Witches were women with a mission who went proudly to the stake. Shuttle and Redgrove were more basic. Witchcraft was 'the subjective experience of the menstrual cycle'. It was this 'womb Knowing and woman Knowing that . . . the *Malleus* wished to expunge from the face of the earth'. Thomas Szasz saw specific attributes in the behaviour of women witches that provoked the establishment. Witches were healers — skilled herbalists and pragmatic psychologists. The poor and powerless turned to the witch for physical and spiritual help. By aiding the sick the witch confronted the professional clergy. Illness was a result of God's wrath which could only be cured by removing the cause — immorality or irreligion — the realm of the cleric. The witch interfered in God's work. She was a blasphemer. As an effective therapist she threatened the authority of the clergy; clergy whose direct methods of healing — prayer and ritual — differed little from the witch. It was inevitable that once the inquisitors were in a position to act they undertook a systematic repression of

11

their more popular rivals. In this way they often received support from the villagers themselves. The local community depended on the witch to provide it with healing and protection. However, her position was highly vulnerable. She was involved by the nature of her work with people in a distressed or hostile state. When things went wrong she was blamed and her socio-economic position gave her few resources to defend herself against local hostility and resentment. The patriarchal establishment if aroused took advantage of such temporary antagonism towards the village witch to destroy her. Barbara Ehrenreich and Deidre English saw in the attack on midwives and female healers in general the hand of an emerging male medical profession.[13]

To Gunnar Heinsohn and Otto Steiger the instigation to destroy the healer or wise woman by libelling her as a diabolic witch did not originate with jealous clergy, distraught villagers or the medical profession. It was a deliberate decision of the political and religious establishment. Witches were persecuted from the late-fourteenth century onwards because of the dramatic decline in population. It was necessary to destroy women who possessed knowledge of birth control. By eradicating contraceptive techniques women would bear more children and replace the manpower essential for the survival of the feudal economic system. Heinsohn and Steiger noted that the *Malleus* directed its most vitriolic attack on those activities of the witch which constituted population control: contraception, impotence, castration, sterilisation, sodomy, homosexuality, abortion, infanticide and child sacrifice.[14]

Perhaps the witches' cult was a gay society. Demos hinted that male witches were victims of a heterosexual community projecting its anti-homosexual obsessions. Tenenbaum saw it primarily as a lesbian cult. Homosexual lust was 'a major reason for the zeal with which older witches recruit . . . younger ones, often at the great personal risk of detection'.[15]

Boyer and Nissenbaum conceived witchcraft as a vehicle through which those who did not adjust to economic individualism and capitalist enterprise explained their own failures and attempted to drag back to the group the successful entrepreneur. Macfarlane and Thomas argued the opposite. It was the upwardly mobile individual who used witchcraft to free himself from traditional restraints. By accusing the needy of witchcraft the moral obligation to assist the poor, sick and elderly was rendered void. Traditional charity was refused and feelings of guilt dissipated. The offending poor and old people could be physically removed from the village scene if legally convicted as witches.[16] Swanson placed the critical emphasis for the rise of witch persecutions on the lack of strong political authority. Where there was no doubt as to the source of legitimate authority, as in Spain, there was little witchcraft. Where there was no doubt as to the effectiveness and ruthlessness of a regime, such as the Swedish military occupation of northern Germany or the Cromwellian government in Scotland, there was little witchcraft. Where legitimacy and power went together, as within the jurisdiction of the *Parlement* of Paris, witchcraft was at a minimum. Witch prosecutions rose in times of crises over political authority — Scotland in the 1590s, England in the 1560s and 1640s, France during the French Civil War and the German principalities during the first four decades of the seventeenth century. Witchcraft became involved in high politics as part of the legitimising process of regimes struggling for recognition and power, and this situation was heightened by the increase in religious tension and the extent of religious conflict.[17]

Munday preferred to see it as an expression of the crisis in ideological or epistemological authority. Between the collapse of religious authority and the emergence of scientific rationalism there was a revival of non-rational magic. Witchcraft was a manifestation of such a development. Leland Estes argued that the origin of the witch craze lay in the medical revolution of the sixteenth century. Medieval Galenic medicine had an answer for everything. Its breakdown left the medical profession and its clients aware of their lack of knowledge and created an insecurity in which the unknown was given a supernatural explanation and the problem handed over to the church. Baroja believed the emergence of witchcraft was a result of the congruence of popular traditions with the views of the articulate elite. Rose suggested that disgruntled wandering scholars, the goliards, used their clerical training and perverted outlook to organise and corrupt peasant traditions into a uniform cult with themselves as the new witch masters.[18]

Explanations of significant developments ultimately relevant to the witch that occurred at various stages from the thirteenth century shed further light on the factual and fanciful aspects of the witch. Most interpretations concentrated on the lack of security. As a result of this, some groups were alienated from society and sought alternative solutions to contemporary problems. On the other hand, the authorities under pressure attempted to enforce conformity by punishing real deviants or projecting their problems

13

onto scapegoats. Alienation as a result of economic dislocation, urbanisation and the plague created a dark mood at discernible periods from 1100 onwards. Urbanisation was seen as a necessary prerequisite to witchcraft. Honegger concluded that 'it was the specific occidental city and not the universal village which was the breeding ground of the diabolical female witch in Europe'. Alan Kors emphasised literacy, which reinforced the 'acute awareness of shared helplessness, danger and constant terror . . .' Consequently the printing press was a significant factor in spreading the concept of the witch and her terror across sixteenth- and seventeenth-century Europe. In addition, the preaching emphasis of both Protestant and Catholic Reformations facilitated the communication of Christian fears and elite ideas on the witch to the populace in general.[19]

The church faced with general insecurity imposed conformity. By the thirteenth century, through the Inquisition and use of torture, it effectively isolated or created its enemies. The adoption of Aristotelianism, which equated the irrational with evil, escalated religious intolerance and persecution. Roman law and the assumption by public authorities of the role of prosecutor intensified the campaign. In traditional Germanic and English law a private individual unable to prove his charge of witchcraft suffered the penalty reserved for the witch. Consequently the legal system was heavily loaded against the accuser. The inquisitorial method widely adopted on the continent by the sixteenth century with its secret evidence, anonymous witnesses, lack of counsel and torture, shifted the balance very markedly in the opposite direction. The most significant factor emerging from the alienation of the many and the efforts of church and state to impose authority and conformity was the growing awareness and importance of Satan. The construction of a complex demonology by the academic elite and its growing impact on the wider community was fundamental. Alan Kors argued that the answers to the problem of witchcraft lay in 'the study of the intellectual, perceptual and legal processes by which 'folklore' was transformed into systematic demonology'.[20]

Before 1100 the Devil was a mischievous evil entity but his power was never seen as threatening that of God. In the twelfth century a more human conception of God and Satan emerged. It brought both into the peasant hovel. At the same time, the intellectuals of the church led by Aquinas and his successors gave Satan a consistent and logical place in the Christian schema. As the church clarified, and in the process popularised, the role of Satan so did the dualist heretical movements that were challenging its power. To the Albigensians the cosmic battle between good and evil was an evenly balanced conflict. The power of evil, Satan on this earth, was more than a match for God. Eliade contended that Satan became a hero for those in rebellion against the Christian institution which had failed to save them from disaster. The church, in the face of this more powerful and effective Satan, found that its adherents increasingly doubted the efficacy of traditional devotional practices. Religious reform movements further undermined the strength of much popular piety by declaring it mere superstition. A stronger and resolute response to Satan was urgently required. His agents must be wiped from the face of the earth. The witch craze was therefore simply a legitimate and necessary response of the church to a serious problem — a genuine increase in the support for or fear of the Devil.[21]

Monter considered witchcraft a potentially lethal form of Western misogyny, and to many historians women, rather than Satan, were the clue to a real understanding of witchcraft. Feminist Selma Williams referred to it as a 'totally unco-ordinated, though murderous war on women'. Most witches were women. Monter argued that neither sorcery nor heresy attracted a preponderance of females although Honegger puts precisely the opposite view. It was the vigorous participation of women in heretical groups that provoked a vehement ecclesiastical counter-reaction manifest in the papal inquisition. Women were of low status, a despised and deprived group who had every incentive to join a subversive cult. The Devil could scarcely be less sympathetic than Christian society and its patriarchal leaders.

There was an increase in misogynistic views in the fifteenth and sixteenth centuries and, as hatred for and fear of women grew, it is alleged that the intensity of the witch craze did too. The reasons why this attitude to women prevailed were complex. Some writers concentrated on contemporary events to show why male fears developed. The plague and the wars of the fifteenth century killed more men than women. There were visibly more women than men. Such demographic changes led to changes within the family structure creating many more unattached women, namely spinsters and widows who were not under the control of fathers or husbands. The decline of the cult of the virgin appeared as another critical factor in the escalation of the witch craze. The innate lust-ful, sexually demanding woman could be made safe by translating

15

her sexuality into spirituality. Patriarchal society tended to polarise women into saints or witches. Given these assumptions, the decline of the former foreshadowed a dangerous increase in and fear of the latter.[22]

A development which dramatically intensified male fear and loathing of women and explained the increase in witch persecution was, according to Stanislav Andreski, the new scourge of syphilis. Here was an illness, painful and often fatal, caught through sin, through the agency of a woman. Andreski concluded that:

> The underlying permanent condition was the prevalence of the belief that Witchcraft works and can cause disease. One of the preparatory conditions was the existence of the machinery of repression forged against heretics by the Church. The second preparatory condition was the demonisation of women which was an exacerbation of an old ingredient of the Christian tradition and a consequence of the tightening up of celibacy. The precipitating factor was the arrival of syphilis at the beginning of the 16th century which evoked panic and a search for scapegoats, chosen with preference (from) the most defenceless members of the subjugated sex.[23]

Rosemary Ruether found the seeds for this misogyny not only in female sexuality but in procreation. If women were downgraded and feared because of their sexuality why was it that most witches were *older* women? Ruether believed that patriarchal society saw the young girl as primarily a tool of male culture but the sexually awakened older woman was sexually autonomous. She was no longer a victim of male desires 'but a sexual initiator in her own right'. This was unacceptable in a patriarchal system in which women were to be sensual when young and inexperienced but as they aged they were expected to lose interest in sex while their ageing husbands satisfied their lust with younger women. Ruether went further. She asserted that the asceticism of patriarchal Christianity not only attempted to repress female sexuality as diabolic lust but also to denigrate procreation and the essential female role. Medieval sculpture regularly depicted women with beautiful faces and torsos of maggots. Immortal man was constantly reminded of his mortality by the ever-present bodily shape through which he entered the world. Monastic misogyny concentrated on women *not* as sensual lust but as decaying flesh. As events constantly brought man's mortality to the fore in the fifteenth

16

century the more he directed a paranoid hatred to older women as demonic aliens who were a constant reminder of that mortality.[24] Some writers focused on the basic misogyny of Christianity itself. Others such as Sherry Ortner argued that all societies were misogynist and female subordination was a universal constant. Men were closer to culture, women to nature. Nature was inferior and woman because of her bodily functions, her social roles and her different psychic structure belonged to it. These writers concentrated on the alleged differences between male and female personality: 'the feminine personality tends to be involved with concrete feelings, things, and people, rather than with abstract entities; it tends towards personalism and particularism'. This polarity taken to extremes yet based on the wisdom of Aristotle equated right hand, rationality, sacredness and maleness; and conversely the left hand, passion, pollution and femaleness. Some scholars, including feminists, rejected absolutely the sex war interpretation of witchcraft. Lucienne Roubin, Michelle Rosaldo, Rayna Reiter and Susan Harding related the witch craze to subtle changes within feminine space, especially the emergence of the never married females. Spinster sisters competed with young wives for the attention of their brothers and control of the household. Witchcraft was an extreme manifestation of the intense infighting between women within the family circle for domestic authority.[25]

From a logical point of view the disparate approaches to witchcraft depicted above can in large measure be reconciled, although the historical validity of any such summation, and the vital quantitative aspect necessary, needs deeper probing.

There was some objective reality and much fantasy in the contemporary concept of the witch. Undoubtedly dreams, drugs and mental illness accounted for much of the latter. Some of this fantasy may have received a special input from frustrated celibate or myopic academic clergy, repressed teenage girls, conniving nobles and inquisitors, or from a more general hedonistic response to austere Christianity. Across Europe amongst those accused of witchcraft there were groups who worshipped the Devil, or partook of pagan practices, or sought escape from or enjoyment of the real world through drugs, sex, dance and drink. Other groups were dissenters or deviants who opposed the political, religious, economic, social or moral values of the establishment. These cults, whatever their nature may have had a special appeal to women, serfs, rural masses, mountain dwellers, the urban poor and racial

17

minorities. Individual accusations may have come from the successful entrepreneur despairing of the parasitic poor, or from the struggling poor upset by the greed of the prosperous, or from within the family, especially from women battling with each other for domestic power.

Political changes created the need for regimes to exert social and, for the first time, ideological control over their population in general. These populations were susceptible to subversive ideas emanating from religious dissent, and spreading rapidly due to the growth of literacy, the advance of the printed word and the new emphasis on preaching. As a result in some jurisdictions witchcraft was seen as a security problem. Changes in the law expedited the persecution and prosecution of suspected deviants and subversives. The crisis of confidence among physicians enabled the demonologist to provide a plausible alternative answer to problems previously considered medical. Sections of the male establishment strove to destroy the female agents of healing and contraception through the demonisation of women, a development which received some impetus from the spread of syphilis. The demonisation of women, indeed of all opponents of the elite, and the power of Satan were major features in the image of the diabolic witch presented at the end of the fifteenth century in the *Malleus Maleficarum*. This was an image which gained considerable establishment acceptance and against which others unsuccessfully struggled for almost two centuries.

Notes

1. Bernard Barnett, 'Drugs of the Devil', *New Scientist* 27 (23 July 1965) p. 222, see also his 'Witchcraft, Psychopathology and Hallucinations', *British Journal of Psychiatry* 111 (1965) pp. 439–45; Michael J. Harner, 'The Role of Hallucinogenic Plants in European Witchcraft', Ch. 8 of M. J. Harner (ed.), *Hallucinogens and Shamanism* p. 128; Linnda R. Caporael, 'Ergotism: The Satan Loosed in Salem?', *Science* 192 (2 April 1976) pp. 21–6.

2. For Weyer see Rossell Hope Robbins, *The Encyclopedia of Witchcraft and Demonology* pp. 538–40; for Pinel, Esquirol, Charcot and Freud and their concepts of hysteria see Thomas Szasz, *The Myth of Mental Illness*, Chs. 1–5; Sandra Shulman, *Nightmare* p. 44; G. Zilboorg and G. Henry, *A History of Medical Psychiatry*; R. E. Hemphill, 'Historical Witchcraft and Psychiatric Illness in Western Europe', *Proceedings of the Society of Medicine* 59 (1966) pp. 851–901, 898.

3. Marvin Harris, *Cows, Pigs, Wars and Witches: The Riddles of Culture*

pp. 167–8; Rossell Hope Robbins, 'The Heresy of Witchcraft', *South Atlantic Quarterly* 65 (Autumn 1966) pp. 532–43.
  4. W. H. Trethowan, 'The Demonopathology of Impotence', *British Journal of Psychiatry* 109 (May 1963) pp. 341–7. 346; Robert D. Anderson, 'The History of Witchcraft: A Review with Psychiatric Comments', *American Journal of Psychiatry* 126 (1970) pp. 1727–35, 1733; Heinrich Kramer and James Sprenger, *The Malleus Maleficarum* p. 121; *The Malleus* quoted in Trethowan, *op.cit.* p. 345.
  5. Richard Kieckhefer, *European Witch Trials: Their Foundations in Popular and Learned Culture 1300–1500* pp. 78–81.
  6. John P. Demos, 'Underlying Themes in the Witchcraft of Seventeenth Century New England', *American Historical Review*, 75 (1970) pp. 1311–26; Demos, *Entertaining Satan: Witchcraft and the Culture of Early New England* pp. 50–4.
  7. Norman Cohn, *Europe's Inner Demons* p. 262.
  8. Montague Summers, *The History of Witchcraft and Demonology* p. xiv; W. B. Crow, *A History of Magic, Witchcraft and Occultism* p. 227; Joseph Tenenbaum, *The Riddle of the Witch* p. 254; Jeffrey Burton Russell, 'Medieval Witchcraft and Medieval Heresy', in E. A. Tiryakian (ed.), *On the Margin of the Visible: Sociology, the Esoteric and the Occult* pp. 179–89, 188. See also J. B. Russell, *Witchcraft in the Middle Ages*.
  9. Margaret A. Murray, *The Witch Cult in Western Europe* p. 12, her *The God of the Witches* pp. 18–19, and her *The Divine King in England*; Sir James Frazer, *The Golden Bough: A Study in Magic and Religion*.
  10. Jean Delumeau, *Catholicism between Luther and Voltaire: A New View of the Counter Reformation* pp. 161–72; Robert Muchembled, 'L'Autre Côté Du Miroir: Mythes Sataniques et Réalités Culturelles Aux XVIe et XVIIe Siècles', *Annales ESC* 40–2 (mars-avril 1985) pp. 288–300; Carlo Ginzburg, *The Night Battles: Witchcraft and Agrarian Cults in the Sixteenth and Seventeenth Centuries*.
  11. Elliot Rose, *Razor for a Goat*; Mircea Elaide, *Occultism, Witchcraft, and Cultural Fashions: Essays in Comparative Religions* pp. 91–2.
  12. Jules Michelet, *Satanism and Witchcraft* (trans. A. Allinson); Emmanuel Le Roy Ladurie, *The Peasants of Languedoc* pp. 203–10.
  13. Pennethorne Hughes, *Witchcraft*; Penelope Shuttle and Peter Redgrove *The Wise Wound: Menstruation and Everywoman* pp. 209, 218; Thomas S. Szasz, *The Myth of Mental Illness*, and his *Manufacture of Madness*; Barbara Ehrenreich and Deidre English, *Witches, Midwives and Nurses: A History of Women Healers* p. 6; Rosemary Ruether, 'The Persecution of Witches: A Case of Sexism and Agism', *Christianity and Crisis* 34 (1974) pp. 291–5, 292–3.
  14. See Jane Sullivan, 'A New Look at Witchcraft', review article from *Der Spiegel*; Melbourne *Age* (26 Dec. 1984) p. 10.
  15. John P. Demos. *Entertaining Satan* Ch. 2; J. Tenenbaum *op.cit* p. 356.
  16. Paul Boyer and Stephen Nissenbaum, *Salem Possessed: The Social Origins of Witchcraft*; Alan D. Macfarlane, *Witchcraft in Tudor and Stuart England*; K. Thomas, *Religion and the Decline of Magic*.
  17. Christina Larner, *Enemies of God: The Witchhunt in Scotland*; Guy Swanson, *Religion and Regime: A Sociological Account of the Reformation*.

19

18. Leland Estes, 'The Medical Origins of the European Witch Craze: A Hypothesis' *Journal of Social History* (Winter 1983) pp. 271–84; J. T. Munday, *Witchcraft in Central Africa and Europe* Chs. 3 and 4; Julio Caro Baroja, *The World of the Witches*; Elliot Rose, *Razor for a Goat*.

19. Claudia Honegger, 'Comment on Garrett's *Women and Witches*', *Signs* 4 (1979) pp. 792–8; Alan C. Kors and Edward Peters, *Witchcraft in Europe 1100–1700* p. 6.

20. Edward Peters, *The Magician, the Witch and the Law*; Jeffrey Burton Russell, *Witchcraft in the Middle Ages*; Kors and Peters *op.cit.* p. 6.

21. Eliade, *op.cit.* pp. 91–2.

22. E. William Monter, *Witchcraft in France and Switzerland: The Borderlands During the Reformation* p. 17; Selma R. Williams and Pamela J. Williams, *Riding the Nightmare: Women and Witchcraft*; Monter *op.cit.* p. 24; Honegger *op.cit.* p. 795.

23. Stanislav Andreski, 'The Syphilitic Shock', *Encounter* 58 (May 1982) pp. 7–26.

24. Rosemary Ruether, *op.cit.* pp. 291–5.

25. Sherry B. Ortner, 'Is Female to Male as Nature is to Culture?' in M. Z. Rosaldo and L. Lamphere (eds), *Women, Culture and Society* pp. 67–88; Susan Carol Rogers, 'Female Forms of Power and the Myth of Male Dominance: A Model of Female/Male Interaction in Peasant Society', *American Ethnologist* 2 (1975) pp. 727–56; Rayna R. Reiter (ed.) *Toward an Anthropology of Women*; M. Z. Rosaldo, 'Women, Culture and Society: A Theoretical Overview' in Rosaldo and Lamphere, *ibid.* pp. 17–42.

2

Shaping the Image: The *Malleus* Tradition and its Critics

Today many feel powerless to influence the course of events. A few dedicated people who believe that the existence of civilisation is threatened by nuclear war have found a simplistic solution to the problem and their own impotence. They seek to deny access to uranium ore, an essential element in the sequence that would produce the holocaust. In the latter decades of the fifteenth century there were equally dedicated men aware that Christian society was in peril and convinced that they could save it. The late-medieval church had compromised with dualism — the belief in an evenly balanced cosmic conflict between Good and Evil. Evil was winning and each misfortune added to its strength. Inexplicable calamities were no longer the result of God testing the faithful, nor reproving the sinner, nor the result of personal incompetence, nor the unaided malice of a neighbour. Nor were the stars, natural causation or chance to be held responsible. It was the Devil. These happenings were manifestations of diabolical evil achieved through the activities of the witch. The authorities, secular and ecclesiastical, had to be made aware of the enormity of the crisis and of the simple solution available. Christendom would be saved, social and political order maintained, and the Devil contained if the witches were discovered and destroyed.[1]

In 1486, two Dominicans, Heinrich Kramer and Jacob Sprenger, attempted to awaken the leaders of society to the diabolical conspiracy. Their work, *Malleus Maleficarum*, stemmed from their experience as inquisitors in Germany. Local officials gave them little assistance — a situation which prompted Pope Innocent VIII in the Bull *Summis Desiderantes Affectibus*, 5 December 1484, to demand support for his inquisitors. He was determined that

21

heretical depravity should be eradicated and described the essential problem as people who had renounced the faith, abused themselves with devils, and by spells destroyed the offspring of beasts and humans, blasted crops and hindered procreation. The *Malleus* reflected some aspects of dualism but orthodoxy was retained by the insistence that the Devil's power was exercised with God's permission, and Satan's especial authority over the witch did not deny free will. It was the witches' exercise of free will in favour of Satan and against God that made their behaviour the ultimate apostacy, the ultimate heresy. The Devil could not command ordinary people. He could only persuade. The witch surrendered her freedom of choice by making a pact with Satan in which she renounced her faith and swore obedience to him. In return the apostate exercised magical powers. This pact was central to the demonologist's image of the witch:

> it is necessary that there should be made a contract with the devil, by which contract the witch truly and actually binds herself to the devil . . . For this indeed is the end of all witchcraft, whether it be the casting of spells by a look or by a formula of words or some other charm, it is all of the Devil.[2]

In this way the *Malleus* linked the traditional peasant sorcery of spells and charms to an organised diabolical conspiracy to overthrow Christendom. It turned isolated, ignorant and often senile elderly women in distant villages far away from the centres of political power into the security problem of the era. It created readily indentifiable subversives in every village in Christendom. As these diabolic witches were not the sorcerers of old but a new and dangerous cult, old attitudes both theological and legal could no longer apply. A streamlined judicial procedure, incorporating contemporary inquisitorial methods and heavily weighted against the accused had to be applied to the situation. Older arguments, based on the Canon Episcopi, that belief in certain aspects of witchcraft was itself heresy could no longer hold. The new heresy was to deny the existence of this new conspiracy.

To some, the *Malleus* was the most important work in the history of witchcraft — a claim based on several of its attributes. It was authoritative, as it appeared to have papal approval. The Bull *Summis Desiderantes Affectibus* was included with the printed editions. However, the *Malleus* never became unchallengeable law or theology and it was not heresy to question its tenets, even though its authors argued to that end. On the other hand, attempts to deny its authority by suggesting that the Pope did not know what it contained, that the inclusion of the Bull was a deceitful subterfuge by the authors to misrepresent the situation, and that the statement affirming its theological orthodoxy was heavily edited are quibbles. Whatever the particular idiosyncracies of the *Malleus*, the Papacy was, and had been for decades, vitally concerned with the basic problem addressed by Kramer and Sprenger. The popes of the early-sixteenth century continued to alert the church to the dangers of the conspiracy so ably outlined by the two Dominicans. The high academic reputation of its authors added to its authority although the historians who depict the friars as academic charlatans totally reject this point. The *Malleus* was considered important also because of its alleged popularity and widespread influence. However, the claim that it was found in every court and read by every judge cannot be sustained. In south-west Germany, not far from the sources of its inspiration, it exerted little influence. The *Malleus* was hardly mentioned in trials or in relevant sermons. One of its key features, impotence, was rarely an issue. Despite being reprinted in 13 editions up to 1520 and another 16 between 1574 and 1669, it remained inaccessible to most lawyers and judges.[3]

Some original features increased its appeal. The basic ideas contained in the *Malleus* were not new. These echoed the views of Johannes Nider written about 1435 but not published until 1475. Significantly, the reworking replaced much of Nider's scepticism with credulity. There were many fifteenth-century writers who clarified the works of earlier authors and, with the advent of printing, together provided a pool of witchcraft theory. There was by the last quarter of the fifteenth century, general agreement on the shape of the witch image. Witches were heretics. Even if witchcraft were an illusion, to believe the illusion constituted heresy. Witches worshipped and obeyed the Devil although Visconti questioned whether the witch formally renounced her faith. Familiars existed but they were not a significant feature of the model. An area of disagreement was transvection. To some it was an illusion created by the Devil, to others an objective phenomenon, although the means of transportation — stick or beast — was hotly debated. On most other aspects of the image — undetected entry into houses, incubi, shapeshifting, the sabbat, sexual orgies and the sacrifice of infants — there was general agreement. Such views were incorporated into the *Malleus*.[4]

23

The originality of the *Malleus* in regard to substance was in the selection from, and emphasis given to, particular aspects of the general theory and detailed advice on the prosecution of the accused. The explicit pact and the detailed linkage of common sorcery and diabolical heresy provided the major thrust in which considerable space was devoted to ligature and the role of women. 'All witchcraft comes from carnal lust, which is in women insatiable'. It was through this lust and the child-like intelligence of women that the Devil was able to undermine Christian society. This emphasis reflected the Pauline misogyny dominant at the time exaggerated by the personal obsessions of Kramer. The appearance of the *Malleus* as a comprehensive manual reflecting on both the theological and legal aspects of the problem enhanced its appeal. The methodology of the authors contributed further to this. It appeared logical and clearly argued through an efficient use of the *quaestio* method and an exhaustive analysis of possible counter-arguments. It was claimed that the cases presented in the *Malleus* were set out with the greatest clarity, argued with unflinching logic and judged with scrupulous impartiality. To attribute logical argument and impartiality to the *Malleus* is totally rejected by many scholars. There were weaknesses in logic — untested assumptions and assertions, circular arguments and *non sequiturs*. Yet to judge the *Malleus* on modern standards is irrelevant to its standing among contemporaries. To expect objectivity, the sustained use of inductive reasoning, the evaluation of evidence, a critical cynicism towards authorities and an empirical testing of hypothesis takes us beyond the world view of the late-fifteenth century. Argument proceeded on the basis of accumulated authority. On this criteria the authority on which the *Malleus* rested could not be better: Aristotle, the Bible, Augustine and Aquinas.[5]

The strongest attack on the *Malleus* was directed against its underlying morality. It was seen as a mad, cruel, hideous and horrifying document. This reaction was provoked by the attitude to the legal rights of the accused, to the denigration of women and its perceived role in the persecution, torture and death of thousands of innocent people. The *Malleus* was written from a preconceived theological viewpoint and with a highly moral purpose — to save Christendom. This preconception contained an inbuilt safety protection against the cries of inhumanity directed against it. By definition, the innocent did not suffer. God would not permit it. The importance of the *Malleus* could be judged against earlier and later treatises and tracts. It was not original but was it the authoritative picture for the next two centuries? Historians disagree. To some it contained the essential elements of the diabolic image and future modifications were minor. To others changes in the image were significant and issues not emphasised in the *Malleus*, such as the Devil's mark and the details of the sabbat, became important while those of the *Malleus* lost momentum.[6]

The revisionist denial of the importance of the *Malleus* is nevertheless incorrect. The *Malleus* reflected contemporary academic views influenced by popular legends and the personal obsessions and experiences of the authors. It had the authority it claimed, although less than has been alleged by both protagonists and opponents. Its relatively wide circulation through printing did not provoke witch hunts in the half-century following its publication. However, the large number of editions in the later decades of the sixteenth and first half of the seventeenth century — the period of intense witch hunting — suggests that its impact may have been felt in that period. It was not, however, the reference manual for the judicial system at large and its impact was exaggerated, nevertheless. The elitist and popular ideas contained in the *Malleus* fermented and developed within society. Although dated in some respects it remained a useful source for later generations struggling against the diabolic cult.[7]

For the next two centuries the image of the witch presented in the *Malleus*, and of the communities' responses to it, were subjected to modification and criticism in one of six ways. Protagonists either hardened or softened the image while critics were either idiosyncratic, conservative, pragmatic or radical in their attack on it. The hardliners accepted the basic thesis of the *Malleus* and with different emphases strengthened its theoretical base and effectiveness of the prosecution stemming from its premisses. The basic thrust of these demonologists was that the phenomenon was real, the accused were guilty, and therefore torture and a sceptical approach to evidence justified. Even if witnesses disagreed on basic facts their evidence should not be discredited because the Devil confused those who spoke against his agents. If facts were unclear they should be interpreted in a way that would convict the accused. Those who complained of such assumptions were witch lovers and enemies of God. An inwardly coherent and logical system developed. The accused were guilty. The evidence proved it. Those who objected were witches. Dominicans, mostly inquisitors — Vicenzo Dodo, 1505, Bernardo de Como, 1508, Silvestro de

25

Priero, 1521, and Bartolomeo de Spina, 1523 — warned Italians of the diabolical conspiracy. Gianfrancesco Pico della Mirandola (1469 – 1533), nephew of the great humanist, raised the issues in a short Latin dialogue, *Strix*, 1523, followed by an Italian version in 1524. Witches flew to the 'game' on a mallet after anointing themselves. At this sabbat they feasted and made love to a male who had the feet of a goose. The witches continued to attend Mass but at critical points of the service they secretly denied its validity and made obscene gestures. They stole wafers which at the sabbat they crushed under their feet and then urinated on the crumbs. They interfered with the weather and murdered babies by pricking them with needles.[8]

The first major restatement of the *Malleus* position was published in response to an attack on it by Johann Weyer. In the growing disorder of the latter half of the sixteenth century in a context of religious wars and the growing assertion of power by secular monarchs, Jean Bodin published *De la Demonomanie des Sorciers* in 1580. Bodin had an unorthodox attitude to both religion and magic. He believed in a transcendent God who ruled the world in a mechanistic way through a bureaucracy of angels and devils who rewarded or punished men automatically in terms of divine law. Evil spread when these laws were not enforced. Laxity in law enforcement explained the increase in witchcraft. Bodin wrote *Demonomanie* to reveal the consequences of this lax administration and of judicial leniency. The witch was a social deviant who deliberately inverted accepted values and the magistrate had a moral responsibility to destroy her. Divine law made it clear that crimes against God should be punished the most severely of all. Bodin strongly attacked conservative opponents of the *Malleus* tradition for selfishly emphasising personal reformation and opting out of their moral duty to enforce rigorously civil and divine law.

Witches were not deluded or sick old women. Exorcism and counter-magic were useless. The issue was not a major battle in the cosmic struggle between Good and Evil. It was a temporary problem arising from failure to implement divine law. The solution was simple: ensure that judicial procedures uncovered and convicted the witch. Most witches would go undetected and unpunished if ordinary procedures continued to apply. Trickery and torture, the use of *provocateurs* and hot irons were especially recommended. Rumour was to be accepted because the public was rarely wrong. The accused must not escape punishment through loopholes in the law or the maladministration of justice. Divine law justified any behaviour designed to achieve a conviction. On this evidence recent attempts to deny that Bodin was a vindictive witch hunter appear misplaced.[9]

James VI of Scotland, concerned with local political order, published *Daemonologie* in 1597. A Christian monarch had the ultimate responsibility to protect God's kingdom and his own. The Christian state in Scotland was threatened when in the early 1590s witches allied themselves with the major political opponent of the monarch. The North Berwick witches revealed a conspiracy in which the great rebel Satan appeared to support the rebellious Earl of Bothwell. The waning of James's enthusiasm for witch hunting in England supported this interpretation. South of the border the survival of the regime seemed assured and the agents of opposition were more readily identified. The *Daemonologie* was unoriginal and was prompted by a political urge to take advantage of the North Berwick experience and by an academic desire to refute Reginald Scot. To James, witches were agents of the Devil and by biblical decree had to die. The mark and swimming were the most efficient means of uncovering a witch. The pact and the sabbat were central to the concept, and trial procedures had to ensure conviction. The evidence of infamous people had to be accepted because honest persons were ignorant of witchcraft. Only the evil would know of evil. No harm would be done through accepting such evidence as God would not permit the innocent to suffer.[10]

Nicholas Remy, Attorney General of Lorraine, was an experienced witch-hunting magistrate. He personally condemned over 900 witches. His work, *Demonolatreiae*, published in 1595, reiterated the *Malleus* argument illustrated by examples from his own experience. When evidence was doubtful it was the work of the Devil and should be interpreted as such and used to convict the accused. Erastus saw in the similarity of the witches' confessions proof of their validity. Imagination was random and therefore confessions would not agree unless they described events that occurred and were witnessed by those confessing. There were too many witches who were not melancholics to accept Weyer's view that these were simply sick old women. Exodus 22:18 gave Christians no choice but to execute the guilty. Martin Del Rio, 1551–1608, high-born classicist and lawyer, and one-time Attorney General of Brabant, joined the Jesuits in 1580. He published an updated encyclopedia *Disquisitionum Magicarum Libri Sex*, 1599, which went through twenty editions. It was probably the least original and most credulous of contemporary works. A soldier fired into the

27

air and a woman fell at his feet. This was proof that witches rode to the sabbat. All the stories recounted he accepted as literally true and his arguments were simplistic. The eating of young babies by witches was permitted by God. The early demise of these infants prevented them committing sins in later life that would have led to their damnation. Any defence of the witch was complicity. Witches defended each other by arguing that witchcraft was an illusion. Any person who argued this way should be treated as a witch.[11]

Henri Boguet, a secular magistrate in the Franche Comte published *Discours des Sorciers* (1602) which went through a number of editions in the following decade — a decade of witch hunting and repression. Boguet ignored the Devil's mark. Not all witches received it and the Devil was smart enough to remove it from his followers when they were captured. Healing white witches were diabolical. They secretly caused illness and received credit from the community for curing it thus increasing the reputation of magic which came from the Devil. Boguet was convinced of the reality of lycanthropy, living as he did in heavily forested country. However his major contribution was in the rustication of demonic possession. French demonologists discovered it in great personages or women in convents. To Boguet it was part of everyday rural life in the Franche Comte. The works of Pierre de Lancre, *Le Tableau de L'Inconstance des Mauvais Anges* (1612) and *Du Sortilege* (1627) were pessimistic, demonic and obsessed. Lawyer and secular witch hunter extraordinary, Lancre was responsible for the deaths of hundreds of alleged witches in the Basque regions of southern France. In bringing his experience to an area rich in witch lore he stimulated panic and spread fear. He saw a world governed by inconstancy. Everything was in flux and on the edge of disintegration. A pluralistic society such as he discovered in southern France was a sign of impending collapse. This situation was out of hand due to lax administration and the penetration by the Devil of aristocracy and church. Lancre was misogynistic, racist and anticlerical. Spanish priests were too tolerant or were themselves witches. Lancre had a divine mission to bring retribution to the offender and cohesion to society. His major contribution was the detailed and sensational account of the sabbat. It was not an illusion and on occasions up to 12,000 witches gathered together and engaged in an incredible ritual. The Devil was often present in the form of a tree, or manifest as a goat with illuminated horns.[12]

Softliners accepted the diabolic conspiracy but modified some of the more extreme features. Some aspects were illusions although the pact and the ability of witches through the Devil's power to cause mischief were real. These deluded women warranted punishment but the Devil deserved the major blame. This emphasis on the Devil led softliners to attack the white witch. It was the exercise of diabolic power that was the heresy, not the manner in which it was used. Protestants removed Catholic underpinnings to the theory. William Perkins' *Discourse of the Damned Art of Witchcraft* (1608) refounded the arguments on a scriptural basis and suggested a little more care in the type of evidence presented.[13]

An idiosyncratic attack on the *Malleus* came from Johann Weyer (1515–88), physician to the Duke of Cleves in *De Praestigis Daemonum* (1563) and *De Lamiis* (1577). Weyer's contribution to an almost non-existent debate was catastrophic. It escalated both the level of confessional bitterness and the obsession with witches. Weyer was seen as a humane man amid a coterie of fanatical demonologists. He denied the pact as there was no Biblical justification for it. The old women were sick. They were melancholics on whom the Devil imposed fantasies. Exodus 22:18 referred to poisoners and not to elderly melancholics. The real collaborators with the Devil were the high magicians. These Catholic clergy and scholars deserved death. Weyer took the argument of the *Malleus* and changed the identity of the victim. From the viewpoint of the peasant women this was a radical re-orientation; with regard to basic principles and theology it was a slight redirection.[14]

The conservative attack on the *Malleus* came from supporters of the traditional position of the Canon Episcopi that to believe in witch fantasies was itself heresy, and from the providentialists who argued that to blame witches for misfortune was the soft option. Christians must take responsibility for their own misfortunes. It was God's response to their sins. This approach directed concern away from the terror of witch hunting to the joys of repentance. Hunting witches was not wrong, it was distractive. Reformation of oneself and of society must be the first priority. To Samuel de Cassini, 1505, the *Malleus*-toting inquisitors flouted tradition, encouraged false accusations and deflected Christians from their proper response. Flight to the sabbat was impossible. The Devil had no power to move people. Such movement would involve a miracle and no miracle would occur in order to facilitate evil. Therefore, if the inquisitors maintained that the Devil flew women to the sabbat, they contenanced heresy themselves.

29

Martin Plantsch's *Opusculum de Sagis Maleficos* (1507) denounced those who blamed the stars, demons or witches for their troubles. People should seek the comfort of the church but if problems persisted they must suffer as did Job, content in the expectation of heavenly reward. Thirty years later, Johann Brenz protested against the moral problem caused by ascribing misfortune to witches. Misfortune was God's way of rebuking people for their sins. These disasters would continue until people reformed. God permitted the Devil to carry out such testing but witches were deluded in thinking they were responsible for what happened. Misfortune was not the work of evil women in league with the Devil engaged in cosmic conflict which required the extinction of such women. It was punishment from God effected by the Devil as a warning to mankind. Alleviation must be sought in personal repentance and a re-ordering of one's life in accordance with God's word. Women who believed that they could do harm might deserve to die but this was a by-product of the problem, not the panacea.[15]

George Gifford, the moderate Puritan cleric in *A Discourse of the Subtill Practices of Devils by Witches and Sorcerers* (1587) and *A Dialogue Concerning Witches and Witchcraft* (1593), also accepted the reality of witchcraft. The Devil did not need women to do his work. 'However, a witch by the word of God ought to die . . . not because she killeth men, for that she cannot . . . but because she dealeth with devils.' This emphasis on diabolic power rather than witch malevolence led Gifford to attack the cunningman, the white wizard. The claims of old hags to magical powers and the recourse of the populace to the cunningman for protection created in peasant eyes a self-sufficient world of magic. As all magic derived from demonic power this was anathema to Christians. There was no need to seek magical protection. As everything depended on God's permission he would not allow harm to come to the faithful. Misfortune was not brought about by the witch. It was the result of God testing or punishing the faithful. 'If thy sinnes have provoked God . . . fall down and humble thyself with fasting and prayer . . . look not upon the witch, lay not the cause where it is not.'[16]

Pragmatic critics were revolted by the slaughter of the innocent and the destruction of communal harmony. Witchcraft was not an exceptional crime that required the presumption of guilt and use of torture to ensure conviction. Ponzinibio, 1520, queried the validity of evidence obtained from the excommunicated, accomplices or condemned witches. He objected to concealing from the accused the nature of the offence and the identity of the accuser. He questioned the reliability of evidence from ignorant rustics and women who readily confused reality with dreams. The phenomenon was an illusion not subject to evidential assessment. A basic premise of the pragmatic opponents was the principle that it was better that a few guilty escape than an innocent suffer. The most damning and perceptive analysis of the psychological and physiological effects of torture to extract confessions to entrap others was provided by a Jesuit confessor to hundreds of victims, Friedrich von Spee.

Spee in *Cautio Criminalis* (1631) argued that the presumption of guilt and the use of torture to obtain confessions propped up the *Malleus* system. The accused under torture had no hope. If she contorted her features with pain she was laughing; if she lost consciousness she had bewitched herself into silence. Both acts deserved conflagration. If she died under heavy torture the Devil had broken her neck to protect his own from further pain. Witch-hunting had become an institution with many vested interests. High fees and the confiscation of the condemned's property in many German jurisdictions made greed a buttress to the system. Spee concluded that 'nobody is safe, no matter of what sex, fortune, condition or dignity, if any enemy or detractor wishes to bring a person under suspicion of witchcraft'.[17]

The radical assault on the *Malleus* image came from Italian scholars and Protestant laymen. Pietro Pomponazzi, a Paduan Aristotelian, rejected miracles and the direct intervention of God in the course of human history. Angels and demons were pedagogic fantasies devised by the elite to explain difficult concepts to the ignorant. There was a natural explanation for everything and all issues must stand the test of observation and experience. In *De Naturalium Effectuum Causis Sinne de Incantationibus* (1566), he rejected basic Christian beliefs such as life after death and the uniqueness of Christianity. Witches could not exist because devils did not exist. The English squire, Reginald Scot, came close to denying the existence of the supernatural. After undermining the props of the *Malleus* argument, Scot concluded that witchcraft was trickery. In *the Discoverie of Witchcraft* he deplored the prejudices of the judges, the idiocy of the charges and the violation of normal criminal procedure, especially in regard to the evidence accepted. Scot denied both spiritual and demonic magic. God would not permit the exercise of his power to fall into the hands of old hags. Those who believed such nonsense were blasphemers and idolaters.

31

God administered his own correction. Scot attacked the magic of the church. It was irrelevant and dangerous. Witchcraft was in essence 'a cousening art'. The myth of the incubi sustained the lusts of celibate priests, deaths were due to poisoning and other apparent feats of magic were sleight of hand or ventriloquism. Demons were no more than evil impulses.[18]

Thomas Ady, *Candle in the Dark* (1656) removed the biblical supports from the *Malleus*. The word translated as witch had multiple meanings and contemporary proofs of witchcraft were not referred to in the Bible. Current witch practice consisted of papist lies and superstition. To the Dutch Protestant cleric, Balthasar Bekker, (in *De Betoverde Weereld*, 1691), spirits had no power over flesh and there was no evidence for a pact. It was an invention of the Papacy to enrich the clergy with the confiscated property of the victims. Protestant attacks on the theological underpinnings of the image were summed up in the argument of Christian Thomasius, *De Crimine Magiae* (1701). No pact between Devil and witch existed. Witches had been killed for a non-existent crime. Thomasius rejected the basic premise that Kramer and Sprenger had sought to establish and on which the concept of the diabolic witch depended.[19]

The enormity of the conspiracy, the validity of the pact, the personal and responsible role of the witch, the reality of the phenomenon and the need for extra legal methods to deal with the crisis epitomised the hardline *Malleus* tradition. To the softliners the conspiracy was no less shocking, the pact was valid but the witch was much more a puppet, some aspects of the phenomenon were illusory and not all the extra-legal procedures were necessary. The conservative opponents saw witchcraft as largely a diabolic illusion which distracted society from its necessary response to misfortune, the need for personal repentance. Johann Weyer's idiosyncratic response denied the *Malleus* tenets as applied to the witch but directed them instead against the high magicians of the Catholic faith, thereby indirectly intensifying religious antagonism and witchly obsession. Pragmatic opponents objected to the judicial processes. The presumption of guilt and the use of torture to obtain confessions often to incriminate others, killed the innocent and disrupted society. Radicals denied the essence of the *Malleus*. There was no pact, there was no conspiracy, there was no supernatural interference in everyday affairs. It was a vast, horrendous hoax.

The diabolic witch of the *Malleus* tradition emerged gradually from the fusion of magic and heresy. Magic in its high, low and folk forms made a major contribution to that image and to its acceptance in the community.

Notes

General references of relevance are: Heinrich Kramer and James Sprenger, *The Malleus Maleficarum*; Sydney Anglo (ed.) *The Damned Art: Essays in the Literature of Witchcraft*; Rossell Hope Robbins, *The Encyclopedia of Witchcraft and Demonology*; Jeffrey Burton Russell, *Witchcraft in the Middle Ages*, H. C. Erik Midelfort, *Witch Hunting in Southwestern Germany 1562–1684: The Social and Intellectual Foundations*; Richard Kieckhefer, *European Witch Trials: Their Foundations in Popular and Learned Culture 1300–1500*; and Edward Peters, *The Magician, the Witch and the Law*.

1. John W. Connor, 'The Social and Psychological Reality of European Witchcraft Beliefs', *Psychiatry* 38 (1975) pp. 366–80.
2. Kramer and Sprenger, *op.cit.* pp. xliii–xlv or Robbins, *op.cit.* pp. 264–6, for *Summis Desiderantes Affectibus*; Kramer and Sprenger, *op.cit.* p. 7.
3. *Ibid.* pp. 20, 74–7; extravagant claims are made by Summers, Kramer and Sprenger, *op.cit.* pp. ix–x, and Andrea Dworkin, *Woman Hating* p. 128; Midelfort, *op.cit.* pp. 20–2 and Norman Cohn, *Europe's Inner Demons* Chapter 12 deny any great significance; Peters, *op.cit.* p. 173 questions whether the Pope was aware of the details; Robbins, *op.cit.* questions the theological endorsement, p. 340, but lauds their academic reputation, p. 337; Dworkin, *op.cit.* p. 128, Midelfort, *op.cit.* pp. 20–2, 113, Peters *op.cit.* p. 173.
4. Cohn, *op.cit.* p. 225; Russell, *op.cit.* pp. 230–1. For earlier theorists see Russell, Chapter 9 'The Classical Formulation'.
5. Kramer and Sprenger, *op.cit.* pp. 47, 44; Russell, *op.cit.* p. 145; Kieckhefer, *op.cit.* pp. 23, 661; Peters, *op.cit.* p. 173; Peters, *ibid.*; Anglo, *op.cit.* pp. 19–22; Robbins, *op.cit.* p. 338.
6. An extreme view in Dworkin, *op.cit.* p. 128 and a more moderate attack in Pennethorne Hughes, *Witchcraft* pp. 178–80.
7. Peters, *op.cit.* p. 174, argues that it contains the fundamentals; Midelfort, *op.cit.* p. 113, that it became outdated.
8. Categories stimulated by Midelfort's classification of 'pragmatic' and 'radical' opponents; Robbins, *op.cit.* p. 484; Peter Burke, 'Witchcraft and Magic in Renaissance Italy: Gianfrancesco Pico and his *Strix*', in Anglo, *op.cit.* pp. 32–52.
9. Christopher Baxter, 'Jean Bodin's *De la Demonomanie des Sorciers*: The Logic of Persecution', in Anglo, *op.cit.* pp. 76–105.
10. Stuart Clark, 'King James's *Daemonologie*: Witchcraft and Kingship', Anglo, *op.cit.* pp. 156–81.
11. Robbins, *op.cit.* pp. 121, 407–8; for Remy, E. William Monter, *Witchcraft in France and Switzerland: The Borderlands during the Reformation* pp. 179–80.

33

12. Monter, *op.cit.* pp. 69–74; Margaret M. McGowan, 'Pierre de Lancre's *'Tableau de l'Inconstance des Mauvais Anges et Demons*: The Sabbat sensationalised', in Anglo, *op.cit.* pp. 182–201.
13. Robbins, *op.cit.* p. 382.
14. Christopher Baxter, 'Johann Weyer's *De Praestigiis Daemonum*: Unsystematic Psychopathology', in Anglo, *op.cit.* pp. 53–75.
15. Robbins, *op.cit.* p. 79; Midelfort, *op.cit.* pp. 30–66.
16. Alan D. Macfarlane, 'A Tudor Anthropologist: George Gifford's *Discourse and Dialogue'*, Anglo, *op.cit.* pp. 140–55.
17. Robbins, *op.cit.* pp. 391–2, 479–84; Midelfort, *op.cit.* p. 28; Robbins *op.cit.* p. 984.
18. Burke, *loc.cit.* pp. 40–1; Sydney Anglo, 'Reginald Scot's *Discoverie of Witchcraft*: Scepticism and Sadduceeism', Anglo, *op.cit.* pp. 106–39.
19. Robbins, *op.cit.* pp. 19–20, 45–6, 496–7; Midelfort, *op.cit.* p. 27.

3

Magic and *Maleficium*

Many attributes of witchcraft were aspects of magic. Magic is a label applied to phenomena which have certain characteristics in common. There is little agreement on the phenomena or the characteristics. Definition is further confused by viewing magic in the context of science and religion. Within this trichotomy of man's confrontation with nature and the supernatural those aspects which appeared irrational, immoral and selfish were deemed magic. Recently this approach has been dismissed as ethnocentric. It reflected a Christian rationalist orientation of Western scholars rather than the attitudes and behaviour of the societies concerned. The subsequent debate on the definition of magic and its relationship with religion revealed four basic positions. The first gave up. The terms 'magic' and 'religion' must be avoided until a consensus was reached. The second saw magic as part of religion. Christianity and magic were subsets of religion, a religion that could be magical or non-magical. A third reasserted the rationalist position in which magic and religion were opposites or at least at extreme ends of a spectrum. Eclectic accumulation of attributes depicted religion as abstract, selfless, communal and pastoral; magic as specific, selfish, individual and professional. Magic was concerned with the immediate wellbeing of the individual, religion with general symbols of life. A variant concentrated on the Frazerian distinction between the manipulative function of magic and the supplicative emphasis of religion. Magic was based on man's selfish desire, will and pride; religion on trust, selflessness and submission.[1]

The fourth view, and that adopted in the context of this discussion of witchcraft, accepted magic as a sensible, coherent system of thought and action in which all objects, human and non-human, were assumed to be alive and endowed with power. As such these related with man. Stars affected man, and man could compel the forces of nature. In this exaltation of man's power lay the appeal of the magical world view. The world was not locked together by scientific laws or religious dogma. It was malleable and subject to change. The outward form reflected hidden reality. Those with knowledge of this concealed reality had real power. The two worlds of outward appearance and hidden reality were linked by symbols — images, physical objects and words. The ability to use these symbols was the magician's art, an art not far removed from Platonic philosophy.[2]

Magic took many forms. High, low and folk magic all contributed significantly to the concept and reality of sixteenth-century witchcraft. The success of medieval high magic undermined the traditional sources of authority, and ultimately church and state, one-time collaborators with high magic, came to see it as a threat to established order. The attitudes formed in their assault against high magic were to be applied centuries later against the lowly witch. Low magic in the form of peasant sorcery, and an urban variant of corrupted high magic, provided sufficient smoke for the authorities to scream fire. The folk magic of every peasant provided tinder for the clerical arsonist to spark the holocaust. High magic originated in Middle Eastern numerology, astrology and religion, and in Greek philosophy and mathematics. It concentrated on the divination of the future, an understanding of the natural universe through alchemy and astrology, and in manipulating cosmic forces through word magic. In this form high magic reflected elements which some scholars would label religion, others science or philosophy. It sought to understand and master the universe and thereby achieve union with the divine.

The ideologues of the early church reacted in two ways to this rival system of belief. Firstly, they equated magic with evil and, secondly, quite deliberately substituted magical elements of their own for those destroyed by Christian evangelism. Old heroic beliefs in newly converted societies were translated into a cult of Christian saints. These new religious heroes worked miracles, i.e. feats of magic achieved through co-operation with God. All other magic was defined as diabolic. This dichotomy was clearly a partisan interpretation. The medieval high magician always claimed God's co-operation. It was God's power that raised the demons necessary for the operation of ritual magic — an operation seen as a Christian religious exercise by its participants. Invocation of demons was but a specific example of the power of prayer. The ecclesiastical hierarchy sought Christian ends by supplicating good spirits; the high magician by coercing evil spirits.[3] Nevertheless, from the sixth to the eleventh century the concept of immanent justice in which a wrathful God directly intervened in human affairs reduced the need for magic other than that provided by the church. Miracles and ordeals to gauge divine opinion sufficed. Dramatic changes during the twelfth and thirteenth centuries enhanced the influence of high magic and the Christian hierarchy's increased concern with it. Christianity, previously directed from within the monastery and concentrating on ritual behaviour designed to assuage God's wrath, changed direction. It broke out of the cloister and facing the problems of the secular world developed an ethic based on intent; and a religion in which emotion, both love and hate, became important. At the same time it became more rational and logic became a major tool of doctrinal clarification; a clarification that became increasingly necessary as a ferment of ideas swept Western Europe.[4]

Penitentials designed to aid confessors indirectly popularised the role of magic, initially among the upper classes. These works stressed the active role of the Devil, defined sin as co-operation with the Devil, and magic as a specific form of such co-operation. Detestation of the Devil and all his works, including magic, became a religious issue charged with emotion. At the same time, reform movements manifesting the same 'new' Christianity opposed the invocation of divine power to ameliorate immediate conditions. This was to debase the sacraments. The church under this pressure modified some of the magical props that had supported its adherents and in the process increased the need for overt magical succour from those so deprived. This could now be supplied from outside the ecclesiastical hierarchy of the church. Two developments made the high magician, the 'scientific humanist', a serious challenger to the church's official monopoly of 'magical' power.

The rise of universities in the twelfth century was seen by conservative monastic ecclesiastics as a very dangerous development. Under the cover of legitimate knowledge the secret teaching of forbidden arts might occur. The success of many graduates of these schools who lacked high birth created jealousy among high-born monastic leaders and led to accusations of magic. Elements within the church were convinced that forbidden knowledge was being

37

spread. They were correct. Arguments giving magic a legitimate place in the academic world were openly advanced. The introduction of many Greek and Arabic sources gave added thrust to the growing importance and acceptability of high magic in academic and political circles.

The emergence of powerful secular monarchs in the twelfth and thirteenth centuries gave the practitioner of magic real power and immense prestige. Courtiers competed vigorously for the King's favour. Anything that would aid such an end was greedily taken up. Many magicians were willing to prostitute their art in the service of ambitious men. The background of some royal advisers gave credence to the suggestion that only through sorcery could such misfits have reached their high position. Stakes were high and courtiers were willing to defend the magician as a learned scientist and to ignore the hardening attitude of some ecclesiastical leaders toward this demonic dabbler. The constant charges of sorcery against the great men of state in both England and France in the thirteenth century and early-fourteenth centuries maintained the fear of, and respect for, the power of magic by the political elite.

As he became more powerful and confident, the magician by the thirteenth century demanded recognition as a member of a professional caste and began to refine and elaborate his techniques. Demons were invoked by name and given precise instructions. With growing sophistication the demon Belial emerged as the overseer of demonic assistance to the fraternity of magicians and the rite of sacrifice involving small animals was used more frequently in the invocation procedure. The church leadership saw an even closer relationship developing between the magician and the demons in the provision of a demonic personal servant for each high sorcerer. However, the magicians maintained their offensive. They attacked their rivals, the church's hierarchy, by suggesting that these godly men were dupes of Satan. In the *Sworn Book of Honorius* they suggested that the Devil and his demons detested and feared the ability of the magician to summon, control and coerce them. The magician was the true enemy of the Devil, acting always in God's name. Opposition by the church to the magician was the result of a crude but obviously successful attempt by Satan to trick the hierarchy into persecuting his real enemies.[5]

These developments were ignorantly misinterpreted, deliberately misconstrued, or acutely perceived as devil-worship by more of the elite. This realisation and the genuine fear that the power of magic incited across the political community finally provoked swift

38

and decisive action from the state. This was followed by the victory within the church, after centuries of agitation, for those who viewed all magic as diabolic. In France, servants of the king were attacked as sorcerers by high aristocrats and disgruntled members of the royal family. The Crown used similar charges to destroy leading clergy and nobility, the Templars, and the reputation of Pope Boniface VIII. It was this legal assault on sorcery by the Crown that destroyed the political power of high magic. In part it was a ploy by the state to solve some immediate problems but the Crown was nevertheless very frightened of unknown magical power. Sorcery had threatened the king. It threatened the succession. Above all, it threatened the kingdom as a whole when it was practised in secret by a large semi-autonomous powerful military organisation such as the Templars. The Crown was vulnerable and used the fear of magic to destroy the power of magic itself. It had outlived its usefulness. It was too dangerous politically to survive.[6]

The church's official response to this growing power of high magic had been slow. Although action from the Papacy was intermittent there had always been a powerful section within the church which pursued a consistent opposition to all magic. The twelfth-century response of Hugh of St Victor in reasserting the Augustine view that all magic was evil and diabolic largely fell on deaf ears. The schoolmen, so often accused of magic by their conservative monastic opponents, approached the issue more rationally. Aquinas argued that magic was not mechanistic. It was only effective with the help of demons. It was this invocation of demons that deeply worried Aquinas. He believed that magicians were deceived into thinking that they controlled the situation. The demons pretended to obey because it suited their evil purpose. The magician's art as it emerged in the time of Aquinas depended increasingly on the ability of the magician to summon up and control the particular demon essential to the task in hand. Books of magic detailed the names of the demons needed to achieve specific tasks and the correct incantations and procedures that were required to bend them to the magician's will. Aquinas saw this co-operation as involving an implicit pact between the magician and the demons. This concept of a pact was to become the essential ingredient in the sixteenth-century legal assault on the witch.

The church in the thirteenth century over-reacted by translating a genuine concern with the invocation of demons into a vision of a devil-worshipping cult. Magicians were Christians. They acted

39

piously, raising demons in God's name after a lengthy Christian ritual. There was no hint of diabolism in their books of magic. Elements in the church were not convinced. The Cistercians in 1240 declared magic to be heretical depravity and in 1258 Pope Alexander instructed the Inquisition to investigate magic if it savoured of heresy. In a concerted campaign of 1277, the Pope, the Archbishop of Canterbury and the Bishop of Paris condemned magic as diabolical. In 1320, following the assault of the French Crown on the magician Avignon, Pope John XXII ordered the inquisitors to treat ritual magic as heresy, a position he endorsed in 1326 in the Bull *Super Illius Specula.* The church proclaimed that magic was not possible without demonic help. This help involved a pact with the Devil. Such a pact was devil-worship.[7]

The late-fourteenth and early-fifteenth-century urban Italian sorcerers helped shape a particular aspect of later witchcraft — an emphasis on sex. In 1375, a Florentine businessman fell in love and neglected his family and business. When he gave large sums of money to his mistress his brother denounced her as a sorcerer. The brother claimed that she put a wax image of her victim in her bed and through this medium exerted her unnatural influence over him. In 1394, to win the love of a neighbour a woman prepared a concoction of bread, charcoal and salt and obtained a coin bearing the imprint of a cross. Another sorcerer used magic to improve the love life of his clients. Female fidelity was ensured by anointing the male genitals prior to intercourse with a secret balm. Hearts could be won by presenting the desired woman with a copy of a psalm. Fertility was achieved through possession of a magically inscribed leaden locket. In commercial Florence it was not surprising that the major case of sorcery in this period was the blatant use of amatory magic to promote the business of the city's most success-ful brothel.[8]

How far these urban sorcerers derived their art from the cor-rupted high magic of the courts and schools or simply adapted rural low magic to the urban environment is difficult to ascertain. This 'middling' level of sorcery has been neglected by scholars but it may yet prove the critical link by which the threat to godly society was transferred from powerful male courtiers to elderly peasant women. The role of unfrocked, discontented, vagrant clergy in this process may have been significant.

The critical shift in the attitude of the establishment towards high magic was to see it as heresy and part of a conspiracy against God and society. It was a slow and erratic process which gained momentum in the late-thirteenth and early-fourteenth centuries. The view that all forms of magic were diabolical gradually gained acceptance, as did the belief following the Albigensian threat that most heresy involved devil-worship. Pope John XXII did much to integrate the devil-invoking propensity of magic and the devil-worshipping nature of heresy into the one diabolical conspiracy. The second major shift in the approach to magic was the fifteenth-century conciliarist development which sought to uncover diabolic sorcery among the lower orders of society. Trials of lower-class persons for sorcery before 1400 were rare. A few women were accused of amatory magic in the late-fourteenth century but there was a rapid escalation in the prosecution of lower-class magic in the early-fifteenth century. Secular authorities, especially the Swiss cantons, sought out lower-class sorcerers and applied to them attitudes and apparatus developed to deal with the high magician and dangerous heretic.[9]

Substance was given to these charges as most of the accused were versed in low magic. The definition of 'low magic' is complex. Contemporary usage solves the problem. The prestige and standing of the actor determined the labelling of the activity rather than the nature of the activity itself. Magic was 'low' when it was carried out by the lower orders. The nature of such low magic was difficult to ascertain. Records detailing peasant sorcery were compiled for the elite. For example, the evidence gathered by the Kirk Sessions in Scotland in response to initial local peasant complaints differed considerably from that which the Commissioners considered relevant for formal prosecution. There were layers of popular beliefs about magic that rarely surfaced. The popular views that appeared in judicial records, treatises and sermons had been modified to meet elitist, academic and clerical assumptions. The problem is highlighted by the central issue under discussion. The peasantry and the elite initially had very different views as to the nature of magic. The peasant believed that the sorcerer had powers of his own and that his magic was effected in a mechanistic manner. The learned increasingly insisted that the magician had no such powers and all that he accomplished was done through the aid of demons. This was important in the developing concept of the witch. To view peasant sorcery as demonic instead of mechanistic was the first step. To see it as diabolic rather than demonic was a small intellectual jump.[10]

Low magic was black or white. The church refused to differentiate but the state continued to treat them differently well into the seventeenth century. In some countries white magicians were rarely troubled by the authorities, in others they provided the main reservoir of diabolic suspects. Miracles, and a late form of magic which substituted angels for demons, are excluded from this discussion of white magic. The evidence for angelic magic is suspect and appears to be an attempt by moralistic clergy to clean up older works. A seventeenth-century version of *Secreta Secretorum* contained a complex spell which could make men irresistible to women. It success was hedged with a number of novel assumptions. The agent had to lead a pious and moral life, and the spell would work only with one woman. This woman had to be the agent's wife.[11]

In early modern Europe low white magic operated in three areas: healing, divination and counter-magic. The intensity of each activity and the response to it by populace and authorities varied in time and space. In England and Wales the healer was popular and untroubled by the law. Healing was not prosecuted *per se* nor was the healer viewed as a potential agent of *maleficium*. In Wales, the new Protestant clergy protested against the power of the healer but given the poor standard of such clergy and the established Welsh magical tradition the wizard maintained his popularity and the tacit support of the local gentry. Healers remained popular because their remedies worked, especially those relying on pharmacology. In the absence of a medical profession willing to minister to the rural peasantry they were essential. To many peasants the effectiveness of white magic in the treatment of animals was even more important and faith in the cunningman continued long after the rise of veterinary science. In Catholic Lorraine the healers faced persecution and unpopularity. The rivalry between the priest and the healer remained strong and most of the latter were eventually accused of witchcraft. In Catholic Europe the church continued to offer its own 'magic', and healer and priest offered similar goods. Competition had to be removed. The populace was often very suspicious of persons claiming the ability to heal. As black witches could remove illnesses which they had caused, anyone successfully healing might really be a black witch. For the peasants of the Rhineland to pay a person to heal an illness they had in fact created was the height of folly. The church may have been cheaper.[12]

Popular suspicion of the healer did not depend solely on elitist or ecclesiastical propaganda equating healers with evil witchcraft. The power exerted by the healer was such that he was a potential source of tension and fear in a village community. In Scotland, the peasants often associated the healer with witchcraft and many Scots healers were tried as diabolic witches. The white healer was placed in a situation where his influence could harm or heal. If the healer failed to cure he harmed and in such a situation nobody could be certain that the failure was not deliberate. This issue highlights a major disagreement concerning the peasant healer and the black witch. The English experience suggested that to confuse the two was alien to popular belief; the Scottish that the realities of communal life did exactly this, while popular evidence from continental Europe was confused by the impact of elitist views. By the sixteenth century the church argued that not only did the use of magical powers to heal involve a pact with the Devil but to attempt a cure by such means when God in his wisdom had allowed an illness to occur was tantamount to blasphemy.

Divination involved fortune telling and the finding of lost property and missing persons. Divination had a long history and most objects were used to obtain the answer. It might be the direction of the wind; the flight of arrows; the casting of pebbles; the activity of water; the random opening of the Bible; the direction of smoke; the use of re-animated corpses; or the interpretation of dreams. In England, the interpretation of dreams and the use of plants were the common media of the peasant diviner. The children's game of chanting 'he loves me, he loves me not' as the petals of a flower are stripped is a remnant of peasant divination. This aspect of white magic came under the scrutiny of the English courts as potential fraud. Yet in Lorraine and French-speaking Switzerland, divination was ignored. Both Protestant and Catholic authorities viewed it as peasant superstition rather than a crime and left its eradication to the preaching agencies of the church rather than the coercive power of the courts.[13]

In the Basque regions of Spain and in sixteenth-century Essex, counter-magic was the primary function of white magic. It was directed toward discovering the source of the *maleficium* and of nullifying its effects. As the witch craze developed, the use of white magic against *maleficium* initially grew, then dropped away alarmingly. Prosecutors too easily confused those who used white magic to counter black magic with the agents of black magic itself. The removal of the 'magic' of the church in Protestant countries left peasants bereft of traditional methods of defending themselves against the onslaught of *maleficium*. In these circumstances it would be reasonable to expect that white magic would remain stronger in

Protestant countries than in Catholic but the evidence is not conclusive. Wales may provide a fertile area of research on this point. The Christian clergy there admitted an increasing appeal of the wizard at a time when the forces of rational Protestantism expected to uproot superstition from this dark corner of Britain.

Protestant peasants, like their Catholic counterparts, retained their traditional defences in *folk* magic. Whereas low magic required the work of a 'professional' sorcerer within the peasant community, folk magic could be worked by all members of the community. 'Amateur' magic was an integral part of the peasant world. The steps traditionally taken to influence key events such as birth, marriage and general survival explain the ready acceptance of powers attributed to the witch. This private magic brought protection by neutralising the effect of evil omens or spells. A newborn child was subject to evil, particularly between birth and baptism. To keep the child safe a crust of bread was put under its head, an upturned knife near its heart, its father's breeches over the end of the cradle and some money sown into its clothes. Its nails were not cut and it had to be carried upstairs before it was carried down. With these precautions the child would survive to baptism. Vervain, dill, St John's wort, horseshoes, ash and rowan trees were used to divert the evils of witchcraft. A stone with a hole in it hung about the neck gave protection from incubi. Urine had protective properties, and gestures with the fingers repelled the evil eye. Private love-charms were divinatory but involved activity that in a suspected witch could be defined as evil. For example, on nine successive nights a girl pricked a shoulder of mutton with a knife pretending it was the heart of the male she desired. The man for those nine nights could not sleep and would in the end come to her. Vervain rubbed on the lips won the love of the first person kissed. An apple inscribed with the names of four demons when eaten rendered the writer irresistible to the consumer. All these activities were unwelcome to a reluctant victim and amatory magic from this point of view could easily be redefined as *maleficium* and its perpetrator viewed as an evil witch.[14]

Maleficium — the use of occult power to do harm — was a fact of peasant life. The lower orders feared *maleficium* throughout the Middle Ages but the law of talion and the disinterest of the ruling classes prevented it becoming an issue beyond the village boundaries. The basic thrust of *maleficium* remained the same across regions and time — the ability to cause death and disease in animals and people, to cause impotence in men and infertility in women, to interfere in the reproductive activities of animals and to use weather magic to destroy crops or sink ships. This *maleficium* was achieved by cursing, contact, image magic, the disposal of a magic substance in the vicinity of the victim, incantations and potions.

Low black magic mainly used image magic. A persistent but unsuccessful sorcerer asked his client to walk around a city block picking up stones and incanting that such stones were the heart of the intended victim. A chicken was killed and the extracted heart penetrated by six pins. This pin-cushion heart was placed in a jar with salt, vinegar and urine, and heated. When this appeared to fail the same procedure was repeated using a frog. The sorcerer then created a wax image of the victim and stuck pins in the vital areas of the effigy. It was then placed in a suffocating mixture of pungent incense in the hope that the victim would be asphyxiated. As a final effort, a special red wax image was created with a magical inscription which was hidden near the residence of the victim.

Ritual incantation was not a major medium for the peasant sorcerer. Nevertheless, words were conceived as possessing an innate power and the malevolent curse was a popular form of black magic. There was often a thin line between the curse and a prayer, both of which might increase in efficacy if uttered at a particular place or time. The curse was a weapon of the poor and deprived against their social betters. The written word was also powerful and in an illiterate society the use of unfamiliar symbols appeared magical.[15]

Traditional peasant sorcery did not invoke demons. Peasant magic was mechanistic and did not require the assistance of spirits. These concepts inbedded in Classical urban sorcery and in high magic had nevertheless infiltrated popular magic in some parts of Europe. The belief that demonic assistance was involved was a major step in transforming the image of the peasant sorcerer into that of the witch.[16]

Other evidence of this transformation was manifest in attitudes to animals and in the changing roles of fairies. Animals were basic in primitive religions in which a physical and psychic affinity between humans and animals was assumed. The worship of animals as totems was imbedded in folk memory with especial prominence being given to the bull and the goat. The violent assault by Christianity against animals was interpreted as evidence that animals were of special importance to the low magician.

Christianity was repelled by nature and obsessed by the demonic assault on man through the agency of sub-human life — women and animals. This fear led Christian elites to attribute to animals human characteristics and even a sense of moral responsibility. Pigs were formally tried for murder after they killed children. The animal partner in acts of bestiality usually suffered the same fate as the human involved. In Paris in 1466 a man and his sow were burned. In Connecticut in 1662 a cow, two heifers, three ewes and two sows were hanged by the Puritan authorities prior to the execution of their lover, a Mr Potter. During trials animals were dressed in clothes, tied in an upright position and treated as if they were human. In 1750 a Frenchman was accused of bestiality with his she-ass. Friends of the animal called character witnesses who testified to her excellent behaviour. The court accepted the evidence; the ass was freed. The man was hanged not for bestiality but for rape.[17]

Animals were especially feared in the sixteenth and seventeenth centuries as familiars, the lesser demons that assisted the sorcerer in his activities. However, familiars were not part of medieval peasant sorcery and probably the assumptions of academics convinced of the demonic assistance necessary in high magic slowly filtered down to the lower orders. Elites assumed, and thereby found, similar animal assistance given to the peasant witch. It was not surprising then that these animal familiars were not fantasy monsters but the normal pets kept by old women — dogs and cats. Lonely old women treated these animals as children. They were talked to, pampered and treated as close personal friends. The fury and hysterical sobbing of a Newmarket women when William Harvey dissected her alleged familiar, a pet toad, was understandable. The affection between old people and their animals was reflected in the names given to such pets — Puck, White, Sugar and Greedigut. In the Basque country it was believed that the witches were allocated a special toad to carry out their malevolent activities — a toad which could transform itself into a human or other animals. Although the authorities in some places chose to emphasise the role of animals as evil familiars the peasantry on the whole saw them as harmless household pets.

The elite redefined another traditional belief related to animals. The strong conviction that magicians could turn themselves into beasts, birds and insects made human confrontation with animals a source of potential terror. Stray dogs, howling cats, toads, rats and flies could all be agents of a malevolent power or a form of

that power itself. The Devil could appear as an animal. This belief
in lycanthropy — wherein humans assumed animal forms temporarily — had a long tradition. The story of a hare being shot or
losing a paw and the village discovering next day that one of its
members had a wound in a similar spot or had lost a hand was
common in European folk culture. Yet metamorphosis was not in
itself malevolent. Lithuanian, Russian and German folklore had
similar traditions of humans transformed into werewolves who as
the hounds of God went into Hell to fight the legions of the Devil.
However, by the sixteenth century metamorphosis was invariably
interpreted as a medium of the Devil.[18]

The reinterpretation of the fairy reflected the general drift of
associating evil with ordinary identifiable peasant women.
Margaret Murray suggested that fairies were the remnants of a
smaller race of inhabitants gradually pushed back into the
inaccessible parts of the realm. In the British Isles they were the
pre-Celtic peoples who by the sixteenth century allegedly survived
only in parts of Wales, Scotland and Ireland. The evidence for this
has never been produced. Yet the slowness of Protestantism to take
a hold in Wales was reportedly due to the power of the wizards
who were known to consult fairies on Tuesday and Thursday
nights. Traditionally the fairy was believed to have certain attributes and behaviour patterns. To transfer these from spirits such
as a fairy to old women was not a great intellectual jump. Fairies
had a reputation for sexual immorality, their gifts could not be
relied on, usually turning into leaves or wood shavings. They stole
children. They could fly. They were guilty of *maleficium* and could
make women sterile and men impotent. They could make crops
fail and animals stop giving milk. By the seventeenth century these
evil attributes had been transferred to more visible agents: certain
women of the village. Fairies now were more likely to create
mischief than cause serious harm. They delighted in overturning
milk pails and tricking travellers into losing their way. They
provided a cover for the carelessness of humans rather than an
explanation of serious misfortune. Where fairies still provided an
explanation of basic human problems such as in Celtic Ireland and
Gaelic Scotland there were no witches.[19]

The magical world view of the sixteenth century emphasised the
unity of nature and the link between microcosm and macrocosm.
The universe was so delicately balanced that chaos, disorder or
immorality in the human microcosm might cause a similar disturbance in the universe. As the universe often reacted ahead of

dastardly deeds, storms and the strange behaviour of animals or heavenly bodies such as comets were accepted as harbingers of approaching evil. Portents were worthy of serious consideration. At a more mundane level ill luck was forshadowed if a person rose first from a table of thirteen, broke a mirror, spilt salt, heard a cuckoo before a nightingale or had a nosebleed. In such a world the charges of *maleficium* levelled against the alleged witch did not differ in kind to the everyday behaviour and attitudes of the whole community. It was not in the exercise and acceptance of magic that the witch differed from her fellow villagers.[20]

The medieval church faced initially with the reassertion of high magic as a respectable science with political influence counter-attacked by reasserting the demonic nature of all magic. This concept of demonic assistance was gradually applied to magic of all types. The creation of the image of witch simply required accepted opinion to move from the concept of magic as involving demonic assistance to one in which the magical practitioner worshipped the Devil. The diabolic cult was the result.

Notes

1. In comparing magic with religion Tylor believed the former was logically wrong, Weber that it was irrational, Marett that it was immoral, Durkheim that it was divisive and Malinowski that it was selfish. For a discussion of these views and the criticism of them as ethnocentric see Murray and Rosalie Wax, 'The Notion of Magic', *Current Anthropology* 4 (1965) pp. 495–518. The first view is expressed by Radcliffe-Brown — see Wax, *loc.cit.* p. 499. The second position is taken by Edward Norbeck, *Religion in Primitive Society* — see Wax *loc.cit.* pp. 500, 510 — and by Jon Butler, 'Magic, Astrology, and the Early American Religious Heritage', *American Historical Review* 84 (1979) pp. 317–46. The third position is exemplified by William J. Goode, *Religion and the Primitives*. See also debate between Hildred Geertz and Keith Thomas, 'An Anthropology of Religion and Magic', *Journal of Interdisciplinary History* VI (Summer 1975) pp. 71–89 (Geertz); 91–109 (Thomas). The Frazerian variant — James G. Frazer, *The Golden Bough* pp. 220–4 — has been adapted by Julio Caro Baroja, *The World of the Witches*; Pennethorne Hughes, *Witchcraft* p. 28. See also Erland Ehnmark, 'Religion and Magic — Frazer, Soderblom and Hagerstrom', *Ethnos* 21 (1956) p. 5.

2. This fourth variant has been advanced strongly by M. and R. Wax, *loc.cit.* and in 'The Magical World View', *Journal for the Scientific Study of Religion* 1 (1962) pp. 179–88; Max Jammer, *Concepts of Force*; Jeffrey Burton Russell, *Witchcraft in the Middle Ages* pp. 5–6; and by E. A. Tiryakian in E. A. Tiryakian (ed.) *On the Margin of the Visible* pp. 5–12. Further arguments for (Charles Galtier and Robert G. Armstrong) and

against (especially David Bidney) can be found in the comments on M. and R. Wax, 'The Notion of Magic', *loc.cit.* pp. 503–18.

3. The discussion on high magic draws heavily on Edward Peters, *The Magician, the Witch and the Law.* Where a specific reference is not given the source is Peters. The other major influence on this topic was Norman Cohn, *Europe's Inner Demons*; Peters *op.cit.* p. xv.

4. For an interesting insight into early medieval attitudes and subsequent changes see the two articles by Charles M. Radding, 'Evolution of Medieval Mentalities: A Cognitive–Structural Approach', *American Historical Review* 83 (1978) pp. 577–97; and 'Superstition to Science: Nature, Fortune, and the Passing of the Medieval Ordeal', *American Historical Review* 84 (Oct. 1979) pp. 945–69; Peters, *op.cit.* pp. 78–81.

5. Peters, *op.cit.* pp. 112–29 and Ch. 5 'The Sorcerer's Apprentice', and Cohn, *op.cit.* pp. 164–79.

6. Peters, *op.cit.* p. 129.

7. Cohn, *op.cit.* pp. 169–77; *ibid.* p. 170; Peters, *op.cit.* p. 57; Cohn, *op.cit.* p. 172.

8. Gene H. Brucker, 'Sorcery in Early Renaissance Florence', *Studies in the Renaissance* X (1963) pp. 7–24.

9. Elliot Rose, *A Razor for a Goat* suggests that the goliards made a major contribution to the spread and organisation of the witch cult.

10. The imposition of learned notions onto popular beliefs is emphasised and exposed by Richard Kieckhefer, *European Witch Trials: Their Foundations in Popular and Learned Culture, 1300–1500* and by Christina Larner, *Enemies of God: The Witchhunt in Scotland.*

11. K. M. Briggs, 'Some Seventeenth Century Books of Magic', *Folklore* 64 (1953) p. 449.

12. Stuart Clark and P. T. Morgan, 'Religion and Magic in Elizabethan Wales: Robert Holland's *Dialogue on Witchcraft*', *Journal of Ecclesiastical History* 27 (1976) p. 45; E. William Monter, *Witchcraft in France and Switzerland: The Borderlands During the Reformation* pp. 173–90.

13. K. M. Briggs, *Pale Hecate's Team* p. 223; Monter, *op.cit.* pp. 177–8.

14. Briggs, *op.cit.* pp. 165–85.

15. Cohn, *op.cit.* pp. 145–63; Brucker, *loc.cit.* pp. 13–17; Keith Thomas, *Religion and the Decline of Magic* pp. 599–611.

16. The role of invocation in low magic is in part confused due to problems of definition. Russell, in attempting to separate sorcery and the new witchcraft, believed that sorcery used both mechanistic magic and invocation while witchcraft used invocation and, in addition, worshipped the devil. Kieckhefer prefers to see invocation as a separate phenomenon. Russell considers invocation of spirits to be essential in low magic whereas Simons believes low magic consisted entirely of mechanistic activity. See Kieckhefer, *op.cit.* p. 6; Russell, *op.cit.* p. 17 and G. L. Simons, *The Witchcraft World* p. 162.

17. Simon, *op.cit.* pp. 98–9; Russell, *op.cit.* p. 255; Thomas, *op.cit.* pp. 626, 771; Simon, *op.cit.* p. 109.

18. Mircea Eliade, *Occultism, Witchcraft and Cultural Fashions* pp. 77–8.

19. Simons, *op.cit.* pp. 83–97; Thomas, *op.cit.* pp. 724–34.

20. Briggs, *op.cit.* p. 187.

4

Heresy and the Diabolic Cult

Magic contributed much to the image of the diabolic witch. The
Christian concept of heresy made an even greater imput. This
concept developed through four stages. In the eleventh century the
most vile abominations were ascribed to all dissenters; in the
twelfth they were invariably accused of devil-worship. During the
church's vigorous attack on dissidents in the thirteenth century
institutions and attitudes were created which exaggerated the
extent of the problem. Explanations of the fourteenth-century
crisis in terms of God's wrath and personal repentance had little
appeal. By the fifteenth a simple and more acceptable cause was
discovered for personal misfortune, and a simplistic picture of
heresy emerged. A diabolical cult was attempting to destroy
Christendom and creating personal havoc in the process.

The church's response to dissent in the eleventh century was to
adapt the sensational exaggeration of monastic pedagogy and to
depict all opponents, even the most austere, as vile perverts.
Puritan mystics in Orleans were described falsely by a contemporary chronicler as engaging in incest, sexual orgies, child
murder and cannibalism. This lurid picture, traditionally used by
the Eastern church against its heretics, was taken up in the West
and the level of vileness attributed to opponents gradually
increased. In subsequent accounts of heretical groups there were
usually descriptions of children burnt alive, sodomy, buggery and
the desecration of the sacraments in the foulest manner. The
arrival of dualist heresies in the twelfth century focused attention
on the leadership of such non-conformist groups. In the eyes of the
church, the Devil was clearly the centre of adoration amidst the
abominations. Heretical groups met in private and their real

beliefs and practices were largely unknown but they were invariably described by the authorities as devil-worshipping cults. The establishment image-makers knew that this was not a truthful account of much heretical behaviour. It was an allegorical and symbolic presentation of heresy for mass consumption. To ascribe abominations and devil-worship to all heretical groups, most of whom were innocent of the charges, was an aspect of the double truth, a feature of medieval mass pedagogy. The truth was too complex and potentially disruptive.

This educational campaign and the intermittent prosecution of the odd heretic did not stop the spread of religious and social dissent. In the last decades of the twelfth century, pope, emperor and secular monarchs agreed that heretics should be excommunicated and if they failed to recant their errors they should be burnt. Innocent III in 1209 launched a military campaign against the Cathars, and in 1215 the Lateran Council asked all secular princes to apply the death penalty to heretics. In 1231 Pope Gregory IX and Emperor Frederick II agreed that the former should appoint inquisitors with special powers to discover and destroy heretics within the Holy Roman Empire. The German church was not happy with this interference and was appalled by obsessional attitudes and arbitrary methods of Conrad of Marburg, the first papal inquisitor. The Pope quickly endorsed the diabolic image of the heretic, replete with some of the more extreme views of Conrad, in the Bull *Vox in Rama*, in 1233. Innocent IV went further in 1252 approving the use of torture, the seizure of property and the reduction of the standard of evidence necessary to convict the heretic. This papal campaign popularised the perceived threat of the heretical assault and its diabolic origins.[1]

During the thirteenth century, orthodoxy prevailed. In the next century old institutions and values received blow after blow — the Black Death, famines, economic decline, the Babylonian captivity, the Great Schism, the decline of the Empire, the weakening of scholasticism and its rational ordered view of society, popular uprisings and disruptions caused by the attempts of secular monarchs to assert their power at the expense of other authorities. When old values crumbled individuals were alienated and developed a sense of anomie. Traditional approaches did not meet the exigencies of the populace. The church failed to adapt to the changing needs of its flock through its conservatism rather than through its incompetence or corruption. The initial reaction to the crisis of the fourteenth century was for individuals to see in it the signs of the last days, and to attempt to assuage God's wrath by personal repentance, often in most gross physical form such as flagellation. Personal repentance and continued heavy penances were difficult options for a populace suffering recurrent reversals. Conciliarists solved the problems of the ecclesiastical hierarchy and saw the cause of popular misfortune in the fifteenth century as a result of a diabolical conspiracy. The Rhineland clergy, in particular, did not limit Satan's agents to the clearly revealed heretic. Academics knew that all magic involved the co-operation of the Devil. The church had for a century or more successfully equated high magic with heresy. It now identified peasant sorcery with the greatest heresy: apostasy, the renunciation of the faith in order to serve the Devil. This development potentially gave Satan agents in every village. It was the awareness of this new menace that provoked the *Malleus*.[2]

By the sixteenth century the diabolic cult was perceived to involve a belief in the power of Satan, an explicit pact with him ratified by sexual intercourse, and regular meetings with him or his representatives at the sabbat at which they indulged in all kinds of perversions. The power of Satan was central to an understanding of the diabolic witch. The development of a complex demonology and its spread through the social order provided the intellectual, and guided the emotional, response to contemporary problems. In early Judaism the monotheism of Jehovah was so absolute that other phenomena were powerless. Isaiah 45:7 saw God as responsible for good and evil, and misfortune a just punishment from God. In the three centuries before Christ the principle of evil within Judaism was expanded and refined under Iranian influences and Christianity inherited a developed concept of Satan.[3]

Satan changed from a rebellious tempter into the manifestation of the principle of Evil — immanent, powerful, approachable and willing to assist mankind for his own ends. The tolerance of the early church towards the Devil disappeared. To Origen, God's mercy was so embracing and His power so absolute that ultimately it would redeem the Devil himself. By the twelfth century a God of justice would not redeem his cosmic antagonist. Satan was the eternal enemy, not a temporary trouble maker. This approachable Devil attracted supporters. Satan's appeal, whether real or in fantasy, reflected both irrational impulses of the subconscious, and rational interests intent on improved conditions — subconscious desires to cope with the terrifying power of God, or inability to cope with the austere demands of Christian perfection and the evident failure of society to meet them. Satan was a hero figure, a symbol of defiance for those who were in rebellion against a church that had failed to meet their spiritual or material needs. To those who believed that God would ultimately win, the Devil offered only short-term solace and assistance. A little amelioration now was rarely worth eternal damnation. One way to guarantee Satan's permanent victory was to redefine the God of the Roman Church as Satan and the Catholic Satan as the true God, as did the Cathars.

The Church denied the Devil real power. He could not create, he simply developed illusions. He could not work miracles but he could use his superior knowledge to work marvels, to impress by using natural methods beyond the comprehension of mortals. Nevertheless, the church contributed most to the power of Satan through monastic pedagogy, the new emotional emphasis on devotion, ecclesiastical factionalism and invective, its reaction to heresy and the rise of scholasticism. Monks guarded Christian truth for five or six centuries. Within the monastery the image of Satan was deliberately developed. This clever and powerful tempter was luridly portrayed and his powers and influence over the world purposely exaggerated as part of the psychological adjustment and intellectual training of the novice. This personification of evil would easily be defeated by strict adherence to monastic discipline. Demonic temptation was a pedagogical device in the training of the monk. When Christianity escaped the monastery the image of a powerful Satan was transferred into the secular world which by its very nature could not adopt monastic discipline. The monks with their lingering monopoly of Christian teaching continued to highlight diabolic power and their devotional literature emphasised Satan's dominance in the secular world.[4]

During the twelfth century the mechanistic worship of a just God was gradually replaced by a theology of redemption and an emphasis on God's love for mankind. This divine love provoked in the faithful an equally emotional response. The negative side of this intense feeling was an irrational hatred of God's enemies — Jews, infidels, heretics and Satan. Reform movements questioned traditional defences against Satan labelling them superstitions. Faced with a powerful Devil, and bereft of effective methods of protection, the church decided to take the offensive and eliminate its enemies. The Inquisition was justified. The church faced a real enemy who appeared to be winning. Ecclesiastical invective and factionalism heightened the belief in this fact. Anyone who opposed the views held by a protagonist was depicted as a diabolical perverter of society. This institutionalised exaggeration of the evil of opposing views and practices within the church helped cry up the powers of Satan.[5]

Dualist heresies contributed further to the rise of Satan. Evil posed a serious problem for elite and masses alike. The Cathars had a simple solution. There was an evil god. This dualism influenced the Christian concept of Satan in two related ways. The role of the Devil was increased within Christian orthodoxy to rival that of the Cathars and, secondly, the very success of the Cathars popularised satanic power. The church's elevation of diabolic power could not arrest the popular slide into Manicheism. Evil, manifest in an individual's misfortune, could stem from human weakness, be caused by the Devil as an autonomous agent or be the result of the Devil acting with God's permission. Orthodox theologians emphasised the third option. However the activities of demonologists and popular preachers, both mainly Dominican, led the population to believe the second.[6]

Apart from the Aristotelian desire to categorise, in which the schoolmen defined the source of human power as either directly divine or indirectly bestowed by the Devil, scholastic theology contributed little to the rise of Satan. The impetus for this came from the popular preachers and moralists. They highlighted in the behaviour of heretics and magicians the basic diabolic motivation. The schoolmen rarely attacked these heretical diabolic cults as such but concentrated on the highly placed practitioners of high magic. The increased obsession with Satan in the latter half of the sixteenth century was also fuelled by fanatical popular preaching now aided by the availability of popular printed material and arising from the anxieties stemming from religious conflict and civil strife. In the Great Catechism of Peter Canisius, designed as a major weapon in the campaign to win back the peasant to Mother Church, Christ's name appeared 63 times and that of Satan 67. In 1581 a French publication revealed there were 7,405,920 demons at work in the world, commanded by 72 efficient generals. The satanic army was on the march.[7]

An explicit pact between witch and Devil was crucial to the image. Of little importance in the early-fifteenth century, the pact had become the basis of legal prosecution, especially in Protestant areas, by the mid-seventeenth century. Calvinists emphasised

God's covenant with his people and therefore the pact was a
perversion of this basic Christian concept. In Scotland the legal
formula stressed the pact, reputation and *maleficia*. The explicit
pact developed from the view that magic involved an implicit
covenant with the Devil. This notion was resisted by the peasants.
To them witches exercised magical powers without demonic help.
In essence the pact imitated feudal relationships. In swearing
fealty to the Devil, he, as liege lord, promised protection in return.
The Devil promised little else. There was no unreal belief that
Satan would bring riches; his help might assist survival. This
explicit pact with the Devil was difficult to prove and most authorities placed little credence on documents that purported to bear the
Devil's signature. However, at Loudun a contract between
Urbain Grandier and the satanic hierarchy was signed for the
latter by Satan, Lucifer, Beelzebub, Leviathan, Elimi and
Astaroth, and accepted as evidence. The arch-demon Asmodeus
had stolen it from the Devil's cabinet. In return for success at
deflowering virgins, destroying the chastity of nuns, and guaranteed sex every three days, Grandier would serve Satan.[8]

The Devil's mark was considered a more objective proof of
apostacy. The Devil sealed his pact with a bite, sexual intercourse,
and sometimes the bestowal of a new name. The mark was insensitive to pain and would not bleed. Some marks were real, involving
cicatrisation or tatooing, most were natural blemishes. The mark
was usually small and very difficult to find. Its form varied. In
France it was an animal shape on the left shoulder, for the Basques
it was revealed in the left eye and visible only under special conditions. It was most commonly any cavity or protuberance usually
discovered in the vagina of a woman and the anus of a man.
Suspected witches were stripped, their pubic hair shaved and long
needles driven into the suspected parts. A new profession of male
prickers developed — although two leading members turned out to
be women in disguise. Pricking attracted not only deviants but
frauds. They were paid according to the number of witches discovered. The more enterprising used retractable needles which did
not cause bleeding but to witnesses appeared to have plunged
deeply into a suspect. This Devil's mark was sometimes confused
with and sometimes seen as quite separate from the witches' teat —
a third nipple from which their demonic familiars suckled. The
witches' teat was also proof of apostacy. In a society in which
partially formed additional teats were not rare a significant number
of women could become suspect because of this abnormality.

55

The pact reflected the changing mode of religious behaviour. The witch entered into an agreement with the Devil of her own free will — recognition that religious commitment involved personal responsibility. Some contemporaries rejected the pact. To Weyer the Devil could not keep it because as a spirit he was unable to confirm it by shaking hands. There were no witnesses to validate it and prior baptism remained the more binding contract. Such views were rare.[9]

The sixteenth century has been described as the period which witnessed the false dawn of the satanic empire when the Devil 'captured the intelligence, harassed the wills, clouded the spirits and attracted a huge following'. Actually the Devil had a meagre following. Devil-worshippers existed but they were few in number. The church defamed most dissenters with such an accusation for centuries. Recent research has clarified the steps in this libelling process. The Orleans canons in 1022 questioned a few doctrines and were branded devil-worshippers. Gregory IX in 1233 gave credence to the view that heretics adored Satan in the form of a black cat. The Templars were accused of revering him as an idol, Baphomet. Pope Boniface was charged with worshipping Satan in the form of a portrait he kept hidden from view. The Pope's idolatry was something more personal; he was gazing at his own portrait. The creation of an exact image of a person, still anathema to Islam, was diabolical to the credulous Christian. In 1335 the Inquisition defined night flying and aspects of malevolent sorcery as manifestations of devil-worship. In the Basque regions satanism was clearly seen as something distinct from witchcraft. In England there was hardly a single case of devil worshipping. In Scotland, although the Devil fornicated, danced and shared meals with witches, there was no form of adoration evident in the image of the sabbatic ritual. The evidence for devil-worship lay in the Christian perception of the pact: in return for help it was axiomatic that the witch must worship Satan.[10]

Demonic possession was a major seventeenth-century aspect of diabolism. Experts disagree as to the scientific nature of possession. Psychologists believe either an alien spirit enters the body, or the self is split and one part takes control, or an entirely new self is created, or the same self masquerades in such conditions as someone different. Demonic possession was a minor aspect of medieval culture. It rose to panic proportions, largely in France, particularly in convents, and also amongst adolescents in England and Massachusetts. The convent outbreaks were psychosexual hysteria, in which nuns exhibited all the signs of sexual orgasm, shouting obscenities, lifting their habits and inviting males to have intercourse with them. Nunneries contained many unwilling novices who found repressive discipline difficult. This alternated with occasional periods of lax discipline and corruption in which attractive males, often priests, had close contact with the women. Imagination and desire did the rest. One of the earliest of the convent outbreaks occurred at Cambrai in 1491. A serious outbreak in a Cologne nunnery took the specific form of nuns arching their backs with their pudenda thrust forward and revealing all of the symptoms of a most vigorous and satisfactory sexual intercourse. These attacks began after the authorities stopped town males visiting the novices at night. They were deprived of physical sex at the moment of their dedication to the one perfect and unobtainable male. Phantom pregnancy was an alternative obsession that arose in similar circumstances.[11]

It was disgusting and frightening that these havens of virginal sanctity should be blasphemed by Satan. By denigrating the genitals, the church created an Achilles heel for the godly. The central figure at Loudun, an ugly Mother Superior, felt rejected by the current sex idol which brought on her hysterical outbursts. Sex was one aspect of the Loudun incident. High politics was the other. The city was under stress. It was a Protestant citadel guaranteed its own garrison under the Edict of Nantes. This right was removed illegally in 1624 and the return of a large number of Catholics, including the Ursuline nuns in 1626, added to the tension. By 1631 the national Catholic government felt secure enough to dismantle the city walls — an instruction opposed by the local Protestant establishment and by many local Catholics, including the priest Grandier. Richelieu and his agents were able to use the convent scandal to discredit both the troublesome priest and the Protestant cause. The obsessed nuns shouted that Calvin was their leader and while possessed proclaimed their love for the Huguenots. Public exorcism was the church's response. It affrighted the populace and its visible success brought credit to the Old Faith. As soon as Catholicism was secure in Loudun and walls demolished the exorcisms became private and the nuns concerned replaced their lascivious visitations from Grandier and demons with beatific visions. The Mother Superior was instructed now by a guardian angel and in later years developed a stigmata.[12]

In France, possession was usually restricted to the upper and middle classes and was not an aspect of common witchcraft. In the

Franche Comte, due to the prejudices of key judges, it became a popular phenomenon. In Salem, the possession of the key adolescents had no overt sexual connotations although its origin remains a mystery. Their behaviour was limited to convulsive fits, exhibitions of demonic non-sexual assaults on the body, muscular spasms and unintelligible language. In the early stages this possession reflected an exhilarating rather than a terrifying posture. After initial strange, erratic and often unique behaviour, most victims quickly learnt to exhibit a stereotype of activity which their viewers expected from the possessed. Children in England vomited pins and wood shavings, foamed at the mouth, became rigid, revealed increased strength, suffered painful cramps, convulsed and passed blue urine. Freud believed that demons were a manifestation of instinctive impulses that had been repressed. Historians have followed Freud in attributing demonic possession to persons who have suffered severe repression or frustration. To be possessed had two advantages. Possession provided an explanation and a legitimisation for normally unacceptable behaviour. A child could hurl a Bible at his stern Puritan father and the Devil would get the blame. The possessed, the French nuns and the girls at Salem, became the centre of attention. In one act forbidden impulses were expressed with safety and attention was gained. Possession did not necessarily involve a witch and it was an area in which the Devil could operate alone.[13]

The cure for possession was exorcism: 'In my name shall they cast out devils' (Luke 17:16). Exorcism was not only a matter of prayers and wordy ritual. It involved vile potions, nauseous smells, and painful probing of the genitals and other sensitive parts of the body. Demons sought the moist areas of the body and privations of the most inhumane type were part of the treatment. The church was often embarrassed by the mistaken enthusiasm of the exorcist and cautioned against its over-use. Too many melancholics, hysterics and lunatics believed they were possessed when all they needed was a good doctor. The church finally restricted the right to exorcise to those with episcopal permission. Nevertheless preventative exorcisms, used to nullify spells affecting flocks and interfering with the breeding of their animals, or the sexual activities of husband and wife, were popular. The rite freed the potential victim of all ligatures, fascinations and satanic witchcraft. Conservative Anglicans viewed exorcists as charlatans or papists, yet some Puritans engaged in the art. Catholic exorcism worked. Possession was a psychosomatic disorder which responded to public therapy. It made overt the explicit elements of sin — temptation and guilt.[14]

Exorcism was not the only defence against the Devil. He could be tricked by mere mortals. His plot to obtain the plans of the great cathedrals at Cologne and Aix was thwarted. The Devil was burlesqued in medieval art and lampooned in medieval plays. The dualist attitudes were deeply engrained on the peasant mind. French peasants saw life as a contest between God, the sun, rain, earth, man, sheep, dog, vine, cabbage and carrot on the one side; and on the other, the Devil, moon, hail, sea, monkey, wolf, fox, brambles and thistles. By keeping the Devil out in the open, by making him the butt of festive occasions he remained a vulnerable folk demon whose hellish terrors could be laughed away. Renaissance France was not dominated by fear of Satan despite bombardment by preachers and printers with the horrific details of the satanic assault and the horrors of Hell. The church used terror to enforce right doctrine and austere morality. Its abolition of mystery plays and of festive occasions was not only to encourage asceticism, but to abolish aspects of popular culture that enabled the individual peasant to relieve his tensions without the assistance of the church. Peasants clung to the concept of a comic devil despite the church's campaign to destroy it. The fear of demons was highly developed by sections of the elite and then partially imposed on the populace. Popular culture was never monolithic and elements of this demonology were readily incorporated into popular thinking only at certain levels and in certain regions. Many French peasants continued to reject this elitist pressure. On the other hand the Scots populace generally accepted the reality of the Devil but played down his sovereignty. They readily accepted the concept of the pact, sexual intercourse between Devil and his followers and the link between ill-fame and diabolic alliance — concepts resisted by the peasantry in other parts of Europe.[15] Yet even the Scottish lower orders did not incorporate adoration of Satan into their image.

Witchcraft at its most fanciful was a highly organised cult. Those who saw witchcraft as a real organisation accepted the confessions of witches detailing its hierarchical structure. Others saw it as a simple response to the expectations of the inquisitors. In England witchcraft was neither a religion nor an organisation. Witches in England showed no signs of co-operation with each other, no continuity or common aspect in ritual. A key aspect of the organisation was the regular meeting of the cultists: the sabbat.

In Catholic Europe persecution was maintained and expanded by insisting that the accused witch describe and name her companions at the sabbat. Deviant groups did meet but confessions regarding the details of the sabbat were largely fantasies. This conclusion is rejected by scholars who accept the confessions at face value and thereby believe in the objective reality of such meetings. This unacceptable view is supported by a number of assertions, mainly *non sequiturs*, designed to cover the obvious weaknesses in the evidence and argument inherent in such a stand. An extreme example is the claim that the confessions must be taken at face value because most of them were given freely, without torture. The countless unproven assumptions involved in this statement, both historical and logical, indicate its unreliability as evidence. On the other hand it was argued that the courage of women subjected to torture was further proof of the truth of their ultimate confession. Their ability to resist torture was due to a psychosomatic insensitivity to pain due to immense feelings of guilt stemming from the enormity of their sabbatical behaviour.[16]

Images of what happened at the sabbat varied. Ritual initiation, eating, drinking, dancing and natural sexual activity were common to most. At one extreme the sabbat was depicted as an occasion for the most perverted range of sexual activities involving men, women, children and animals; child sacrifices and cannibalism, homage to and adoration of the Devil, black Masses and lessons in *maleficium*. Basque witches concentrated on child vampirism, the violation of graves, and the devouring of corpses at the sabbat meal. The brains of children were considered a special delicacy. German witches had a penchant for the scatological. All human waste — menstrual blood, semen, faeces, vomit, urine and pus — had magical properties. They were often mixed with cereals to produce a cake of aphrodisiacal qualities. Sacrilege played a major part at other gatherings. The host was desecrated and some witches prepared especially large hosts with a convenient slit that could be used as an artificial vagina. In Geneva witches specialised in spreading the plague. In England sabbats did not exist and in Scotland they were peasant jollifications lacking the horrendous aspects. Eating, drinking and dancing were the major ingredients and sex was an extension of normal peasant bawdry. The Scottish sabbat did not invert the natural Christian order of society. It reflected simple peasant needs under an austere Calvinistic regime. The loss of communal jollification permitted under the laxer morality of Catholicism, which had provided a safety valve

60

for pent-up peasant frustrations, reappeared in fantasy, at least, in what the witches did or were thought to do at the sabbat.[17]

How did witches attend the sabbat when reliable witnesses saw them sleeping peacefully in their beds at the time of the alleged meeting? They flew, often invisible to the naked eye of any potential witness. Flying at night was not an alien concept to either elite or populace. Angels and devils flew. The early-medieval church tried to stamp out the traditional Roman and Germanic beliefs in night-flying deities who with their followers flew abroad. The idea proved difficult to eradicate. When the church itself began to discover in the thirteenth century that these flying persons were not devilish illusions but fact, popular folk beliefs gradually received official sanction. Witches had to fly to the sabbat if the church was to explain how people met so often and so far from home without being seen travelling to the rendezvous. With this form of transport there was no limit to the numbers and geographical areas involved in the conspiracy and consequently its potential political and social threat. While many witches were certain that they flew to the sabbat on a broomstick or on the back of an animal, they were in most cases dreaming. The broomstick has been interpreted as a symbol of peasant womanhood, or as a ritual or symbolic phallus. It was most probably a drug applicator. The witches fasted before they went to the sabbat and drugs applied to the more sensitive parts of their body would have had a rapid effect. Many women did not distinguish between waking and sleeping. They dreamed, and believed what they had dreamt to be true. Authorities countered this view that women were merely dreaming. The real woman left the locked bedroom to go to the sabbat but the Devil left a duplicate in her place so that watchers would believe that she was still there. The Devil could also create illusions creating clouds to cover the flight of women on their way to the sabbat. Sexual orgasm, as well as drugs, may have provided a sensation of flying for these women. A strong supporter of the objective reality of sabbats believed that the women walked. Surprisingly, apart from Salazar inquisitors did not probe witches very closely on this aspect of their confessions.[18]

The sabbat was accepted generally as a real and dangerous meeting of the enemies of society. This reflected the social fears of the establishment. Meetings of dissidents in secret, in isolated places and engaged in activities subversive to law, order and morality, became the focus of communal anxiety and individual fears. In the tradition of medieval parodies such as the Feast of

Fools and a history of attributing to a variety of heresies the most abominable behaviour, the populace had enough fuel for the imagination to create a whole range of fearful and dangerous secret meetings of a diabolical enemy. Population growth and the creation of a large number of unemployed and under-employed caused hundreds of vagrants to wander the countryside. These vagrants gathered each evening as a group in someone's barn where drinking, dancing and often more scurrilous behaviour occurred. The secret but riotous behaviour of the vagrant made plausible to the settled villager, alarmed by such proceedings, the objective reality of the sabbat.

This contemporary view that witchcraft was, or was thought to be, a diabolic cult is still advanced. Montague Summers had no doubts that the inquisitors were engaged in a genuine struggle against a satanic army. Although dismissed with innuendo and sneer by the sceptics, Summers was far from repeating the extreme credulity of the demonologists. To him the treatises, trial records and confessions were full of ignorance, malice, imagination, deception, fantasy and fraud. Transvection was impossible — very few confessions alluded to it — and those that did were attempts to gain attention. An overdeveloped imagination of the witches turned their ritual dances using broomsticks into a belief that they were actually flying, a belief validated perhaps by genuine cases of levitation. Some images were framed under the influence of drugs; an explanation accepted at the time by many conservative demonologists. Summers also dismissed metamorphosis. People wore masks and skins of animals and often behaved as such — activities with a long tradition in primitive religions. Death after an argument with a witch sometimes had psychological causes but most probably resulted from poisoning. The Devil at the sabbat was usually a local identity.[19]

Yet this was not always so. The Devil could be present. There were cases which could be explained in no other way. Despite all the qualifications there was evidence to support the existence of a diabolic cult. The basic thrust of the demonologists had to be accepted at face value. They were the experts. Summers differed from his critics not so much on his critical approach to the evidence but on the assumptions underlying his interpretation of it. To him the eternal conflict between good and evil was self-evident and paramount. Evil was planned, marshalled and directed so skilfully that it reflected the mind of a genius — the Devil. With conviction Summers looked at the evidence as proof that the witch existed and that she was 'a member of a powerful secret organization' and 'an evil liver . . . battening upon the filth and foulest passions of the age'. Most critics simply denied Summers' basic assumptions and justified this by pointing up his ignorance of folklore and his consequent tendency to define a wide range of traditional human activity as demonic.[20]

Jeffrey Russell also believed in the reality of the demonic cult. Witchcraft had to be taken seriously by the church because witches worshipped the power of evil. It was a heresy which emerged from Christianity and became its antithesis. In a society in which the spiritual world was real, frustration, alienation, discontent and hostility were invariably expressed in religious terms. Witchcraft was therefore the ultimate expression of social discontent. The witch was the complete rebel. Witches deliberately inverted Christianity as a dramatic repudiation of society. To escape dissonance and despair these rebels accepted a new symbolic order. In rejecting God they found their identity in the Devil.[21]

To those scholars who rejected the objective existence of diabolic cults it was the establishment who inverted Christian values and projected them onto a range of deviant and dissenting groups. Whatever the actual behaviour of these minorities they were depicted as inverting Christian principles and practices and therefore diabolic. This creates a major difficulty in affirming the existence or not of real diabolists. Inversion applied in general and with specifics. The Christian Mass involved bread and wine; the witches' ritual used excrement and urine. In fruit growing areas a major disaster was the hailstorm. Diabolic evil in those regions consisted of provoking such storms. Inversion had a long pedagogic tradition and cosmic purpose. Good could not be taught by comparison with absolute good. Man would always fall short of such impossible ideals and become disillusioned. Society could only be instructed comfortably and with a reasonable chance of success by comparing itself with absolute evil; that is with the direct inversion of the dominant values of society. The witch personified these inverted values and her existence and persecution affirmed and strengthened the basic mores of society.[22]

Norman Cohn argued that the phenomenon was more complex. The witch cult was a delusion, a complex reflection of the darker and baser emotions of mankind reacting against the austerity of Christianity. It was a collective fantasy that became part of the individual psyche. Tension between conscious beliefs and rational ideals on the one hand and unconscious desires and resentments on the other was found an outlet in an obsession with Satan and with the creation of a group of licentious apostates. Society created a mythical group which did horrendous deeds and in turn excited, indeed projected, the lascivious subconscious which it could then punish in conformity with its conscious rules and requirements. This witch fantasy satisfied the deep stirrings of natural man and the necessary reinforcement of ordered austere mores. The legend of the wild man who lived as beast relying on instinct and passion reflected a similar need.

Others saw witchcraft not as a manifestation of the Christian Devil but as a reflection of a long-established paganism.

Notes

1. Four sources basic to the medieval developments are Jeffrey Burton Russell, *Witchcraft in the Middle Ages*. Russell believed that heresy made the major contribution and that many of the aspects were objectively real; E. Peters, *The Magician, the Witch and the Law*. Peters plays down the role of heresy and plays up the contribution of the high magician; Norman Cohn, *Europe's Inner Demons*, in which he contends that magicians played an important role but that the development was fantasy; R. Kieckhefer, *European Witch Trials: Their Foundations in Popular and Learned Culture* — apart from the argument Kieckhefer lists the actual trials conducted during the period; for a quick reference to the issues raised concerning the diabolic cult, although his interpretation is strongly anti-church, see Rossell Hope Robbins, *The Encyclopedia of Witchcraft and Demonology*. An excellent survey of medieval heresy which provides a salutory balance to the above (witchcraft and sorcery receive only two references in the index) is Malcolm Lambert, *Medieval Heresy: Popular Movements from Bogomil to Hus*.

2. Gordon Leff, 'Heresy and the Decline of the Medieval Church', *Past and Present* 20 (1961) pp. 36 – 51; Robert E. Lerner, 'The Black Death and Western European Eschatological Mentalities', *American Historical Review* 86 (1981) pp. 533 – 52; Russell, *op.cit.* p. 234; Monter, *Witchcraft in France and Switzerland* pp. 22 – 3.

3. Peter Brown, 'Sorcery, Demons, and the Rise of Christianity from late Antiquity into the Middle Ages' in M. Douglas (ed.) *Witchcraft Confessions and Accusations* pp. 17 – 46; C. A. Patrides, 'The Salvation of Satan', *Journal of the History of Ideas* 28 (1967) pp. 467 – 79.

4. Peters, *op.cit.* pp. 40 – 5, 92 – 5.

5. *Ibid.*

6. Russell, *op.cit.* pp. 193 – 8; Cohn, *op.cit.* p. 74; Peters, *op.cit.* p. 94.

7. David Nichols, 'The Devil in Renaissance France', *History Today* 30 (Nov. 1980) pp. 25 – 30.

8. Russell, *op.cit.* pp. 238, 249; Larner, *Enemies of God* p. 172; Gustav Henningsen *The Witches' Advocate* p. 11; Thomas, *Religion and the Decline of*

Magic p. 533, Roger Baker, *Binding the Devil: Exorcism Past and Present* p. 75.

9. Hughes, *Witchcraft* pp. 99–101; for Weyer see Christopher Baxter, 'Johann Weyer's *De Praestigiis Daemonum*: Unsystematic Psychopathology' in Anglo; Sydney Anglo (ed.) *The Damned Art: Essays in the Literature of Witchcraft* pp. 53–75.

10. Henningsen, *op.cit.* p. 4; E. Brouette, 'The Sixteenth Century and Satanism', in C. Moeller (intr.) *Satan* p. 310; Paul Bernard, 'Heresy in Fourteenth Century Austria', *Medievalia et Humanista* 10 (1956) pp. 50–63; Cohn, *op.cit.* pp. 56–9; Robert E. Lerner, *The Heresy of the Free Spirit in the Later Middle Ages*; Russell, *op.cit.* pp. 17, 130, 160–3, 178–9, 153–4; Thomas, *op.cit.* pp. 614, 528; Baroja, *The World of the Witches* pp. 74–5, 88, 122; Larner, *op.cit*, p. 152; Russell argues for a considerable degree of devil worship but Bernard, Lerner and Cohn disagree.

11. Anita Gregory, Introduction to T. K. Oesterreich, *Possession Demoniacal and Other Among Primitive Races in Antiquity, the Middle Ages and Modern Times* p. x; Baker, *op.cit.* p. 70; R. E. L. Masters, *Eros and Evil: The Sexual Psychopathology of Witchcraft* Ch. 12. 'Devils in the Convents', pp. 104–10.

12. Baker, *ibid.* p. 76; I. M. Lewis, 'Spirit Possession and Deprivation Cults', *Man* 1 (1966) pp. 307–29; P. J. Wilson, 'Status Ambiguity and Spirit Possession', *Man* 2 (1967) pp. 366–78.

13. Monter, *op.cit.* pp. 71–2.

14. F. X. Maquart, 'Exorcism and Diabolical Manifestation', in C. Moeller, *loc.cit.* p. 180; Baker, *op.cit.* pp. 80–2.

15. Nichols, *loc.cit.* pp. 28–9.

16. Master, *op.cit.* p. 86; Hughes, *op.cit.* pp. 89–92, 116–26; Baroja, *op.cit.* p. 174; Thomas, *op.cit.* pp. 616–27; Cohn, *op.cit.* p. 11.

17. Midelfort, *op.cit.* p. 106; Henningsen, *op.cit.* p. 627; Larner, *op.cit.* pp. 153, 155, 169, 200.

18. Hughes, *op.cit.* pp. 129–30.

19. Montague Summers, *The History of Witchcraft and Demonology* pp. 4, 8, 13.

20. Montague Summers, *Witchcraft and Black Magic* pp. 19–20; see also his *The History of Witchcraft and Demonology* pp. xiv–xv, and *The Geography of Witchcraft*; for criticism of the Summers position see Henningsen *op.cit.* p. 3 and N. Cohn *Europe's Inner Demons* pp. 121–2.

21. Jeffrey Burton Russell, *Witchcraft in the Middle Ages* pp. 29, 266–7, 19, 278–9.

22. For inversion see Peter Burke in Anglo *op.cit.* pp. 29–40; E. William Monter, *Witchcraft in France and Switzerland* p. 170; Baroja *op.cit.* p. 170; Henningsen *op.cit.* p. 74; Larner, *op.cit.* pp. 134ff.

23. N. Cohn *op.cit.* pp. 262–3; Richard Bernheimer, *Wild Men in the Middle Ages: A Study in Art, Sentiment and Demonology*.

5

Paganism and Popular Religion

Margaret Murray equated witchcraft neither with magic nor heresy but with a pre-Christian fertility cult which originated among the hunting and pastoral peoples of Western Europe. She traced the worship of the horned god from its palaeolithic origins to its confusion with the two-faced Janus or Dianus. In medieval England the great mass of the people and many of their monarchs, she alleged, followed this god and it was not until the Reformation that Christianity dominated. Michael Harrison recently reframed the Murray thesis. He described how religious beliefs developed through animism and shamanism to that of a phallic cult in which the tumescent phallus was identified with divine revelation. This concept was modified when the role of female fertility was recognised. The newly recognised dual origins of life found their logical compromise in a hermaphrodite deity Diana/Dianus. This phallic–fertility cult acknowledged a supreme deity, believed in the immortality and transmigration of the soul, and practised magic with especial emphasis on the prediction of the future. With the coming of Christianity the cult absorbed Christ, the rural shepherd, into its orbit.

The Christian consensus soon split into three conflicting sects. Urbanisation, wealth and influence led Roman Christianity to depict God as the political overlord of the universe. A darker side of Christianity, diabolism, emerged and separated. God was both a giver and taker, creator and destroyer, but these destructive and negative aspects of the one deity were more easily envisaged as two separate gods. Some cultists recognised this dualism and accepted the dominance of the evil deity, whom they served through an obsession with death by providing clients with poisons and destructive spells to hinder and harm their rivals. By the fifth century the old fertility cult which had absorbed many Christian attributes competed with Roman Christianity and diabolism for popular acceptance.[1]

In Britain the fertility cult won. English paganism was so strong that Christian chroniclers did not refer to it, refusing to recognise its strength. English monarchs after the Norman Conquest were themselves leaders of a cult coven and were sacrificed personally, or through surrogates. Under royal patronage the Old Religion developed unchecked by Rome. Churches displayed scarcely concealed fertility and phallic symbols and the clergy were in reality devotees of Janus. Rome could not act because the Papacy had its hands full elsewhere. The Empire challenged its temporal power, Islam was a major threat to its survival in the Mediterranean, and the Normans in southern Italy threatened the political independence of the papal states. The Crusades against Islam led to further problems and fed into Western Europe new ideological forces that threatened to undermine the church's position. The Cathars and the Templars became powerful. Finally the church found an answer. It unleashed a new weapon — the Dominicans. The witches in France deserved their fate at the hands of these mendicant shock troops. Their simple fertility faith had been corrupted by dualist ideas imported from the East through warfare, trade and urbanisation. Diabolism re-emerged and dominated the cult in southern France. Despite the Dominican and diabolic assault on traditional witchcraft — that is, the old fertility religion — it recovered its appeal when the church failed to cope with the immediate aftermath of the Black Death. Nevertheless, this recovery was short-lived. Within a century the Dominicans, through popular preaching and learned treatises culminating in the *Malleus* and by the efficient use of inquisitorial methods, discredited the re-emerging pagan witchcraft by equating it with diabolism. In part the Dominicans were right. Some leaders betrayed the fertility cult and became diabolists leaving the true believers unprotected with little but their faith. In a mood of quiet resignation these Dianic witches went to the stake as martyrs praying in the language of the cult, which Harrison identified as a variant of Basque. There is little evidence to support this selective thesis.[2]

Pennethorne Hughes also accepted the existence of the Old Religion although his history of its medieval development differed from Harrison's. By then it had lost many of its pristine beliefs and faced a powerful Christianity dominant in the cities and centres of power. Even in the countryside the populace was ambivalent and uncritically accepted either or both religions as the circumstances dictated. In its thirteenth-century degenerate form the cult was a mixture of phallic Druidism, Mediterranean ritual, Scandinavian magic and Christian parody. It was composed of fairies, feminists, Eastern dualists and those with personal and political interests in the survival of the cult.[3]

These interpretations of witchcraft as the remnant of a specific pagan fertility cult were effectively destroyed by Elliot Rose in his analysis of the Murray thesis. Rose limited his assault to medieval Latin Christendom and focused on whether witchcraft was essentially Dianic or diabolic. The evidence on which Murray based her argument was manufactured centuries later and was essentially trial material, and tracts and treatises, themselves offshoots of hysterical and neurotic behaviour. This was stimulated by the laity and have-not clergy misinformed through the spread of printing. Behind these developments was the anti-witch lobby within the church that had finally achieved dominance and through works such as the *Malleus* had imposed a uniformity and behaviour pattern on its opponents that did not exist in reality. This faulty early modern material was projected into the past and indiscriminately used by later historians. Earlier evidence does exist but it concerns sorcery, the evil eye and diabolic possession. None of these relate to organised fertility cults. Evidence of a pagan cult was the most recent, hopelessly confused, and confusing. The picture became 'explicit and detailed only as culprits, witnesses and the judges themselves learned with the increasing volume of trials, sermons and pamphlets, what kind of crime they were expected to confess, reveal or unmask'. The judicial process of the sixteenth century now stimulated latent superstition and fixed in the popular mind the picture of the witch as a member of a cult.[4]

Rose found little evidence one way or the other to show whether the object of veneration within the cult was Satan or Dianus but he demolished many of the props on which the Murray argument rested. There was no link between earlier fertility cults and British druidism. There was no Dianus cult in the Celtic provinces of the Roman Empire. There was no link between pre-Roman paganism and that of Scandinavia. Nordic paganism had no impact on English beliefs and human sacrifice was not part of this paganism. England was Christian. Although the populace was ignorant of much of Christianity and retained many customary beliefs woven

68

into a Christian framework, they had long forgotten the paganism of their ancestors. Picts, dwarves and fairies could not be equated. Fairies, traditionally with no religion, could not be adherents of Dianus. The English aristocracy were not crypto-pagans although many of them indulged in activies frowned upon by the church. The Christian church, through its missionary activity and the role played by clergy in the legal and social structure of Anglo-Saxon England, was extremely powerful. Monastic chroniclers attacked delinquent monarchs and subjects alike.

They did not attack the old Religion simply because it did not exist. The cases used by Murray to prove the existence of a pagan cult were dissected and dismissed. In Inverkeithing the phallic activities of the parish priest and the young girls of the parish, if they were anything more than an oversexed cleric enjoying himself, substantiate only the survival of dance rituals and not the existence of a pagan cult. The Bishop of Coventry and Alice Kyteler were defamed in the course of political and financial battles between powerful Irish factions, and the foundation of the Order of the Garter resulted after all from an act of chivalry and not from a reprimand hastily contrived by the leader of the coven. To consider Thomas à Beckett as a surrogate sacrifice for Henry II was historically naïve. These men were bitter enemies and given Plantagenet family relations one of Henry's sons would have been a more obvious and acceptable choice. This theory of royal sacrifice was nonsense from beginning to end — the thesis made no sense, the mathematics were incorrect and the evidence did not exist.[5]

Murray made much of the Canon Episcopi dating from around 900 AD, and its reference to women riding out at night on beasts with the Goddess Diana. The Canon argued that this was a delusion that Christians must not accept. Murray accepted it as proof of a Dianic cult. Rose interpreted it as an attack on the inadequate Christianity of the populace and not as a warning against rampaging paganism. Murray's thesis was weak. The links between women riding out on beasts at night with Diana, a fertility cult and the later image of the witch were too tenuous to hold together. Stories did become confused over centuries of telling and a picture that might approximate to a witches' sabbat could have developed from these composite sources. Yet such sources would only support the existence of a fertility cult according to Rose if they referred to Herodias and not to Diana. In all, the Canon was poor evidence for the survival of a Dianic cult and especially of one devoted to fertility. Rose raised two further objections. In the eleventh century, according to Murray, there was a fertility cult worshipping a female deity. In the sixteenth century there was a cult which showed no evidence of promoting fertility and it worshipped a male god. Surely the latter could not be a descendant of the former. To Rose, witchcraft *was* a cult but a drug-induced Dionysian cult in which frenzied dancing and phallic orgies produced an ecstasy in which direct communion with the Divine was achieved. Such a cult had no need of magic, dogma or deity. Divinity was immanent in the ecstasy itself. This, in time, became temporarily manifest in the leader of the dance. With this diverse ritual leadership there was no regional let alone international cult but a variety of independent local groups seeking psychic release. The individual was abandoned to something greater than self. Eliade argued that similar but sex-induced ecstatic groups existed in Roumania. In this ecstatic state critical faculties were numbed and the unconscious accepted a range of images that transported it to the limits of human awareness. In a highly suggestible state the participant felt divinely inspired or conversely paralysed and inhibited. This intense emotional release was followed by inner contentment.[6]

Harrison and Hughes believed that witchcraft was a fertility cult — the Old Religion — but both admitted that a diabolic aspect came to the fore in the later Middle Ages. Rose agreed. Up to 1215 witchcraft was for him decentralised groups of ecstatic release cults. The satanic element was introduced by the educated goliard — the wandering scholar. Hundreds of unemployed, over-educated minor clergy frustrated and angry about their situation, parodied the newly formed mendicant orders. Idle, often immoral, and fed up with the pretensions of the hierarchy who spurned them, the goliards evolved their own structured order. This unofficial order, begun as casual buffoonery, developed into a well-organised secret society of embittered forced drop-outs. Cells of thirteen were set up and the members parodied not only mendicant organisation but Catholic ritual. Satan, a popular character in medieval morality plays, became the focus of goliard attention. These spoiled clergy already linked with each other found themselves by virtue of their education welcomed in the rural villages in which they were forced to move to eke out a living. They were welcomed by local dance leaders who impressed by their superior knowledge gave way to them as leaders of the group. Independent ecstatic groups were linked by the pre-existing goliard structure into an organised cult — a cult in which Satan played a significant role. This organisation did not last for long and although some groups retained their framework during the course of the next century or two, most degenerated into simple orgiastic sects or others disappeared altogether. The Black Death, in which the clergy suffered disproportionately, created employment for the would-be leaders of such subversive societies. However, the heightened religious feelings of the next century, intensified even further by the Reformation and Counter Reformation, gave some local groups a new lease of life.[7]

There was no Christendom or even a nationwide witch organisation. At times there may have been regional groups of cultists and there were certainly local sects of an organised and secretive nature. In the sixteenth century some of these groups may have worshipped Satan. It is also clear that many other groups followed age-old traditions that included not only remnants of paganism but accretions from earlier partly understood Christianity. Most clearly of all, these groups had a magical view of the universe, an animist view that fitted uneasily with establishment Christianity.

Witchcraft was not a pagan cult. To many who accepted witchcraft as objectively real it was an aspect of popular religion. Christianity was still a veneer over the basic animist mentality of the peasant and the first attempt to remove such a mentality had to await the Reformation and Counter Reformation. Animists accepted that all objects contained matter and spirit and that whim and emotion rather than law and reason governed the universe. The animist mind did not distinguish between image and model, visible and invisible, or part and whole. Consequently the world could be manipulated by the concepts of contact, similarity and contrast. Contact included direct physical touching and indirect contact through eating herbs on which the shadow of the relevant person had fallen, the wearing of talismans, the evil eye, and the consumption of parts of, and waste from, the body. The human body and its waste material was held in special awe. Similarity was an endemic concept in peasant thinking. Men could be made impotent by tying knots in a shoe lace. Rain would fall if a still pond was stirred vigorously. Contrasts, the concept of antipathy, enabled people to take counter-measures. Evil could be neutralised by evil. The mechanics of this magic depended on correct procedures. Words had powers of their own and without the correct incantations rites would be useless. Christianity camouflaged this mentality. The Christian message was processed through an animist frame of reference creating a Christian folk religion significantly different from the faith espoused by theologians. With peasants continually on the edge of survival this animist folk 'Christianity' was primarily designed to bring plenty, fend off illness and postpone death. Parallel with the visible world there was an invisible world of anthromorphic figures. They intervened in the real world to help or hinder mankind. Saints or demons, the occult powers for good and evil, were equally part of this system which made the diabolic witchcraft of the establishment so plausible and believable.[8]

This folk religion developed its idiosyncracies through the failure of the church to meet basic religious needs in an immediate sense through the absence and incompetence of the parish priest. Spiritual and doctrinal guidance through learned preaching, catechisms and the sacraments did not exist for the vast majority of European peasants. The populace adapted older, more primitive remedies to fill the gaps in Christian instruction. The wives of sailors and fishermen swept the local churches, gathered up the dust and threw it into the air to procure favourable winds for their husbands. Others took the statues of saints and threatened them if their requests were not fulfilled. These peasant women acted aggressively. Several statues were whipped or thrown into the sea when the saints failed to deliver. All containers of water were emptied in houses in which someone had died for fear that the departing soul might slip into the water and drown. Praying to the new moon, making offerings to springs and wells and providing extra seats around the fire on the eve of St John the Baptist for dead relatives to rejoin the family circle were all aspects of early-seventeenth popular Breton 'Christianity'. The origins of such beliefs and responses lay deep in a pagan past.[9]

In Lorraine a dislocated hip was to be cured by filling the breeches of the patient with the manure from nine stables and hanging them in the church. A saint was expected to cure another patient when he was presented with a stocking containing five eggs (the bribe) and three handfuls of horse dung (representing the sickness). Pagan concepts were also seen in the attitudes to suicide. Bodies were not allowed to be carried out over the threshold. If they were these unhappy souls would find their way back and haunt the inhabitants. It was necessary to throw the body out of the window.[10]

It was not only a question of the peasantry filling the gaps in Christian instruction with pagan practices. Their basic animist mentality actually modified the major Christian festivals and tenets. Delumeau concluded that such a development led to 'a relapse into paganism'. At the feast of St John the Baptist fires were lit to ward off evil spirits and in Paris cats (agents of evil) were burnt alive. At Metz, it was a custom to bathe before the dawn of this same feast day and immunity from the fever would be achieved for one year. An aspect that brings the world of popular 'Christian' religion close to that of witchcraft was the concept of the maleficient saint. Saints were seen as jealous, often spiteful persons who if displeased could cause illness even death. The Virgin herself was not above such unfriendly behaviour.[11]

Some local clergy found it expedient well into the seventeenth century to pander to such popular expectations. Processing around fields to ensure fertility and carrying the host through vineyards to deter destructive insects were common occurrences. The peasants were not simpletons. This supernatural assistance was for a specific purpose in exceptional circumstances, usually in times of crisis when all else had failed. The basic attitude to agriculture was well expressed by the Italian peasant Niccolo Pellizzaro in 1595. He declaimed that 'the benedictions which priests pronounce over fields, and the holy water which they sprinkle over them . . . in no way help the vines and trees to bear fruit; only dung and the industry of man do that'. The *Parlement* of Paris granted permission for the relics of St Geneviève and St Marcellus to be paraded around Paris in 1605, 1611, 1615 and 1654 to encourage rain and in 1625 and 1675 to stop it. The Bishop of Geneva exorcised a glacier for the inhabitants of Chamonix. After this episcopal intervention the dangerous glacier began to retreat.[12]

Such clergy were becoming rare. The godly, Catholic and Protestant, had begun a campaign to destroy popular culture and with it these pagan aspects of popular religion. This process of reform was begun prior to the Reformation but gained increasing impetus in the latter quarter of the sixteenth and first half of the seventeenth century. It was systematic and persistent. Popular culture was attacked because it was pagan and immoral. Miracle and mystery plays, popular sermons and religious festivals were aspects of folk religion to be abolished, usually by Protestants, or seriously modified by Catholics. Religious drama contained too much that was unacceptable. It encouraged confusion between the sacred and the profane and a familiarity between peasant and God that was blasphemous. Paris banned them in 1548 but they were allowed to reappear in 1574 and 1577. They ceased in Florence in the 1540s and in Milan in the 1560s. They were abolished in the Spanish Netherlands in 1601 because they depraved and corrupted the morals of the populace. St Carlo Borromeo, Archbishop of Milan, banned all theatre. The Devil was the master of illusion and theatre was illusion. Religious festivals were either abolished or reformed by depicting them as pagan remnants. The Carnivale was a Bacchanalia, Twelfth Night the Feast of Phoebus, and the May games the Feast of Flora. The pagan goddesses involved were known to be demons. Such activity, although indirect, was nevertheless worship of the Devil. The simple method of the reformer was to paganise folk religion and then demonise the pagan.[13]

Boy bishops and Abbots of Misrule were abolished. They blasphemed God and his episcopal and abbatical servants. Popular initiation rites using water were banned as this mocked the sacrament of baptism. The Charavari was forbidden as this was a mockery of marriage. Popular sermons had to conform to a rigorous code. The sermons must not play on the emotions. To cause crying or laughter was anathema. The preacher must refrain from colloquial terms, coarse words, gesticulation and the telling of stories for entertainment. The continuation of such practices could lead to accusations of witchcraft. The many clergy who found themselves in such a position were largely the rural parish priests and the urban friars. Popular culture was also attacked because it encouraged immorality, created occasions for violence (football) and wasted time and money (taverns). The extent to which the assault on popular culture concentrated on religious aspects, for example, in an attack on witchcraft or on excessive drinking or excess holidays depended on the priorities of the godly and their influence with the political establishment. The different regional levels of witch hunting reflected the varied importance of witches within the broad spectrum of the popular culture that provoked reform.[14]

The process by which aspects of popular culture which drew from a pagan past were redefined by the authorities as diabolic and subsequently destroyed was illustrated in the case of the benandanti of the Friuli region of Italy. The case of the *benandanti* highlighted the inability, or deliberate refusal, of the elite to understand the peasant mind.

Carlo Ginzburg's thesis on the *benandanti* was misinterpreted by Russell and Midelfort as giving support to the Murray thesis. Murray argued that sabbats were objectively real and that these were meetings of a fertility cult. The *benandanti* did not actually go to the sabbat bodily but they were vitally concerned with fertility. Their activities are described by a confessed member, Battista Moduco:

> I am a benandante because I go with the others to fight four times a year . . . I go invisibly in spirit and the body remains behind; we go forth in the service of Christ, and the witches of the devil, we fight each other, we with bundles of fennel and they with sorghum stalks . . . we fight over the wheat and all the other grains, another time over the livestock, and at other times over the vineyards . . . and for those things won by the benandante that year there is abundance.

The vital point was that peasants believed that what the spirit (soul) did when it left the body was real. The *benandanti* knew their fight with the evil witches was real even though they attended in spirit only. The soul itself was real and often took the form of an animal, usually a mouse, when it left the body. It had to return to the body by dawn or the person would die and the soul become lost. This peasants' view of the reality of the 'dream world' was understood by many fifteenth-century 'witch hunters' such as Alfonso Tostado but was academically unacceptable to most later investigators. What the fifteenth-century elite was content to discard as diabolic illusion the sixteenth and seventeenth accepted as objective reality.[15]

The *benandanti* raised the question of the relationship of Christian and pagan ideas. When asked why they fought the witches they claimed that they did so for the Christian faith and the fertility of their fields. This answer probably reflected a genuine syncretism rather than an attempt to protect themselves from ecclesiastical investigation. Ginzburg isolated three sets of ideas within the group: Christian, fertility, and aspects capable of being related to witchcraft. He argued that the inquisitors rejected the Christian nature of the cult, could not understand the agrarian fertility elements and therefore concentrated on the other aspects as they 'uncovered' what they knew they would find, a diabolic cult of witches.

The *benandanti*, drawn from those villagers born with the caul, were only active between maturity, sometime in their twenties, to their mid-forties. In addition to their nocturnal spiritual battles with the evil witches they were also healers, and the women communicated with the dead. Their healing role was concentrated on diseases of children. The speciality of the witches of Friuli was to bewitch children and as a result they wasted away. Florida Basili in 1599 proclaimed that 'if it wasn't for us benandanti witches would devour children even in their cradles'. Women *benandanti* believed that when they went into a trance they processed with the dead, with those that had died before their time. This concept of the wandering dead, or 'the furious hordes' was a long-established pagan tradition which the Canon Episcopi had highlighted centuries earlier. It was a tradition strongly entrenched in the Rhineland, Alps and northern Italy. Nider (1380–1438) attacked the belief, which he explained as a diabolic illusion but associated with the pagan goddesses Diana, Herodias and Venus, of women who 'during Ember days, out of their senses, boasted of having seen the souls in purgatory and many other fantasies'.[16]

There was a well-established tradition across this region of Europe which clearly separated the night walkers from diabolical witchcraft. A Court chaplain in 1475 in the Upper Palatinate wrote of a dangerous sect of sabbat attending diabolical witches and of another very different cult of women who travelled during the Ember days, provoking storms and casting non-fatal spells. The confession of a 37-year-old Bavarian peasant indicated that three groups of people were believed to have the ability to travel at night by supernatural means: witches attending the sabbat, the lost souls of the dead, and certain women during Ember days. The Swabian eccentrics, the *clerici vagantes*, in the mid-sixteenth century claimed to visit Venusberg, the world of the dead, and offered to call up the aid of the wandering dead to assist in the fight against the Devil. The dead needed to be controlled by such people because left to their own devices they could be destructive. An Italian woman confessed to the Inquisition in Modena in 1601, 'I do believe and consider true that when someone dies before his appointed time on earth, he is compelled to wander, inclined to do evil and remains lost until he reaches the appointed day'.[17]

If inquisitors wanted to discover diabolical witchcraft in such attitudes it was not difficult. The alleged ability of the *benandanti* to recognise witches made it easier. Initially, the *benandanti* refused to name their opponents claiming an agreement between both sides to keep the conflict in the spiritual world — an attitude essential if village harmony was to be maintained. Pressure from the authorities and perhaps changing perceptions by those claiming to be *benandanti* gradually reversed the situation and in the end brought the cult into disrepute and tarred it with the brush of its traditional opponents. Distressed villagers now called in *benandanti* such as Girolama Cuechuil to name the witch afflicting a sick relative. On one occasion he accused the sick woman's daughter-in-law's mother, explaining that with the patient dead the witch's daughter would become mistress of the house. Not only was Cuechuil beaten by the male relatives of those involved but the local cleric denounced him to the Inquisition:

> I accuse . . . my parishoner, as one who publicly professes to be able to identify the bewitched and heal them, to know who are witches and even their names, without ever having seen them. And he spreads this around with the danger that the relatives of the victims might try to kill a person who may well be innocent. And he has done this time and again in many places.

In time, *benandanti* such as Cuechuil under inquisitorial pressure confessed to participation in a diabolical cult. The *benandanti* fighters for Christ and fertility had within a century been successfully categorised by the Inquisition as their own opponents — witches of the Devil.[18]

In summary, witchcraft was not the fertility cult of Dianus. Many groups accused of witchcraft may have been small cults retaining some pagan attributes. More importantly, the ingredients for the elitist concept of witchcraft were inherent in the popular religion of their day. Animist ideas not only filled the gaps in the Christian message itself. The campaign against witchcraft was but part of the general assault by the godly against most elements of popular culture. To redefine the pagan aspects of society as diabolical was an effective method to achieve their end. The case of the *benandanti* revealed the entrenched position of key 'pagan' concepts in the peasant mind and in his very concept of reality which the elite through such a process was able to destroy.

The belief in an international witch cult of horrendous design and immense proportions was a fantasy. However, there were groups in a society of only partially Christianised peasants who provided some real fire beneath the inquisitorial smoke. There were cults which ranged from devil-worship, through a range of pagan responses to sexual, dream and drug cults, and others of deviant or dissenting moral and political minorities. Together they sought either to escape the world or to enjoy it. A major ingredient in this process was sex and major participants in such organisations were allegedly women.

Notes

1. Margaret Murray, *The Witch Cult in Western Europe*; and her *The God of the Witches*; Michael Harrison, *The Roots of Witchcraft* pp. 9, 43, 58, 64, 69, 95–108.

2. Harrison *op.cit.* p. 209; see Margaret Murray *The Divine King in England*; Harrison *op.cit.* pp. 281–9, 225, 235, 260–1, 147–73.

3. Pennethorne Hughes, *Witchcraft* pp. 72–3, 86.

4. Elliot Rose, *A Razor for a Goat* pp. 25–32, 34–5.

5. *Ibid.* pp. 40–79.

6. *Ibid.* pp. 108–16, 131, 141–8; Baroja *op.cit.* p. 217; Russell *op.cit.* p. 277; Eliade *op.cit.* p. 65; John Allegro, *Lost Gods* pp. 41–55.

7. Rose *op.cit.* pp. 154–70.

8. Jean Delumeau, *Catholicism between Luther and Voltaire: A New View of the Counter Reformation* pp. 161–9; Nichols *op.cit.* p. 25; Larner *op.cit.* p. 57.

9. Delumeau *op.cit.* p. 162.

10. *Ibid.* p. 163.

11. *Ibid.* p. 166–8.

12. *Ibid.* p. 169; Carlo Ginzburg (trans. J. and A. Tedeschi) *The Night Battles: Witchcraft and Agrarian Cults in the Sixteenth and Seventeenth Centuries* p.23.

13. Peter Burke, *Popular Culture in Early Modern Europe*, especially Ch. 8 'The Triumph of Lent: the Reform of Popular Culture' pp. 209–10.

14. *Ibid.* pp. 210, 212–13.

15. Ginzburg *op.cit.* pp. xii–iv, 4, 16.

16. *Ibid.* pp. 25–6, 64. 42–3.

17. *Ibid.* pp. 52, 55, 60.

18. *Ibid.* pp. 92–5.

6

Gender, Sex and Misogyny: I

Four-fifths of those prosecuted for witchcraft were women and a considerable proportion of their alleged activities were sexual. Both the gender bias and sexual emphasis have been seen by some historians as accidental by-products of economic and social conditions. Others found the explanation for these, and the key for understanding the nature of witchcraft itself lay in aspects of gender conflict and sexual obsession.

Gender bias existed. The total number of women persecuted as witches will never be known but the ridiculous claim that nine million persons, mostly women, were slaughtered as such, and that male society deliberately concealed the truth, can be dismissed on both counts. Only a minority of reputed witches were formally tried but few of those informally persecuted were killed. At the most, 200,000 people died in Western Europe between 1450 and 1700 as a result of formal investigations, and one-fifth of these were men. On this basis, two women were executed each day over that period somewhere in Western Europe for the crime of witchcraft. In a century and a half of the most intense period of witch-hunting Scotland tried 1500 women, the Jura jurisdictions 1370, the principalities of south-western Germany 1050, the Venetian Inquisition 430, the English Home Circuit 406 and the Castilian Inquisition 324. On an average, nine women were tried each year in each of Scotland, the Jura and south-west Germany but in most other jurisdictions between one and three women appeared before the courts. Assuming half of those tried were executed, four or five women died each year for witchcraft in the three areas named and in the others from none to one. Such averages have limited value and provide only a broad sketch that can look very different when more specific statistics are examined. The average of nine women charged each year in Scotland becomes meaningless when 212 women were tried in the two-year period 1649–50, 149 in 1658–59, and 326 in 1661–62. Total numbers are an insecure foundation on which to base conclusions.[1]

The proportion of women among those tried is a much more reliable statistic although it varied over space and time. In Essex and the Spanish Netherlands county of Namur 92 per cent of those formally accused were women. The English Home Circuit 89 per cent, Scotland 86 per cent, south-west Germany 83 per cent, the southern Spanish Netherlands (later the French Département du Nord) 81 per cent, the Swiss canton of Solothurn 81 per cent, the New England colonies 80 per cent, the Venetian Inquisition 78 per cent, the jurisdictions of the Jura 78 per cent, and the Castilian Inquisition 71 per cent indicate the range. These generalised regional figures conceal further variation. Trials were conducted by specific jurisdictions, large and small. In the Jura region the proportion of women accused ranged from the diocese of Basle (95 per cent), through Geneva (76 per cent) and the Franche Comte (76 per cent), to Fribourg (64 per cent) and the Pays de Vaud (58 per cent). In New England, Massachusetts, 83 per cent, and Connecticut, 76 per cent, reflected less marked variations.[2]

The proportion of women tried also varied over time. In the Nord between 1451 and 1500 91 per cent were women, between 1501 and 1550 only 70 per cent. In New England a decade-by-decade summation revealed a much higher proportion of women in the last three decades of the seventeenth century — 90 per cent in the Seventies, 95 per cent in the Eighties and 91 per cent (excluding Salem) in the Nineties. In the earlier decades, the Forties, Fifties and Sixties, the proportions were 67, 80 and 65 per cent. In Scotland, decadal differences were marked. The 1680s, 96 per cent, and the 1660s, 93 per cent, were at one extreme; the 1590s, 78 per cent, the 1690s, 75 per cent, the 1610s, 75 per cent, and the first decade of that century, 64 per cent, at the other.[3]

Division by decade was not necessarily a useful analytical device. The proportion of women accused in Scotland changed according to the panic nature or otherwise of the investigation. In most panic years the percentage of women rose — 1658–9 (95 per cent), 1661–2 (93 per cent) — compared with the non-panic, 1652–7 (64 per cent). In south-west Germany the difference between panic and non-panic years was also evident but in the opposite direction. There the proportion of women dropped during panic periods. In Scotland there was a limited number of male healers who had built up an evil reputation. Reputation was a key factor and it took years to develop. When the number of witches had to be expanded rapidly the accusation of the familiar female stereotype was more plausible and convincing. In the more urbanised and smaller jurisdictions of the German south-west, the use of torture to obtain from the female witch the names of the accomplices who attended the sabbat with her destroyed the gender bias. The normal stereotype of the old woman collapsed as the shape of the next witch was determined by the imagination, spite and terror of the victims, often strongly influenced by the financial greed and political ambition of the magistrates. With more wealthy and powerful male opponents of these prosecutors indicted, the percentage of women among the accused dropped. The English situation in which the proportion of women among the accused remained high provided support for these explanations of male increase. The key factors present in Germany and Scotland were missing. There were few multiple trials or panic situations. The sabbat was hardly mentioned. Torture was illegal. The attempt by judicial authorities to implicate others was rare and consequently the trial of an individual female witch rarely escalated into an investigation of her male kin and friends. In addition the English magistrates, unlike the Scots, ignored the male cunningman as a potential witch. Therefore the supply of male suspects remained low and the proportion of women unusually high.[4]

This was not the case in the New England colonies where males were deemed guilty through their association with suspect women. Half of the men tried for witchcraft were secondary targets as husbands or associates of a female witch, the major subject of the investigations. In trying to effectively assess gender bias these males should be discounted. The proportion of women singled out for trial as prime suspects in the New England colonies would then be similar to that for the old country, nearer 90 rather than 80 per cent. This suggests that the gender bias against women may be greater in other jurisdictions than the raw figures indicate. Whatever the variations, women were normally four times — and in England, Basle and possibly New England nine times — more likely to be formally charged with witchcraft than men.[5]

Gender and sex may have had little to do with this preponderance of women among the accused. The bias may have been an accidental result of the interplay of quite different factors. Nevertheless, the conviction that gender and/or sex were basic not only to the apparent bias in prosecution but to the witch phenomenon itself was deeply held by the protagonists of four very different interpretations. To the first the phenomenon and bias arose directly from the misogynistic fantasies of males; to the second it stemmed from the desperation of powerless men confronted by forceful women; to the third it developed from a conflict which only involved women seeking domestic power and therefore most of the casualties were of necessity female; to the fourth it reflected the actual dominance of women in allegedly subversive movements, correctly or incorrectly labelled as diabolic cults.

In part, at least, witchcraft was a 'uniquely lethal form of Western misogyny'. Misogyny is the dislike and fear of women, the belief that they are inferior and the conviction that they must be controlled by men. A constant medieval theme was that the great men of history — Adam, David, Solomon and Samson — were ruined by women. Clerical misogynists argued that the fondling of women destroyed the mind. To love any woman too passionately, too physically, including a wife, was adultery — a view reasserted recently by Pope John Paul II. The basic principles with regard to women were to avoid them and to control them. This male fear of women had a long history, much of it expressed in myth and explained by unprovable psychological concepts. An underlying and constant cause was attributed to man's sexual inadequacy. The sexual act created the impression that women were insatiable, whereas man after ejaculation was exhausted and unable further to satisfy his partner. Castration and the loss of potency were symbolised in the sexual act. The penis, the manifestation of rampant masculinity, was reduced by women to a powerless appendage. Man lost control over his body even at the earliest stages of love-making. From a distance a woman by words and gestures could effect an erection. This loss of phallic control reinforced the impression of feminine power and masculine weakness.[6]

Women's control of the strange and mysterious powers relating to procreation and birth increased male anxieties. Conception created further concern as man could never be certain that he was personally responsible. Menstruation was a magical act that terrified the primitive male. Birth was a fundamental mystery denied him. What was not understood had to be degraded in order to be controlled. Menstruation and travail were therefore equated with pollution. Childbirth was a time of disgrace and labour pains a just punishment for indulging in the sins of the flesh. Inherent in such views was the denigration of nature. Men envied the female's natural creative role and tried to compensate for this inadequacy by a frenetic attempt to create and dominate in the political and cultural spheres. It was argued that it was this dichotomy between nature and culture, and the underlying difference between female and male personalities, that was fundamental to the understanding of misogyny.

The significance of these factors was explained by a story built on myth, selective archaeology, controversial psychological assumptions and historical trends generalised to the edge of, if not beyond, validity. In the beginning men stood in fear of nature: of volcanoes, storms, earthquakes and women. The mysteries of childbirth were like other natural mysteries invested with magical powers. Women were man's link with nature. Society was dominated by the Mother Goddess and by fertility beliefs. Man ultimately realised his role in the procreative process and a major psychological and subsequent socio-political change occurred. A patriarchal revolution reversed the power structure and symbolism of society. The sun, a linear concept of history and the individual replaced the moon, a cyclical pattern of history and the community. This change had a biological base. The male principle was aggressive, analytical and categorising. It was intent on creating abstract thought, ethical and legal systems. The feminine principle was passive, stable, receptive and synthetic. Man concentrated on the external result; women were more concerned with motives and feelings. The male dominance of Greek civilisation established the mode of logical thought that emphasised that contradictions were incompatible. Although this formed the basis of Western philosophy, it was alien to Eastern philosophies and religions in which these were mutually compatible options along a spectrum. For women, nature determined the major stages of their life — menarche, pregnancy and menopause. For man, the watersheds were culturally contrived and conditioned. Logical thought replaced feeling, religion became ethical and the concept of good and evil developed. Good was no longer an intellectual choice but a moral imperative. Women were associated with evil, with mystery, passion and pollution; the male with ethics, rationality and sacredness.[7]

Imbedded in these developments were two attitudes, both detrimental to women, that emerged in particular cultures and individuals with varying degrees of intensity. The first was an ambivalent attitude by males to their mothers and the transfer of hostility from mother to women in general. The second was the pervasiveness of the patriarchal system which became the cultural norm. Women may not be hated but they were inferior and must remain subject to men.

The unprovable myth of matriarchal society followed by the dominance of the male principle assessed along the nature – culture spectrum and the subsequent association of women with evil was one encapsulated view of pre-Christian Europe. The contribution of Christianity was clearer and more complex. It rejected the analytical logic of the Greeks and the stern monotheism of Judaism. The Trinity would cause problems for both. Christianity displayed aspects of the fertility cult and adopted basically feminine principles in the concept of death and resurrection, and of salvation through a redeemer. It appealed to women through such cult mysteries. Christ's death and resurrection, the essence of Christianity, were neither Greek logic nor Judaic ethics. In the beginning the church protected women and gave them significant authority within the family. The Byzantine Church continued to give them high status and its concentration on ritual, pomp and community involvement and its lack of emphasis on ethics reflected feminine interests. Doctrine, preaching and ethics were masculine attributes best expressed in the Middle East in Islam. This balanced treatment of women stemmed from the Eastern theologians' emphasis on the equality of the sexes. Clement of Alexandria wrote: 'One only is the God of both . . . Nature is the same in each individual . . . Woman does not have one human nature and man another. They both possess the same nature.' St John Chrysostom denied the basis for much of the subsequent misogyny when he argued, 'the woman sinned and so did Adam. The serpent deceived them both, and one was not to be found stronger and the other weaker . . . Christ saved both in His passion.' While Christianity remained an Eastern phenomenon the status of women remained high, and secondly sex was considered an enjoyable natural act. The genitals were created by God and were not to be devalued.[8]

Nevertheless, from the apostolic church onwards Christianity contained the seeds of misogyny. Planted by St Paul these ideas gradually became more important, heavily fertilised by an ascetic view of sex. Such a view saw woman as temptation. She was prone to evil and easily led by the Devil. St Augustine considered women were morally and mentally inferior to men. Deadly sins were given feminine characteristics. Erigena argued in the ninth century that mankind was originally sinless and sexless. With Eve-induced sin came sex and the distinction between genders. Sex was born in sin and a manifestation of evil. To enjoy sex was doubly sinful. To Aquinas, following Aristotle, women were inferior to males: 'the woman is subject to the man on account of the weakness of her nature — both mind and body'. Woman was essentially sexual appetite (to be avoided) and a vehicle for procreation (a necessary evil for some). Even her role in this was limited. Some theologians claimed that the male through his semen deposited a complete little person who was simply incubated in the female womb. The *Malleus* epitomised this clerical misogyny in its claim that Christ died for men — and not for women.[9]

These views were expressed with more vicious invective and gradually became more widely accepted by the political, academic and ecclesiastical establishment, and less certainly within popular culture from the twelfth century onwards. With the commercial revolution trade and commerce slowly replaced agriculture and urban centres became dominant features in political and cultural life, feeding their values into the ideology of the church. Agriculture and its associated symbols and values lost their influence. The powerful abbess disappeared. The Earth Mother in her various Christian guises became irrelevant. The cult of the Virgin Mary, its popular replacement, was gradually transformed. Virginity, not fertility, was the ideal and woman could only free herself from evil and sensual temptation by renouncing her sexuality. This new development was a means through which men exerted control over female behaviour and in the process played down their own sense of sexual inferiority. They failed to satisfy the carnal woman. The virgin saved them from this humiliation. All good women must emulate the virgin as far as their circumstances permitted. Even married women should avoid sex except for procreation. Women who did not conform exhibited their sensuality, their devotion to evil.

This ascetic view and idealisation of virginity was gradually imposed on a cult which in its beginnings had been an embodiment of feminine values. Courtly love and the cult of the virgin were both aspects of an attempt to bring about a more emotional and a less physical and intellectual culture. Its initial popular appeal forced the intellectual leadership of the church to compromise. They reluctantly incorporated into the ritualistic calendar festivals including Annunciation, Visitation and Assumption dedicated to the Mother of God. Popular pressure elevated a woman to the level of the all-male Trinity. It was to Mary the understanding, warm, sympathetic woman, to Mary the mother, that the people responded. In time the male-dominated church adapted this popular adoration and directed it toward the archetypal virgin rather than the compassionate mother; away from fertility to virginity. The moralists argued that this new emphasis on the Virgin, and the principles of courtly love, were designed to enable men to achieve higher spiritual comfort. Through the unobtainable men understood the true meaning of love. Female virginity and noble platonic love were simply means for the spiritual advancement of the male. More cynically, both courtly love and the cult of the Virgin were manipulated by the secular and ecclesiastical male elite for their own purposes — to cover adultery or to control the sexual behaviour of women. By the fifteenth century many academic clergy had lost touch with real women. The complex female gender had been simplified into the ideal and its opposite. The reverse image of the virgin was emerging. It was the witch.[10]

The role played by women in medieval heresies hastened this dichotomy and increased the underlying anxieties concerning women. It was not a question of relative gender proportions within these heresies but the opportunities which membership gave women — opportunities unavailable in orthodox society. If women were a despised and deprived group most alternatives would be more sympathetic than established patriarchal Christianity. Women played a major role in the heretical movements of the twelfth and thirteenth centuries especially within the Cathars and the Waldensians. These groups, *inter alia*, highlighted the corruption of the male Catholic clergy. These clergy were lambasted for failing to reach the ideals which lay women outside of the church's jurisdiction could obtain. Women heretics living better Christian lives than the professional caste created to encourage such behaviour rankled with the ecclesiastical community. The appeal of these heresies forced the church to embark on a rigorous counter-offensive and, given such female participation, retaliation involved a concerted attack on women. The only concession granted to females in this resolute assault on the enemies of the church was the papal decision in 1376 that pregnant women should not be tortured. Even this was for the sake of the foetus and not the woman. In reality, the role of women in heretical organisations decreased in the fourteenth century as these groups began to reflect the patriarchal bias of the world around them. But the church continued to exaggerate the role of women in such movements. Monter may be correct when he concluded that in the Swiss borderlands in the fifteenth century neither sorcery nor heresy attracted a preponderance of women. He believed that it was a libel applied by the church in its campaign to mutually denigrate women and heresy. In reality it may have been a label in that region by that time but to many male clergy, given the developing misogynist environment, it appeared a just label.[11]

There were ascetic intellectuals who idealised the virgin and held other women in contempt. Men of this ilk over five centuries regularly discerned a breakdown in sexual moral standards and attributed the cause to women. Life appeared a continuous sexual orgy and religious females led the way. Convents became brothels, nun and whore were synonomous. To the godly this was irrefutable proof that the Devil ruled this world and that women and sex were the source of his power. This was nonsense. It was not nonsense that some religious authorities, determined to impose a more rigorous morality, voiced man's atavistic fears of women and concentrated on the sexual act as sinful and corrupting. The stereotype of feminine evil was a well-entrenched constant and a simple explanatory model especially for the mendicant orders confronted with popular anxiety. The female membership of unorthodox and heretical groups confirmed the image. The Jews could not be held responsible for every disaster. As crises waxed and waned so did mendicant-inspired misogyny.[12]

This misogyny manifested as witchcraft has been seen as a deliberate attempt by late-medieval patriarchal society to bolster male domination and confidence by a more effective subordination of women. Although a small group of clergy may have seen the situation in such terms there was no evidence that male society in general recognised such a need. Male oppression appeared constant and male dominance secure. If women needed to be suppressed further direct means were available. Islam offered, and Portugal at least copied, a range of effective methods and an appropriate value system. In the peasant world a good beating was effective. Political leaders were not yet prepared to swallow the misogynistic paranoia of a few clergy.

However, demographic changes slowly strengthened the clerical argument. In the early Middle Ages men outlived women by over a decade. There was a population shortage. Women were needed as breeders and consequently they were valuable assets. In

Germanic codes, a woman capable of bearing children was valued three times that of a younger or older woman and the loss of a female child brought double the *wergild* of a male. The demographic revolution of the twelfth century and the accompanying improvement in the lifestyle of women removed this differentiation. The status of women dropped. The curtailment of violence and the exclusion of women from warfare, the general imposition of law and order and the development of sedentary trades involved females in less strenuous work and increased their life expectancy to just beyond that of men — 30 years for women, 29 for men.[13]

The Black Death increased the imbalance. It killed a greater proportion of men creating a glut of women, especially in the towns. The increased age at marriage and the refusal of many men to marry at all created a large surplus of unattached women. Females without husbands or fathers were a new phenomenon which adversely affected the image of women in numerous ways. Some unattached females sought identity or economic security by entering convents. A few of these who lacked religious dedication found temporary solace in sexual activities which justified the ascetic's fears of a breakdown in morality. Others were attracted to unorthodox cults and as potential heretics stimulated a response from conservative religious leaders. The survival of such a disproportionate number of women in the plague prompted popular preachers to suggest that the Devil protected his own. This was an effective misogynistic arrow in highly emotional plague-ridden communities.

The growing number of unattached women stimulated panic in the area vital to the peasant, economic survival. In periods of economic difficulty these women became a burden on the community. Economic changes created pools of dependent women. Children left villages to seek jobs in neighbouring towns and left their elderly relatives to fend for themselves. The creation of the nuclear family in parts of Western Europe and late marriages added to the problem. The decline of the extended family and the kin tended to put more and more old and female relatives outside the area of immediate family concern. These people perforce became dependent on a potentially hostile community. Within the nuclear family, unsoftened by sympathetic relatives, conflict between daughter and mother-in-law, and husband and wife, occasionally forced one or more of the partners out of the family into a dependent position in the community. In a Norwich survey in the late-sixteenth century one in twelve of the married women in the city had been deserted by their husbands and as a result were dependent on their unenthusiastic neighbours. The dependence of these women, and for some their recourse to magical means of revenge, accounted for a large number of women being accused of witchcraft independent of any elite feelings of misogyny. They were an economic burden on the community. Nevertheless, links were being forged. Economic survival, the primary aim of a peasant society, the recourse to popular sorcery by dependent women to assist survival, and elite misogyny, filtered through the mendicant orders, were coming together. The dependent old woman was not only an economic parasite; she was an evil and diabolical witch.[14]

The major Renaissance contribution to anti-feminist attitudes was in the reaffirmation of classical misogynist ideas. The Ancients were the authorities and the 'opposites' of Aristotle and the 'dualities' of Pythagoras were the unchallenged assumptions of most academic debates. In essence, male, right, square, straight, light and good were superior to female, left, oblong, curved, darkness and evil. Man was linked with the active, perfection, completion and possession; woman with the passive, imperfection, incompletion and deprivation. From this most of the scholastic concepts of female inferiority and subordination were reasserted by the humanists. Humanism was a code for the male elite and the few concessions to the education of the gentlewoman were in the interests of that elite. The impetus given to homosexuality and hedonism further denigrated women. Women did not reflect true love as did men. They were so inferior spiritually and intellectually that their only possible service to mankind was the provision of their bodies. This might ease some of the distress for those unfortunates unable to obtain the true love of another man. To other Renaissance writers provision of those bodies was their *raison d'être*. Women were primarily an instrument for man's pleasure. A prostitute filled a more natural and useful role than a nun.[15]

Given the already low opinion of women and the belief that witchcraft could cause disease, the arrival of syphilis at the end of the fifteenth century significantly increased male anxieties and antagonism towards females. Syphilis was a painful, often fatal disease that in the process caused physical wasting and mental deterioration. At the tabetic stage it caused hallucinations and depression, both usually dominated by a sense of persecution. This debilitating and deadly disease was caught through sexual intercourse, often illicit, with a woman. Guilt and anxiety combined to create both a genuine fear of a female carrier and the need for a scapegoat who must be punished for the agony the victim suffered.

Stanislav Andreski has plausibly suggested that syphilis was the trigger to heightened misogyny and to the witch craze itself. Such an interpretation explained key features of both. Obsessive writing against women and witches in the sixteenth century, such as that of the later Bodin, reflected persecutory hallucinations and general mental deterioration indicative of syphilis. Malaria was a cure for and a protection against syphilis. It was widespread in southern Europe and much less so in the north. Syphilis made a greater impact on northern Europe and this was the region of intense misogyny and witch hunting. There was no hunt in the malarial areas of southern Italy or southern Spain. Witch hunting appeared most prevalent in areas in which there was a high ratio of single women who provided a large pool of casual sexual partners and potential agents of the disease. Witch hunting also occurred in the wake of military campaigns. Soldiers carried the disease and forced their attention on local women. The ultimate victim, the local male, sought a scapegoat. Syphilis caused abortions, still-births and malformations in babies and the increase in these directed bitterness toward the midwife who became a prime suspect as a witch. The wasting quality of the disease severely affected the appearance of the victim and this may explain the 'ugliness' of many accused witches. It also created insensitive areas in the body which were immune to pricking and to some aspects of torture. Andreski concluded that syphilis explained the timing and class-lessness of the witch fear, and the especial concern of celibates and puritans with it.[16]

Misogyny was further boosted by the religious reforms of the sixteenth century. The Protestant Reformation emphasised the individual rather than the community, and ideas rather than feeling, strengthening the male principles within Christianity. The abolition of convents and the confessional forced women back into the home and kitchen, back under the absolute authority of father or husband. Luther believed that women must 'stay home, keep house and bear and bring up children'. The leading Protestant reformers reaffirmed basic scholastic attitudes to women. The heavy emphasis by some on asceticism and the growing ability to enforce this anti-sexual ethic generated anxieties regarding women and sex while the abolition of the confessional made it more difficult for men who fell from the high ideals required to assuage intense feelings of guilt. Calvinism developed the masculine principle to the utmost. Symbolism and allegory gave way to hard rational logic. Intellectual, austere and efficiently organised religion replaced one in which there had been some room for symbolism, ritual, and emotion. The Protestant translations of the Bible had a direct impact on the prosecution of witches as well as reflecting dominant academic attitudes. The traditional Latin translation of Exodus 2:18 used the neutral term *maleficos* for the entity which cannot be suffered to live. German, French and English Protestant rendering was the feminine — *leben, la sorcière* and 'witch'.[17]

After Trent, the Catholic Church officially moved in a similar ethical and ascetic direction. That which it now defined as diabolic was traditional peasant sexual behaviour, which was the antithesis of the new model of Catholic piety. In highlighting 'diabolical' sexual deviance — a woman giving Satan some of her pubic hair or another woman marrying the arch-fiend — the church was symbolically demonising peasant attitudes that were to be eradicated by deliberate misinterpretation and exaggeration. Another major contribution to the growth of misogyny and the formation of the diabolical sexual image of the witch was the gradual imposition of clerical celibacy. It received considerable impetus from the conciliar movement in the fifteenth century and from the Catholic Reformation. Although the open marriage of priests ceased in the thirteenth century, concubinage and casual sexual encounters were widespread until the effects of Tridentine reforms were felt. The Protestants, while permitting the marriage of priests, adopted a harsh ascetic line and pre-marital sex and marital infidelity of their pastors was not acceptable. The attempt to impose an ascetic ethic on an unwilling lay population through the agency of the clergy, subject to the same hedonistic impulses yet now required to set the highest moral standard, imposed considerable stresses on such men. Robert Muchembled described the effect of such stress in Cambrèsis, a situation probably typical of much of rural Catholic Europe:

> the seventeenth-century reformers were able to superimpose an atmosphere of moral anxiety and guilt upon the substructure of very real fears . . . The interplay of these anxieties could touch off the witchhunting. But it was first that this moral insecurity should profoundly trouble certain elements in the village, that it should in effect, be hammered home by

91

the local priest. He would tend to project his guilt upon his parishioners all the more strongly if he was uneasy in his conscience about his own conduct . . . The Counter Reformation was making slow but steady progress, converting one after another, sowing its message of guilt amongst the priests, who in turn passed it on to their flock, and together they looked for an expiatory victim, a witch — a woman that is, the very symbol of sexuality. The burning of witches could thus provide a means of wiping out one's own sins.[18]

To some, the hatred of women stemmed from the very specific fears of particular male interest groups. For example, it has been suggested that the attack on women as witches was inspired by the male medical profession to destroy the village healer who monopolised the treatment of the ordinary peasant. Women healers were seen as victims of both a sex and a class war. The witch craze was part of the ruling elite's campaign of terror against female peasant leaders — a role often filled by the healer. She gave women relief from pain in circumstances such as childbirth, in which the church considered such relief sinful. One aspect of this interpretation is invalid. The male medical profession had lost confidence in itself in the sixteenth century, becoming aware of how little it knew. It was forced to attribute insolvable problems to witchcraft and to seek help from the clergy. Physicians and healers were hardly rivals in the villages of Europe as peasants could not afford the urban doctor. It was not until the eighteenth century, long after the witch craze had vanished, that the medical profession sought the monopoly of healing and broadened its services both socially and geographically.

However, the thesis may be more viable when applied to the clergy. They resented the healer and led the campaign against them. The village healer had wide knowledge — insights into telepathy, hypnotism and the use of drugs, especially hallucinogens capable of controlling and influencing the moods of clients. The witch-healers were the repository of traditional lore. They were counsellors and comforters. Yet their role was dangerous. If they failed their activities could be interpreted as harmful by distraught and angry clients. Opponents of the healer need only wait their opportunity to gain popular help in their assault. As has been seen, healers were treated differently across Europe: heavily persecuted in Catholic France, occasionally harassed in Scotland and ignored in England. Another major flaw in this explanation is that it has not been established that the majority of healers were women. Both in Scotland and England the craft appears to have been exercised predominantly by males, although quantitative proof either way is lacking. If it was the healer that was the primary target then the biased treatment of female healers must be due to factors other than their knowledge of healing.[19]

The suggestion that the attack on these women was a deliberate attempt to destroy the knowledge of contraception by the authorities anxious to rebuild the labour supply after the Black Death cannot, given the communications and organisational structures of the fourteenth and fifteenth centuries, be given much credence. Assaults on individual women by local authorities obsessed on this point was not impossible. Interference in the process of procreation was anathema to many church leaders and the sins of the witches described in the *Malleus* were connected with this process. However, by the sixteenth century circumstances had changed and woman's insatiable lust was being blamed by Martin Luther for the unwanted population explosion experienced in Germany. Regional depopulation in Catholic Europe into the seventeenth century reactivated the issue. The agent immediately responsible for birth was the midwife. She could be blamed by both the public and the authorities for death and deformation. Often incompetent and superstitious, some of these women undoubtedly increased the hazards of childbirth. A few may have murdered infants at birth at the request of one or more of the parents and they may have supplied the bodies of stillborn babies to others. Most of them, however, were ordinary village women, middle-aged and experienced in childbirth. Yet, like the healer, their position made them very vulnerable. Their role, real or fantasised, was another potential source of male fears and anxieties.[20]

The foregoing arguments have emphasised the impact of particular ideas and events in increasing the fear of woman — woman viewed as an evil sexual creature. The common stereotype of the witch as elderly initially appears to undermine the sexual thesis that underlines much of the misogynist approach. In Geneva, the median age was 60. In New England in normal circumstances the witch was middle-aged. Three-fifths of witches (excluding Salem) were in their 40s or 50s, one-fifth under 40, and one-fifth 60 or over. In the panic situation of Salem this age stereotype gave way. Less than half were in their 40s and 50s, and nearly two-fifths were under 40. Menopause rather than senility may have been the key factor in behaviour which provoked accusation. The older woman incited attention for reasons both overt and subconscious. It will be argued later that it was the older woman's vulnerability rather than her gender that encouraged her persecution. The growing number of dependants in the village community were targets of public antagonism. These were largely the aged, but the elderly women did have additional characteristics that invited attention. The old body was more likely to reveal the Devil's or witches' mark than that of a younger woman. With the onset of menopause or senility the older woman was depressed, talked to herself, grumbled and felt generally cross with the world that had turned against her. She often found comfort in the companionship of a domestic pet which could be easily defined as a familiar. Such women living along on the edge of town without sufficient means of support and without direct patriarchal control created fears in the minds of the local peasant establishment. If subject to informal persecution these women had no means of avenging themselves against an uncaring society other than by arson or by accepting the attribution of diabolical powers.[21]

The demonologist had linked these older women with sex and apostasy. No woman was content without sex. Those that were most deprived, the isolated elderly, would do anything for sex — even to selling their soul to the Devil. The Devil deliberately chose the old and, by implication, the ugly for his sexual pleasure. It degraded sex and revealed to the world the depth to which sex-crazed women would sink. Women became more evil the older they became. Old women, having failed as sex objects in their youth and vindictive against men, led young girls into the joys of lesbianism. Others, remembering the delights of heterosexual lust, vicariously enjoyed the deflowering of innocent young maids in the group orgies of sabbats. These concepts and assumptions revealed the obsessive sexual fantasies of the authors rather than any real assessment of female sexuality.

It was this perceived assault by elderly women on innocent maidens that deeply shocked patriarchal society. Rosemary Ruether believed that it was the sexual autonomy of these women that infuriated the male establishment. In this male-dominated society, women were sexually repressed until marriage. After a brief sexual experience as a wife the male then expected the motherhood role to dominate and her sexual desires once more to be repressed. In reality, many older women ignored the social conditioning that they should lose interest in sex as they aged and were potentially, and in some cases actually, autonomous. Both their interest and possible initiative in this area terrified the male. Ruether suggested that the older woman was also subjected to innate fears concerning mortality, especially in the eyes of the male ascetics that unduly influenced establishment attitudes. Asceticism attempted to transcend mortality, to see the body and the process by which it came into being as alien and inferior. These processes were through women who were therefore equated with fleshly corruption. They symbolised the mortality of birth and, as they aged, this symbol with sagging breasts, bulging belly and scarred body was increasingly an infuriating reminder of flesh and its decay.[22]

Notes

1. Andrea Dworkin, *Woman Hating* p. 130; M. Harris, *op.cit.* p. 147; P. Hughes, *op.cit.* p. 195; C. Larner, *Enemies of God* p. 91; H. C. Erik Midelfort, *Witch Hunting in Southwestern Germany 1562–1684* p. 179; E. William Monter, *Witchcraft in France and Switzerland: The Borderlands During the Reformation* pp. 11, 22–4; Hugh V. McLachlan and J. K. Swales, 'Witchcraft and Anti-Feminism', *Scottish Journal of Sociology* 4 (1980) pp. 141–66; J. K. Swales and Hugh V. McLachlan, 'Witchcraft and the Status of Women: A Comment', *British Journal of Sociology* 30 (1979) pp. 349–58, 351.

2. McLachlan and Swales, *op.cit.* p. 160; John P. Demos, *Entertaining Satan: Witchcraft and the Culture of Early New England* p. 61.

3. Demos, *op.cit.* p. 61; McLachlan and Swales, *op.cit.* p. 162; Robert Muchembled, 'The Witches of Cambresis: The Acculturation of the Rural World in the Sixteenth and Seventeenth Century', Ch. 6 of James Obelkevich (ed.), *Religion and the People 800–1700* pp. 221–76, 228.

4. Swales and McLachlan, *op.cit.* p. 351; C. Larner, *op.cit.* pp. 91–2; H. C. Erik Midelfort, *op.cit.* pp. 179, 175; Keith Thomas, *Religion and the Decline of Magic*, p. 568.

5. Demos, *op.cit.* p. 60.

6. H. R. Hays, *The Dangerous Sex: The Myth of Feminine Evil* pp. 106, 117–19, 152, Ch. 10; Monter, *op.cit.* p. 17; Ferdinand Mount, *The Subversive Family: The Alternative History of Love and Marriage* p. 23.

7. Larner, *op.cit.* p. 92–3; Hays, *op.cit.* p. 111; Selma R. and Pamela J. Williams, *Riding the Nightmare: Women and Witchcraft*, Introduction; Amaury de Riencourt, *Sex and Power in History* pp. vii–vii; Sherry B. Ortner, 'Is Female to Male as Nature is to Culture?', in M. Z. Rosaldo and L. Lamphere (eds), *Women, Culture and Society* pp. 67–88; Susan Carol Rogers, 'Woman's Place: A Critical Review of Anthropological Theory', *Comparative Studies in Society and History* 20 (1978), pp. 123–73; Riencourt, *op.cit.* I–3, I–5.

8. Riencourt, *op.cit.* II–6 pp. 154–5.

9. Hays, *op.cit.* Ch. 10; Riencourt, *op.cit.* p. 219.

10. Williams, *op.cit.* Ch. 1; Riencourt, *op.cit.* III–2; Hays, *op.cit.* pp. 105, 115.

11. Williams, *op.cit.* p. 19; Claudia Honegger, 'Comment on Garrett's *Women and Witchcraft*', *Signs* 4 (1979) pp. 792–8, 795; Monter, *op.cit.* Ch. 1; M. Lambert, *Medieval Heresy: Popular Movements from Bogomil to Hus*.

12. Riencourt, *op.cit.* II–6.

13. David Herlihy, 'Life Expectancies for Women in Medieval Society', in R. T. Morewedge (ed.), *The Role of Women in the Middle Ages* pp. 1–22.

14. Alan D. Macfarlane, *Witchcraft in Tudor and Stuart England* Ch. 10; Ralph A. Houlbrooke, *The English Family 1450–1700* pp. 207–10.

15. Riencourt, *op.cit.* III–3, III–5; Ian Maclean, *The Renaissance Notion of Women: A Study in the Fortunes of Scholasticism and Medical Science in European Intellectual Life* Ch. 2.

16. Stanislav Andreski, 'The Syphilitic Shock: A New Explanation of the Witch Burnings', *Encounter* 58–5 (May 1982) pp. 7–26.

17. Maclean, *op.cit.* Ch. 2; Williams, *op.cit.* p. 51.

18. Andreski, *op.cit.* pp. 16–18; Muchembled, *op.cit.* pp. 266–7.

19. Barbara Ehrenreich and Deirdre English, *Witches, Midwives and Nurses: A History of Women Healers*; Leland Estes, 'The Medical Origins of the European Witch Craze: A Hypothesis', *Journal of Social History* (Winter 1983) pp. 271–84.

20. Larner, *op.cit.* pp. 101, 138; Thomas Forbes, 'Midwifery and Witchcraft', *Journal of the History of Medicine and Allied Sciences* 17 (1962) pp. 417–29; Thomas R. Forbes, *The Midwife and the Witch*.

21. Monter, *op.cit.* p. 122. Demos, *op.cit.* pp. 65–6.

22. Thomas, *op.cit.* Chs. 16, 17; A. Macfarlane, *Witchcraft in Tudor and Stuart England*; Rosemary Ruether, 'Persecution of Witches: A Case of Sexism and Agism', *Christianity and Crisis* 34 (Dec. 1974) pp. 291–5.

7

Gender, Sex and Misogyny: II

It was morality rather than mortality that was the primary obsession of the misogynist. The fantasies developed over centuries reached an extreme form in the *Malleus Maleficarum*. Women were 'feebler both in mind and body' and 'intellectually like children'. As such they were 'more credulous' and 'naturally more impressionable'. They had 'slippery tongues', were avaricious and always deceived, finding it difficult to 'hold and preserve the faith'. A woman was an imperfect animal in whom lust was insatiable. She was 'more bitter than death' and 'a wheedling and secret enemy' who when she thought alone thought evil. Dominated by bestial lust she was a willing partner of the Devil. Gone were the days when he had to force himself upon her. The hidden irony for this diabolic witch, and perhaps an unconscious salve for the misogynistic demonologist, was that she gave her loyalty to Satan, a male.[1]

The sexual emphasis in the misogynistic view of diabolical witchcraft was reflected in three main areas: activities at the sabbat, the role of the incubi and the misuse of sexual magic. The sabbat was given the attributes of heretical cults: perversion and the adoration of the Devil. Images of the sabbat differed and the balance of activities varied. Blasphemy and sacrilege in the worship of the Devil, the renunciation of the faith, and in the desecration of the host, usually in the most scatological manner, were important. At some there was cannibalism, sacrifice and infanticide. At all there was eating (often the most nauseous objects), and dancing (in a group rather than with a partner). It was sexual activity that appeared most important in many French, German and Basque images of the sabbat.

An inquisitorial enquiry at Logruno, Spain, in 1610, summed up the confessions made to it by accused Basque witches:

> When the Devil has finished his Mass, he copulates with everyone, men and women, carnally, and after the fashion of Sodom . . . He, with his left hand (in the sight of everyone) stretched her face downwards on the ground, . . . placed her against a tree and there had knowledge of her in the manner of the Sodomites, while her said husband . . . made music. And while still in the said act, she gave a very shrill scream which everybody heard . . . like a bull roaring. And when they had finished the shameful acts she went away very proud and satisfied . . . Maria Irarte . . . declares that when her mother sent her for the first time . . . the Devil entered her carnally by both ways, and deflowered her, and she suffered much pain and returned home with her shift all bloody . . . Martin Viccar Bruno . . . reports that the first time the Devil had knowledge of him after the fashion of Sodom, he suffered great pain and returned home all bloody, and to satisfy his wife (who asked him what the blood was) he pretended a branch of a tree had struck him in the leg.[2]

At the same time, just across the Pyrénées, De Lancre recorded and commented on the confession of sixteen-year-old, Jeanette d'Abadie:

> The Devil often made her kiss . . . his member, then his behind . . . As for the coupling . . . she saw everybody having incestuous intercourse against all the dictates of nature . . . She accused herself of having been deflowered by Satan and having had intercourse an infinite number of times with a relative of hers and with others who had condescended to demand her. She shrank from intercourse with the Devil because, as his member was covered with scales, it caused extreme pain, besides which his seed is extremely cold, so that it never makes a woman pregant, nor does that of the other men at the Sabbath, even though it is natural. Outside the Sabbath she never did anything wrong, but at the Sabbath she had a marvellous delight in this intercourse, apart from that with Satan which she said was horrible. She even seemed to us to take a marvellous delight in telling it and talking about it, calling everything by its name more freely and boldly than we

dared ask of her . . . it is more probable that she copulated at the Sabbath with the people she named than that Satan made them appear to her in bed by illusion, or that he carried them physically to her; she would not have been able to feel this natural sperm a hundred times (as she says) except by copulating physically and actually with a real man whom she named to us.[3]

The witches had sex with the Devil or with the other participants. This included heterosexual intercourse, anal and oral sex, homosexuality, bestiality, mutual masturbation, group sex and incest. The nuns at Lille were encouraged to confess that their sabbat organised these activities into a regular timetable so that specific activities occurred regularly on a particular day of the week. On the one hand, the details of the sabbat reflected the corpus of fantasies developed over centuries by demonologists and was manifested in the assumptions and specific questions and interpretations placed on answers by the investigators. On the other hand, the hundreds of willing confessions made by women who never left their own beds showed that it also met the needs of some accused women. It provided a fantasy fulfilment of the needs and desires left unsatisfied in their sexual life. Yet the reactions as confessed to the witch hunters by those claiming to have been participants in sabbatical orgies ranged from sadistic and masochistic to the openly hedonistic.[4]

Scholars, and many of the accused women, were fascinated by the genitalia of the Devil. An Italian humanist believed witches preferred sex with the Devil because his penis was larger (23 inches by one account) than a mortal's, and his technique of agitating it within the vagina was beyond the wildest imagination of any male peasant to rival. Others claimed that the Devil's penis was three-pronged, permitting him to engage in coitus, sodomy and fellatio simultaneously. Rival traditions emphasised the smallness of the demonic penis and the power of demons to tighten up the vagina of their female partners in order to make the experience enjoyable. Consequently the mortal acquaintances of these women could no longer have intercourse with them. The lack of a physical relationship between a husband and wife, whatever the real reason, could be explained in these terms.[5]

Another problem was the common confession that sex with the Devil was painful. He was cold, hard, rough and his instrument hurt. Voluntary resubmission to diabolical lust, even when the payment offered on the previous occasion had turned to dust, was the norm. Perhaps this pain was a small price to pay for skill of his love-making in general. A Françoise Fontaine with obvious pleasure confessed that the Devil made love to her on two occasions for over half an hour before he had intercourse and although it hurt he never left her afterwards without continuing to make love to her. The evidence suggests that few male peasants engaged in fore- and after-play. The Basque witch Maria de Zozoya's confession was a eulogy of sexual pleasure. In the twentieth century the Devil would take the form of a pop star, television personality or sporting hero. He would bring pleasure into the dull lives of disturbed, bored and frustrated women, even if only in the imagination. In fact the whole emphasis on pain may have been a gloss developed by phallic–sadistic males. Women who had sex with the Devil, the ultimate of sexual perversions, should not be seen to have actually enjoyed the experience. Women may have acquiesced in this assumption because this was what the investigators wanted to hear. On the other hand it may have been a psychosomatic response of women arising from guilt and anxiety about what they believed they had done. Yet even the *Malleus* cannot hide that some women enjoyed it. It noted that while coition was usually painful the incubi could make it very pleasurable on special occasions, especially at Easter and Christmas.[6]

Sex with demonic agents need not await a sabbat. The imagination of the Christian ascetic had created the ultimate manifestation of sexual evil, and of woman's willing association with it — the incubus. This sex demon, often Satan himself, copulated with women at any time, in any place and in any form. Some experts argued that the incubi copulated in any manner but there was a strong school of thought that argued that God had not granted the incubi permission to have intercourse in the missionary position. Man on top of a woman with the partners facing each other, the symbol of man's domination and superiority, was restricted to married couples. The incubi must make love dog-fashion. Neither the incubi nor their human partners seem to have been bound by this rule. The incubi were outrageous, bedding down beside women while they were in bed with their husbands. The earthly males were heavy sleepers. Most claimed that they noticed nothing. The *Malleus*, however, recalled that 'husbands have actually seen incubus devils swiving with their wives, although they have thought that they were not devils but men'. Yet when 'they had taken up a weapon and tried to run them through, the devil has suddenly disappeared, making himself invisible.'[7]

Adult demonic possession was often sexual. In French convents in the seventeenth century attractive male confessors were seen as the Devil's agents and the subsequent possession of the nuns took the form of simulated intercourse. The initial seduction of these women was often by a real male, for example Urbain Grandier at Loudun. When this real male was no longer available he was replaced by an incubus who often took the form of the original seducer, or other desirable males known to the women. Women in these situations lay on their back and exhibited all the signs of the most erotic physical relationship, climaxing in a series of orgasms. The nuns at Loudun spoke in the most obscene language, lifted their habits and in the most depraved manner invited males to copulate with them. Demonic possession provided an outlet for frustration and anxiety and enabled the victim to indulge safely in behaviour normally unacceptable to a Christian society, especially one in the throes of an ascetic revival. Similar gyrations viewed in field, forest or home gave credence to the belief in the incubus. The women were obviously being brought to orgasm by an invisible demon. Intercourse between women and demons was of long concern to theologians. Academics debated how a non-material demon could have intercourse with a material woman and in what manner the diabolical lover gathered the semen it expelled during its lascivious activity. The answer solved the problem of wet dreams. Demons in female form aroused the sleeping male to ejaculation and used the semen so obtained in their male form when they seduced women. Semen provided further problems in the sexual life of the witch. The promiscuous orgies at the sabbat and regular visits from an incubi rarely led to pregnancy. The sceptics saw this as proof that the whole concept of a sexually depraved witch was sheer fantasy. The women involved claimed that semen ejaculated at the sabbat or by an incubus was not fertile or that certain drinks were taken at sabbat or preferred by the incubus that rendered them infertile. However, if they wished to get pregnant it was possible. The sixteenth-century Catholic demonologists argued that such conceptions, which they believed were quite common, were likely to develop into monsters or people such as Martin Luther.[8]

Sex with incubi was not a major part of English witchcraft and it was almost exclusively an activity conducted in private by the alleged witch and Satan. As this took place most often in the woman's bed and usually at night there were few independent witnesses. The confessions of these women, probably formed out of dreams, were entirely fanciful and reflected the level of psychosexual disturbance suffered by the women concerned. The exact condition would be difficult to diagnose as many confessions were obtained under coercion — usually enforced sleeplessness which influenced the fantasy. Other confessions were consciously or subconsciously adjusted to mollify the prosecution, to reframe events in a form that would be more acceptable to the accusers. Nevertheless, it is possible to discern that some fantasies reflected mild and explicable problems, usually the absence of sexual activity. More significant disturbances were manifested in the statements of depressed women, most often following the death of a husband. A few extreme cases reflected the confused world of seriously disturbed women, or more commonly, advanced cases of senility.

For example, the women who believed that the Devil changed into a mouse or an insect and sucked their thighs, nibbled their private parts or created a feeling of butterflies in these genital areas were simply seeking a concrete explanation for their sexual arousal and its physical consequences. The lonely woman accosted on her way home from market and drawn into a thicket and seduced by the Devil in the form of a comely gentleman may have been creating in fantasy a major element missing at home. A large number of accused witches found themselves in bed with the Devil. One group made it clear that they escaped his lascivious attentions despite the tricks he used, for frequently he pretended to be their husbands. Perhaps they were rejecting their real husbands. Once the Devil claimed he was the prophet Daniel and he was well advanced with heavy petting before the woman realised who he was and what he intended. He was sent on his way. Another woman when the Devil became too aggressive called her husband and the incubus fled. This group of alleged witches appeared to have treated the Devil's sexual advances as would any respectable woman. Perhaps they found it easier to confess to the Devil's visit as it was difficult to disprove and concentrate their defence on their Christian response to such a visitation.[9]

The second group of women who found themselves in bed with the Devil consented to his advances. He was so attractive and persuasive. This explanation and their subsequent defence revealed much about the attitudes of peasant women to sex. When the Devil first visited them as a cat, a calf or a crab they refused his attentions. When he returned as a golden-haired gentleman they succumbed. Yet even these women did not always give him what he really wanted. The Devil wanted their souls; they only gave their bodies. A considerable number of witches who admitted sex with the incubi denied they signed a pact with him. As the latter was seen as the basis of the crime of witchcraft on the Continent and in Scotland, and considered by some English magistrates as important, the witches were exceedingly prudent.

The death of a husband with resulting depression, often to the point of attempted suicide, appeared to be the spark for more significant fantasies. An Abigail Briggs confessed that a month after the death of her husband 'there came one to her in the shape of her husband and lay heavy upon her and she asked him if he would kill her and he answered in the voice of her husband, no, I will be a loving husband to you'. She consented to his sexual advances because 'he promised her she should be revenged of all her enemies but . . . she found Satan a liar'. Perhaps this was the typical case of the vulnerable unprotected widow. A confession that fitted the mould of the demonologist was made by Mary Skipper after three days of being watched by gaolers, probably involving sleep deprivation. Skipper stated that 'the devil appeared to her in the shape of a man after her husband's death and told her if she would enter a covenant with him he would pay her debts and he would carry her to heaven and . . . she would never want'. She signed and 'the devil have constantly the use of her ever since but she felt him always cold'. Far more serious appeared the condition of an Ellen Driver whose fantasy involved marriage with the Devil and the bearing of his children:

> She confessed . . . that the Devil appeared to her like a man and that she was married to him . . . and that he lived with her three years and that she had two children by him in that time . . . It was sixty years since the Devil wooed her to marry him and it was the next time of his coming before (she) agreed to him. After she married he had carnal use of her but was cold . . . she did not know that any of his neighbours did ever see him . . . and being in bed with him she felt his feet and they were cloven, and he lived with her two years and then he died as she thought, and that it was her pride was the cause that made her consent to him.

This account is rambling, contradictory and confused. The woman concerned was over 80 and the condition reflected may have been an advanced stage of senility.[10]

The third area of sexual emphasis was the use to which the witch put her powers. In addition to the sexual feats traditionally attributed to low and folk magic — making people fall in and out of love — the witch concentrated with destructive intent on the sexual act and its consequences. She created infertility and impotence. The witches used a variety of approaches to create sexual malfunction. They prevented physical contact between male and female, froze sexual desire, made the lover appear loathsome, prevented the penis from becoming erect, stopped the flow of semen, and created the illusion that his penis had disappeared. Male castration fears were evident in this belief that witches cast glamours over men and convinced them that they had lost their penises. The usual method to achieve this was the ligature, the sympathetic tying of a knot in a cord. The courts and the church took the results of ligature and the casting of glamours seriously. Two Scots women were convicted in 1590 of removing the penises from men and bestowing these on strangers. In parts of Catholic Christendom ligature was a cause for annulment of marriage and in Aquitaine it was abused as the easy option. Women produced their husbands before the courts to prove their impotence. In some cases the examination was made by physicians, in others by attractive women who were permitted considerable freedom in trying to stimulate an erection.[11]

Some of the elite minds responsible for the witch image were morbidly obsessed with sex and as a consequence the image has been seen primarily as a manifestation of the sexual anxieties, guilt and frustrations of celibate clergy. Repressed sexuality sought vicarious expression and in the subconscious of the ascetic cleric the death of a witch became a temporary symbol of victory against intolerable tormenting lust. This simplistic explanation has many weaknesses. Although some individuals might react in such a way to sexual anxieties there is no evidence that it was the norm. To suggest that the proportion of those who did respond in this way was high among the ideologues of the church is impossible to prove. A large number of clergy, including those who contributed to the ideas and attitudes of the church, were not celibate. The majority of investigators and prosecutors in the sixteenth and seventeenth centuries were laymen, most of them married. However, some demonologists were celibate and may have unduly influenced the witch image. Parts of the *Malleus* reflected the sexual obsessions of its authors. Yet works such as the *Malleus* were simply extreme manifestations of a basic problem in a society intent on enforcing an ascetic ideal. The imposition of celibacy or marital fidelity on Catholic and Protestant clergy respectively during the late-sixteenth and seventeenth century intensified the position. It took the problem out of the elitist universities and cloisters and spread it through the parochial clergy. These men now depended upon strict conformity to the new ideal for status and professional preferment. For the priests of peasant stock any form of sexual deviance destroyed their newly won status. Conformity to the ascetic ideal under such circumstances increased the tensions.[12]

Yet some succumbed to lascivious lust. A priest in the Cambrèsis in 1626 had his own form of exorcism. He visited a 20-year-old woman, who later recalled:

> He took a rather strong drink, and after hearing her confession, he told the girl that she was bewitched and that if she would be willing to let him get into bed with her and to make love to her she would be cured, all of which she refused. However he redoubled his efforts in order to gain his objective, putting his hand under the covers to touch her breasts and even more, which modesty prevents her mentioning.

Exorcism, even in Puritan New England, created opportunities for clergy to fondle female breasts. Cotton Mather was accused of such activity and he did not proceed with a libel action to clear his name.[13]

A method of witch discovery that the sceptics saw as an excuse for males to satisfy their sexual fantasies was the search for the Devil's mark. In many societies this was carried out by respectable married women of the community, in others by lascivious minor officials and in a few by the prosecuting officers themselves. The development of a profession of male prickers who made a living by examining every inch of a woman's body, particularly her vagina, anus and breasts, certainly raised questions, even among some contemporaries, as to its propriety and the individual motivation involved.[14]

This discussion of the misogynyist fantasies and sexual imagery that surrounded the witch taken in isolation, can be misleading. The attitudes described existed and the factors discussed to varying degrees increased the breadth and depth of their appeal. Yet how typical were they? Misogyny was present in the attitudes of ascetic academics, celibate inquisitors and syphilitic demonologists.

Princes and peasants were not necessarily in agreement. Misogyny did not need to take a sexual form. In secular literature of the sixteenth and seventeenth centuries it was female extravagance not wayward sexuality that received most attention. Catholic and Protestant puritans rehashed the old theme but with far less viciousness and prurience, and with an emphasis on pride and avarice as well as sensuality. Misogyny was the negative side of man's attitude to women and in most cases did not dominate. Ferdinand Mount correctly warned us that 'To take the anti marriage, anti women stuff as showing the attitude of the times is to miss out half the evidence; it is also to miss the whole atmosphere of the debate — combative, ironic, indignant, passionate, playful'. The evidence also supports Kathleen Rogers in her view that:

> Men's prevailing attitude toward women, in their writings as well as their lives, has been positive: this is the natural result of human biology and nurture; it is equally necessary for the happiness of the individual and the continuance of society. Men's love and respect for women, however, have always been accompanied in the culture as a whole and sometimes within a single individual by some degree of fear, dislike or contempt.

This was revealed in the continuing debate on the value of marriage and the relevant position of men and women within it. Chaucer raised both sides of the issue and there are many examples of love and equality and respect by the male for the female. In the Renaissance the neo-Platonists argued that women were in fact superior to men because beauty and love, attributes of women rather than men, mirrored Divine Love. Other writers took up the theme enunciated centuries earlier by St John Chrysostom that women have the capacity to reach greater virtue and greater vice than men. By concentrating on the former, women were painted as potentially spiritually superior to men.[15]

The letters and diaries of the nobility and the court records and wills involving the peasantry revealed the respect and love of man for woman. The life of Honor Lisle, wife of Henry VIII's noble Governor of Calais, revealed 'in quite a remarkable manner the difference between the theory of woman's place in the scheme of things as set forth in the mass of sixteenth century treaties' and her real role. Honor Lisle ran the estates, negotiated with Henry and his ministers as an equal and partner of her husband. The misogynistic proverbs of the peasants, part of the give and take of village and family life, was not reflected in the wills and depositions of the peasant community. Love and respect were manifested in the transfer of property to wives and daughters. The peasant farm needed a happy working partnership to survive economically.[16]

The concerted effort of church and state in this period to impose a strict patriarchy, in which the woman was to be subjected to father and husband, suggested a genuine fear that such was not always the case. Yet this concern to keep women in their place did not spill into biased treatment of them in the judgments of the courts. The southern provinces of the Spanish Netherlands executed nine of every twelve men charged with witchcraft but only seven of every twelve women. One in ten women were acquitted, and no males. The Calvinist states of Scotland and Geneva were open-handed. Geneva executed and acquitted a greater proportion of males than females, two-thirds of whom were banished compared with 50 per cent of men. In Scotland a little over half of both sexes were executed and one-fifth acquitted. Bias against women was evident in the Franche Comte where the same proportion of each gender was banished (27 per cent) but four-sevenths of the women and only three-sevenths of the men were executed, and the reverse proportions acquitted. Most strikingly anti-female was England. Three-quarters of the men were acquitted and half of the women. A quarter of the women were executed and one-eighth of the men. An Englishwoman had nine times greater chance than a man of being accused of witchcraft and double his chance once accused of being executed. All jurisdictions enforced female subordination in matters of public life, excluding women from politics (with the embarrassing exception of female monarchs), the professions and the priesthood. Within the private sphere, both in the sense of attitudes within the family and of areas of domestic concern, husbands and sons did not necessarily relate to their wives, mothers and daughters in this superior manner. Attitudes varied from individual to individual. The private role of women may have been very different to that prescribed by the authorities and this is basic to a second type of explanation of gender and bias.[17]

Many interpretations rest on the assumption that women were subordinated and powerless. Witchcraft may not have been the response of powerless women kicking against a male-dominated

107

society because women had the real power hidden under mutually accepted myths of male dominance. Women were primarily associated with the domestic aspects of existence. Society itself was domestic oriented and informal power relationships dominated village life. Men had access to formal power and prestige but the real decisions were made by women. The myth of male dominance salved his wounds but consolidated the real position of women. Man was linked with formal overt power and women with *de facto*, informal and covert authority. In practice, this was exercised in the allocation and disposal of family resources which in a peasant subsistence society were basic. In such circumstances powerful peasant women exercised real power in the village community and did not need diabolic help. This might explain why accusations of witchcraft were made against women by male relatives. The powerless male with no means of effectively taking revenge on dominant women within the accepted structures, myths, and mores of the village resorted to such accusations as the only means available. In a Scottish case the source of the accusation against the woman came from her husband and his drinking companions. There were powerful peasant women such as Mary Combe in Somerset who held such sway over the community that local vicar and magistrates refused to become involved.

This concept of female power underlies a third explanation of the gender bias in witch accusation. It was not a sex war but emerged from the battle between women for control of this feminine space, a conflict intensified by the increased number of non-married females. Witchcraft was seen as the manifestation of vicious infighting among females within the family circle for dominance. Men and women in this peasant domestic society were interdependent and it was not until industrialisation that female power crumbled and effective male dominance occurred. Both explanations based on female power must be seen in the context of the village community. These may explain specific choices in a particular village but local tensions and feuds were much more complex and will be examined later. At the most, dominant females or intra-gender conflict were contributing factors to gender bias in a few situations where relevant conditions, impossible to quantify, prevailed.[18]

The Christian ethic repressed natural sexuality. There were three ways to deal with the tension created. The sufferer attributed sexual hedonism and perversion to others and then tried to prosecute them for these attributed characteristics — the misogynist fantasy approach already discussed. Secondly, the tension-ridden victims might fantasise that they were engaged in such activity — the plight of many women who confessed. The third approach was to reject the ascetic ethic and indulge their sexuality. The fourth explanation of gender bias was that it reflected this reality. More women were accused because more women were witches. The low status of women convinced some writers that witchcraft was a feminist movement. Witches were women who refused to conform to patriarchal society. They refused to show deference to existing authority figures. They were independent adults who refused to play a subservient role whether in the household or in society. Such subversives were attacked by men, and by the majority of women who willingly conformed to the role allocated to them. This argument taken further suggested that witches were members of an alternative society with different values to that which pervaded patriarchal Europe. They were laying the basis of a new society. There is scant evidence for this other than the fundamental point that most female witches were strong personalities unwilling to be cowed by circumstance or society. This thesis is little more than a backward projection by extreme feminists of their idealised future.[19]

Evidence of either a feminist cult or a devil-worshipping sect of sexual perverts was psychological assumption rather than verifiable historical data. These groups must have existed given the ascetic sexual ethic and male domination. Some women would reject both as unnatural and strike at the authority that imposed them. Their sexual repression once released could become destructive, distorted, and eventually perverted. To meet together with like minds, naked, in darkness, under the hypnotic influence of dancing and music, and indiscriminate sex of incredible variety would be explicable. Undoubtedly there were groups of satanists, as there are today, but they were insignificant among the diverse groups labelled as such by the witch hunter.[20]

Many such groups met in isolated places at strange times. As ascetic Christianity increased its strength and severely modified popular culture many of these assemblies were illicit peasant jollifications in which the traditional attitudes to sex were given free rein. In Scotland, such meetings concentrated on feasting and dancing with some casual sex — activities openly acceptable in pre-Calvinist days. Other groups performed old fertility rites, often gathering on specific nights to dance naked in the church-yard, performing rituals in which sex was reduced in most cases to symbolic gestures. There were a few ecstatic groups in which dancing and sex led to a heightened state of religious experience. By concentrating on man's basic sexual nature his psychic essence was activated to an advanced degree of spiritual ecstacy. Coition became the highest spiritual experience. Sex was not lustful gratification but a means to recover a lost perfection. Many political protesters and strange religious groups in which no sexual activity occurred were defamed by the witch hunters. By definition, any unorthodox group meeting in secret were devil-worshipping, sex-crazed witches. All five views of the nature of sexual activity engaged in by small groups — moral deviance, peasant bawdiness, cult ritual, ecstatic release and defamed dissenters — were valid. Somewhere, at some time a particular group reflected one of these patterns of behaviour. The extent of each is impossible to determine. In the totality of witchcraft accusations, however, none appear significant.[21]

Such patterns were not exclusive and many groups combined two or more of the approaches suggested. A sex cult which blended peasant bawdiness and extreme moral deviance accounted for some meetings described as sabbats. Pedro de Valencia, a seventeenth-century investigator concluded that 'evidence of all my senses leads me to feel that the meetings have been between men and women who have come together . . . to commit sins of the flesh.' Sexual behaviour at the lower end of the social scale in some European villages and towns was not very different from that attributed to the witches. In all, sex was not a major activity or prime purpose of secret meetings. Peasants were interested in sex. Sex, viewed as illicit by the authorities was readily available in the peasant community and enjoyed. Arguments that postulate witchcraft as a sex cult reacting against Christian asceticism assume incorrectly that asceticism had permeated the lower classes. Ethical Christianity did not reach the peasantry until the sixteenth and seventeenth centuries as a result of the painstaking efforts of the Protestant and Catholic Reformations.[22]

To believe that secret groups were necessary to engage freely in sexual activity accepts at face value the ascetic view. As this view permeated isolated villages the inhabitants of those villages may have been forced into such clandestine activity. This appeared to be the case in parts of Scotland, and probably in the Cambrèsis. Yet, in general, until well into the seventeenth century a witches' sabbat was not necessary for the peasants to experience sexual licence. The flexible structures which the authorities created to deal directly with illicit sex reflected a realistic approach to sexual deviance. This is not to deny that in order to strengthen reform movements the authorities did not deliberately confuse peasant orgies with witches' sabbats. The link between evil and sex was too strong a weapon for Christian reformers to renounce its use.

One piece of evidence that would support this fourth interpretation of gender bias as reflecting the predominance of women in deviant cults would be the sexual profile of the witches accused. According to the accepted elite image witches were perverted creatures who delighted in every form of sexual deviance. Most of this occurred at the sabbat or alone with the Devil and was difficult to substantiate. The verifiable facts revealed that most women accused of witchcraft had no record of sexual deviance. Rarely were witches women who had defied the sexual mores of the community. Illegitimate children were the trigger in some accusations at Salem but witches did not belong to the bawdier elements in a peasant community. There was no correlation between women who were bastard-bearers or casual prostitutes and those accused of witchcraft. John Demos has shown that in New England the sexual deviance of the witch was less than one-third that of the female 'criminal' population in general. Of women 'criminals', 32 per cent were charged with sexual offences compared with only 10 per cent among the future witches. The witches' previous misdemeanours lay elsewhere: in assaultive speech (41 per cent), theft (20 per cent) and lying (12 per cent). The actual sexual proclivities or otherwise of the designated witch were largely irrelevant to her subsequent prosecution. Their readiness to confess to a gamut of sexual activities confused the situation.[24]

The key feature which increased the impact of the witch on contemporary Europe was the partial and intermittent acceptance by the political establishment of the diabolic image.

Notes

1. Heinrich Kramer and James Sprenger (trans. Montague Summers), *The Malleus Maleficarum passim*.
2. G. Zacharias, *The Satanic Cult* p. 57.
3. *Ibid.* p. 65.
4. R. E. L. Masters, *Eros and Evil: The Sexual Psychopathology of Witchcraft* Ch. 1; Rossell Hope Robbins, *The Encyclopaedia of Witchcraft and Demonology* pp. 414–24; Montague Summers, *The History of Witchcraft and Demonology*, Introduction.

5. Masters, *op.cit.* Ch. 2; H. R. Hays, *The Dangerous Sex: The Myth of Feminine Evil* p. 155; Robbins, *op.cit.* pp. 254–9, 461–8.
6. Masters, *op.cit.* Ch. 7; Hays *op.cit.* Ch. 15; Julia Caro Baroja, *The World of the Witches* Ch. 13; Masters, *op.cit.* pp. 22, 61.
7. Robbins, *op.cit.* pp. 254–9.
8. Masters, *op.cit.* Ch. 1 pp. 4, 18; Robbins, *op.cit.* pp. 461–8, 312–17; Robbins, *op.cit.* pp. 254–9.
9. C. L'Estrange Ewen, *Witch Hunting and Witch Trials*, Appendix VI pp. 291–313.
10. *Ibid.*
11. Kramer and Sprenger, *The Malleus* pp. 121, 156; Robbins, *op.cit.* pp. 305–7.
12. W. H. Trethowan, 'The Demonopathology of Impotence', *British Journal of Psychiatry* 109 (May 1963) pp. 341–7; Robert D. Anderson, 'The History of Witchcraft: A Review with Psychiatric Comments', *American Journal of Psychiatry* 126 (1970) 1725–35; R. Muchembled, 'The Witches of Cambrèsis: The Acculturation of the Rural World in the Sixteenth and Seventeenth Century', Ch. 6 of James Obelkevich (ed.), *Religion and the People 800–1700* p. 266.
13. Muchembled, *ibid.*
14. Robbins, *op.cit.* pp. 299–301.
15. Ferdinand Mount, *The Subversive Family* pp. 226–7; Katherine Rogers, *The Troublesome Helpmate: A History of Misogyny in Literature* p. xvi Ch. 8; Ian Maclean, *The Renaissance Notion of Women* pp. 20–7.
16. Mount, *op.cit.* p. 236.
17. J. K. Swales and Hugh V. McLachlan, 'Witchcraft and the Status of Women: A Comment', *British Journal of Sociology* 30 (1979) pp. 349–58 and McLachlan and Swales, 'Witchcraft and Anti-Feminism', *Scottish Journal of Sociology* 4 (May 1980) pp. 141–66; Larner, *op.cit.* p. 94.
18. Susan Carol Rogers, 'Female Forms of Power and the Myth of Male Dominance: A Model of Male/Female Interaction in Peasant Society', *American Ethnologist* 2–4 (1975) pp. 727–56; Susan Carol Rogers, 'Woman's Place: A Critical Review of Anthropological Theory', *Comparative Studies in Society and History* 20 (1978) pp. 123–73; Rayna R. Reiter (ed.), *Toward an Anthropology of Women*, especially Paula Webster, 'Matriarchy: A Vision of Power' pp. 141–56, and Gayle Rubin, 'Traffic in Women: Notes on the "Political Economy" of Sex' pp. 157–210; G. R. Quaife, *Wanton Wenches and Wayward Wives* pp. 155–8.
19. P. Hughes, *Witchcraft* Ch. 6.
20. Joseph Tenenbaum, *The Riddle of Woman: A Study in the Social Psychology of Sex* Ch. XVIII; Judith H. Balfe, 'Comment on Clarke Garrett's *Women and Witches*', *Signs* 4 (1978) pp. 201–2.
21. Margaret A. Murray, *The Witch Cult in Western Europe* Parts IV–VI; Summers, *op.cit.* Introduction; Mircea Eliade, *Occultism, Witchcraft and Cultural Fashions: Essays in Comparative Religions* Ch. 5.
22. Julia Caro Baroja, *op.cit.* p. 113.
23. Peter Burke, *Popular Culture in Early Modern Europe* Chs. 7–8; Muchembled, *op.cit. passim.*
24. Demos, *op.cit.* pp. 76–8.

8
Ideology and Authority: The Establishment and Witch Hunting

The belief in a diabolical conspiracy against society would have been limited and action against it impossible without acceptance of the problem, and of its urgency, by sections of the political establishment. This acceptance was related to problems of ideology, and of power and its legitimisation — issues complicated by the religious upheavals of the sixteenth century. The varying intensity of these problems from state to state reacted with the particular composition of the relevant establishment and with the diverse nature of interplay between aristocracy and middle class, national monarch and bureaucracy, central and local administrations, and secular and ecclesiastical officials to differentiate the structure and fervour of each witch hunt.

The Reformation, Protestant and Catholic, linked political survival to popular beliefs. This link was not a new phenomenon but a conjunction of factors in the sixteenth century accentuated the situation. The first was the more thorough indoctrination of the masses with a Christianity, in its several forms, which emphasised individual responsibility for salvation and the reflection or achievement of this through conformity to a strict code of behaviour. This code of behaviour was of vital concern to the political elite because the Reformation split the establishment creating a new source of internal dissent and external threat. The legitimacy of a regime rested on its defence of the godly society. Both confessions claimed the exclusive monopoly of Christian truth. The loyalty of the subject and the legitimacy of the regime were therefore reflected in the total acceptance of one version of Christianity. The populace showed their loyalty to the regime by conforming to a specific pattern of values. Nonconformity, by definition, was deviance

113

from God's way, subversion of the state and rejection of the godly values of society. In the one act the dissenter was heretic, traitor and social pariah. The removal of such deviants strengthened the regime's social control and reinforced its claim as the legitimate godly authority. With heightened religious feeling, intolerance of nonconformity was a moral virtue and eradication of the dissident a moral duty.[1]

Political and moral thought in the sixteenth century used the concepts of contrariety and inversion. The basic contrasts were the religious God–Satan; the political, order–disorder; and the moral, good–evil. In attacking evil, a godly regime enforced Christian ethics, imposed political order and confirmed itself as the legitimate authority. For a regime, the diverse forms of popular deviance would most economically and effectively be contained by an assault on a deviance which subsumed all others. This ultimate evil would manifest in an inverted form the basic values of society. If these manifestations took human form they were, by definition, agents of the Devil.[2]

A diabolic agent manifested an evil that was self-evident, a clear threat to society, whose eradication by the regime was both possible and rewarding in terms of popular approval. Identification of such agents in the form of elderly peasant women appeared plausible. The struggle to bring Christianity to the populace in the sixteenth century was largely a struggle against traditional animist beliefs in which peasant sorcery appeared a major obstacle. At this time, when the establishment decided on their eradication, the sorcerers increased their popularity with the populace. Protestantism, Catholic humanism and many of the Tridentine reforms destroyed the magical props of medieval Christianity and deprived the populace of their traditional defences against evil. Their level of insecurity increased as did their fear of the Devil and they sought protection from the peasant magician. Without the protective ritual of medieval Christianity, black magic appeared more dangerous and white magic more necessary. The apparent resurgence of sorcery amongst the peasants only confirmed in the minds of segments of the establishment the danger and diabolical nature of the situation.[3]

The Scots, in particular, linked ideology, legitimacy, social control, popular conformity, contrariety, inversion and popular sorcery. The Calvinists imposed a social control based on the kirk which required a considerable degree of conformity by the masses, enforced a tightened criminal code and regulated aspects of popular life, such as drunkenness, sex and violence. The Reformation saw the overthrow of a pro-French elite by a new crop of landowners supported by lawyers and Calvinist clergy who took decades to establish their legitimacy. James VI finally used the Berwick witches to consolidate his position. He depicted the witches as supporters of his dangerous rival the Earl of Bothwell with himself as the prime target of the Satanic conspiracy. The attention paid to him by the Devil and his resolute action in destroying God's enemies verified his claim to be God's vice-regent and the legitimate power. The witch hunt in Scotland served the twin purposes of a godly regime: it enforced an ethical Christianity against traditional popular values, and it consolidated and legitimised the position of the regime.[4]

However, formal witch hunts which could escalate into popular panics and judicial mayhem were not usually initiated by a political elite succumbing to popular pressure nor imposed on an unwilling populace by a cynical or pathological magistracy. Hunts developed in periods of general community crisis when the magistrates, convinced that society was under threat, believed that only resolute action could save it. Magistrates had more than a legal responsibility to act against witches. It was a moral duty. Christian society was a manifestation of God's will and those who threatened it were agents of the Devil. Persecution of such agents was not an act of hysterical frenzy. It was a righteous, rational, required response to a clearly perceived problem.[5]

The nature of a regime's response to witchcraft in the sixteenth century was similar in Catholic and Protestant areas; the *Malleus* approach dominated. In the seventeenth century, Protestant regimes more readily adopted a providential approach by attributing misfortune to God rather than diabolic agents — an attitude most clearly seen in Puritan Massachusetts where God himself was held accountable for the day-to-day misfortunes of the Puritan father rather than an elderly female neighbour. Calvin's emphasis on morality eventually cleaned up the fantasies of the sabbat and his concentration on the sovereignty of God limited the Devil to creating illusions and thus undermined the extreme *Malleus* position.[6]

The political elite operated through different types of institutions which exercised varying degrees of effective power. The nature and effectiveness of this political authority shaped the course of the witch hunts. Witch hunting was affected by situations in which there was no clear political authority; where authority was divided between powerful groups; where powerful authority believed itself, often mistakenly, under pressure; and where powerful authority wished to extend its area of control. The geographical extent of the authority, the political effectiveness of the authority, the level at which that authority was exercised (local, regional, national or international), and the nature of that authority in terms of secular or ecclesiastical jurisdiction were relevant considerations.

The actual size of the political unit was itself irrelevant to the incidence of witch hunting. However, in the larger territories there were usually many institutions acting as checks and balances against each other. This made it difficult for witch hunters to make effective use of the total political and judicial power of the state. Spain allowed episcopal and secular courts as well as the Inquisition to prosecute witches. The conflict between such authorities at regional and central levels prevented popular panics receiving total establishment support. This is not to suggest that a large territorial state could not overcome such limitations if the issue was considered vital. In Spain, the relapsed Christianised Jew was the ultimate evil and the Inquisition was given extra-ordinary judicial power to override all other jurisdictions in its ruthless investigation of these most dangerous and often high-placed deviants. Large territorial states could mount major witch hunts if such extraordinary judicial power was effectively utilised.[7]

The French government used such extra-judicial authority in areas where normal jurisdictions were unsympathetic to its cause. It created a special tribunal to override local and regional courts when it sent Pierre de Lancre to the Pays de Labourd in Bearn to eliminate witches. At Loudun, Father Urbain Grandier was not tried before the normal courts, and was not given his right of appeal to the *Parlement* of Paris. A special investigating tribunal with arbitrary power was set up by Cardinal Richelieu which *inter alia* undermined the political autonomy of the city. These events led to the reassertion of ultra-Catholic dominance in the area and confirmed the illegal destruction of the city walls, a physical protection which had been guaranteed by the Edict of Nantes. However, in those areas of France where the central administration was strong, such as the Seine Basin, there was no witch hunting. As the power of the French monarch expanded and new areas were brought under control, witch hunting ceased, and formally ended with the edict of Louis XIV in 1682. This had been a progressive development over centuries. With a few exceptions, such as Labourd and

Loudun, the French monarchy under the guidance of the *Parlement* of Paris adopted a sceptical approach to witchcraft and considered it a provincial superstition. In 1589, Henry III and the *Parlement* freed on appeal thirteen condemned witches from Tours. Throughout the seventeenth century the *Parlement* of Paris upheld most appeals against the death penalty for this crime. In the 1670s, the *Parlement* at Rouen, which had consistently convicted witches in Normandy, was finally overruled by the king who reprieved those found guilty, much to the annoyance and protest of the local magistrates.[8]

In small political units exercising *de facto* sovereignty there were often no other institutions to check the obsessions of those in power. The individual or small group could readily use the coercive power of the state for witch hunting ends, as did the Prince-Prebend of Ellwangen, the Abbot of Obermarchtal, the Bishop of Eichstatt, the Prince-Bishops of Bamberg and Würzburg and the Abbot of Fulda. These men presided over the most extreme cases of witch hunting. Ehrenberg, Bishop of Würzburg, had his own young and able heir tortured and executed as a witch while an Abbot of Fulda allowed his witch hunter, Balthasar Ross, to poke red-hot skewers into women as they hung in strappado. The reality of the power exercised by these petty sovereigns was underlined when, with the accession of the new abbot, Ross was incarcerated and witch hunting ceased.[9]

Where small principalities and towns were subject to a superior jurisdiction anti-witch outbreaks at the local level were usually tempered by the sovereign power. The witch craze in Calw was modified by the intervention of a commissioner from the Duke of Württemberg. Inferior jurisdictions were more likely to promote witch hunting than the superior or sovereign power but the latter was not always willing or able to intervene. The Habsburgs, both as dynasts and emperors, were weak beyond their Austrian homeland. The imperial cities had more than their share of witch hunting. The distant Habsburg territories of Ortenau, Hohenberg and Bressgau hunted zealously, ignoring the moderation of their nominal sovereign. There were constant appeals from throughout Germany by lesser jurisdictions or against lesser jurisdictions asking the Emperor to enforce the Carolina Code against witches. Some appeals hoped its application would soften the campaign, others that it would strengthen it. The Vice Chancellor of Bamberg, the senior secular judge under the Prince-Bishop, was executed as a witch despite the direct orders of the Emperor to the contrary. It was only a barrage of complaints from highly placed courtiers that forced the Emperor to act against Bamberg.[10]

There is no pattern in the relationship between the local and central or inferior and superior jurisdictions in moderating or inflaming witch hunting. The French, Danish, Spanish and English governments often acted through their superior courts to modify the decisions of local jurisdictions. Between 1564 and 1640, 43 per cent of the appellants against witchcraft convictions before the *Parlement* of Paris had been sentenced to death by an inferior court, 38 per cent to the galleys and 21 per cent to banishment. In reconsidering these cases, the *Parlement* condemned 10 per cent to death, 12 per cent to the galleys, 36 per cent to banishment and released 37 per cent. The Viborg Landsting (the Danish High Court responsible for northern Jutland) acquitted 114 of the 225 capital appellants between 1612–37. In Germany, the more nominal superior jurisdictions usually did not bother to act, allowing local fanaticism its head. In southern France and in Bavaria the superior jurisdictions promoted the witch hunt against local inaction or moderation. In 1619, Duke Maximilian I of Bavaria personally intervened in a trial at Ingolstadt when the local judge dropped charges against a woman and her three children. His subsequent *Instructions on Witchcraft* (1622) spelt out a hard line that was to be enforced by local judges. Occasionally the central authority was overwhelmed by local pressures. This occurred where appropriate local authorities did not exist and the central body had to act *de novo*. Tensions built up in the local area affected the judgement of external authorities. This happened at Salem. The village elite had no institution to express their authority. The *ad hoc* bodies that arose in the village — the regular meeting of householders, the elected village committee and the local church organisation — had no authority to resolve differences and take resolute action to prevent discontent growing. This power rested with the government of Salem Town which was seen as unsympathetic to the needs of the village and the partisan supporter of one faction. Salem Village's separate existence was recognised but it was denied political autonomy. This forced the petty issues of the village to be translated into matters of principle by their protagonists in order to obtain outside support. In this way the central authority of Massachusetts was dragged into local issues that having been raised to fundamentals became emotionally charged.[11]

Sometimes superior jurisdictions failed to control their own local representatives. Witchcraft in Sweden experienced one major hunt which resulted from Charles IX setting up a special commission in 1670. It came to an end when Charles belatedly revoked the commission. The interim witnessed a fanatical witch hunt when the King failed to control his officers. In Scotland, the local desire to hunt witches was firmly harnessed to the interests of the central authority. After 1597 witchcraft could only be prosecuted with permission of the central authority. The local power of the lairds was effectively curtailed. As they were the most prominent witch hunters, the situation in Scotland indicates the moderating influence by the centre on local fanaticism.[12]

It was not the level of the jurisdiction that governed its impact on witch hunting, however; it was its effectiveness. The central administration operating in Massachusetts in 1692 was an *ad hoc* authority awaiting a new regime. In these anxious circumstances it lacked the courage to override local obsessions. The new Governor stopped the hunt. Witch hunting did not occur where a strong authority so determined. Military goverment, especially of foreigners, ended witch panics in Germany and Scotland. The military authorities had effective power and their priorities did not include pandering to local concerns. The locals, on the other hand, could find immediate scapegoats in the soldiery for their misfortunes. This was not a sudden change from a diabolic to a providential view of misfortune. Given the confessional nature of the Thirty Years War, the Protestant Swedish troops could be equated with the agents of the Devil as easily as local women. In Cromwellian Scotland, the occupying power imposed conformity with the sword and freed nine-tenths of the indicted witches. Yet as soon as the English troops left in 1658 witch hunting began anew — in panic proportions. Military occupation suspended rather than abolished the hunt. In January 1627 the town magistrates of Offenburg in Baden burnt five wealthy women. For six months Swedish troops occupied the town putting an end to the hunt. When they left in late June the town council immediately offered two shillings for every witch apprehended and within the fortnight four more wealthy women had been arrested, tried and burned.[13]

Strong superior authority prevented witch hunts if it so determined. This was the case in both England and Spain. These effective administrations did not permit local fears to manifest themselves in this way or, where they did (as in the Basque areas), used their central authority to contain and control the problem. In England, on the rare occasions when local magistrates encouraged hunting and effected a prosecution, the central authority often

119

intervened and quashed these activities. John Smith of Leicester, who for a decade had accused persons of witchcraft leading to many executions, found his activity stopped by the fortuitous visit of James I. James ordered the Archbishop of Canterbury to investigate the matter. In a retrial under the influence of an archepiscopal representative Smith was revealed as a fraud and the accused released.[14]

The effectiveness of a central authority depended on the ability and attitudes of its own officers and the resistance of existing local institutions to its authority. Central judicial officials could by their personal attitudes strongly influence approaches to witch hunting. The Chief Justices of England in the latter half of the seventeenth century gave the lead. Sir Matthew Hale supported witch hunting and it flickered on; Sir John Holt opposed it and it ceased. Central governments were also affected by the layers of judicial authority through which their power had to filter. Until 1600 in the Franche Comte the local Inquisition had a free hand in dealing with witchcraft, which it did with moderation. In 1604, the Archdukes centred on Brussels, who exerted authority over the Spanish Netherlands and Free County of Burgundy (Franche Comte), gave all seigneurial courts exercising high justice the right to pronounce the death sentence for witchcraft. This decree could have opened up the Franche Comte to the fanatical witch hunts seen in south-western Germany. However, the depth of legal institutions permitting appeals slowed down any panic and acted as a brake on the obsessions of seigneurial justice. Convicted witches could appeal from the seigneurial court to that of the *bailli* and from this to the *Parlement* of the Franche Comte. Most often each superior court was more lenient than the inferior jurisdiction although in times of panic the superior courts sometimes endorsed, if not increased, the penalties of the lower courts. It was probably the acquiescence of the superior court itself in a particular series of convictions that created panic which in more stable moments it would nip in the bud.[15]

The resort to, or acquiescence in, witch hunting by the political establishment was related more to its sense of security than to its actual power. Where elites felt secure there was little witch hunting. In England, the few outbreaks that did occur took place in periods of political tension. Extreme anxiety led to the passing of new Witchcraft Acts as well as to the pursuit of witches. In the early years of Elizabeth's reign the regime saw plots at every turn. In 1562, the Countess of Lennox was condemned for consulting wizards as to the longevity of the queen, and in the following year Sir Anthony Fortescue and two nephews of the former Catholic strongman Cardinal Pole were arrested for treason for the same activity. Later that year, a new Witchcraft Act, strong against the conjuration of spirits, was passed and prosecutions followed. Other periods of increased prosecution occurred in England during the crisis of the Spanish threat and its aftermath, and in eastern England at the conclusion of the First Civil War where the lines of authority were not clearly re-established. In Scotland, major outbursts occurred in the 1590s, when James was concerned to establish his position; in the late 1620s, where difficulty in adjusting to a rigorous Caroline regime were exacerbated by Protestant setbacks in central Europe; in the late 1640s, when the Covenanting party was determined to retain power; and in the early 1660s in the difficulties associated with the Restoration. When the Christian state appeared insecure it lashed out at its enemies, defining them as diabolic.[16]

The German principalities led the way. Those which had just changed their confessional allegiance — the newly Protestant imperial cities in the 1560s and Baden following its return to Catholicism in the 1630s — experienced severe witch hunts. Regimes which were constantly under threat of a rival confessional coup or who experienced such coups — Helfenstein or Lowenstein — were prominent witch hunters. The insecurity did not need to stem overtly from ideological differences but any anxious political elite could construe any form of opposition as a threat to the ideology of the regime. The imperial city of Rottweil was obsessed with outsiders, and the dominant factions in Offenburg and Reutlingen with their local rivals. In each case a witch hunt was directed against the opposition. In the imperial city of Offenburg the town boss had the three daughters of his major opponent arrested and one of them cruelly tortured. In Nordlingen, in Swabia, in 1590 a similar move resulted in a holocaust involving 32 women, the wives of opposition burgomasters, senators and other civic officials. Such activities not only reflected attempts of one faction in the establishment to gain supremacy over others but were often part of a campaign to centralise their administrations. The bitter attack and ultimate execution of the Vice Governor of Treves, a defender of the traditional rights of the secular courts, on the charge of witchcraft and the subsequent decline of those courts, suited the administrative rationalisation of the Prince-Archbishop. The execution for witchcraft by the Prince-Bishop of Bamberg, of

his Chancellor and five of the burgomasters served a similar end.[17]
Witch hunting was more pronounced where the elite linked their
position to a strong confessional commitment, typified by the
resurgent Catholic states of southern Germany, many cities of
France during the Wars of Religion, the Spanish Netherlands and
Scotland. This ideological commitment was most pronounced in
four of the largest Catholic states of Germany: Austria, Bavaria,
and the Prince-Archbishoprics of Cologne and Treves. Until the
last quarter of the sixteenth century Austria was free of witch hunts
due to the tolerant attitude of the Spanish-educated Emperor
Maximilian II. Even the Carolina was largely ignored and in the
Tyrol witchcraft was punished lightly with a fine; one-quarter
went to an informant, one-quarter to the judge and one-half to
charity. This moderation disappeared with the accession of Jesuit-
dominated Rudolf II who immediately issued instructions for the
resolute suppression of witchcraft and replaced the more sceptical
judges of his predecessor with fanatics of his own ilk. Four decades
of resolute hunting culminated in the codification of imperial
practice and policy by the Attorney General of Innsbruck in 1637
which set Austrian attitudes in a *Malleus* mould for another
century. Bavaria did the same. Duke William V was informed by
the Jesuits of the presence of witches and he consulted their new
university for advice. They suggested that the crime of witchcraft
was new to Bavaria and therefore the magistrates must receive
especial instruction. Between 1590 and 1630 the Dukes threw their
weight behind an intensive campaign to educate the magistrates
against witchcraft. This campaign was closely associated with the
advance of Catholicism against pockets, and later principalities, of
Protestantism in southern and central Germany. The Bavarian
witchcraft laws of 1611, 1612 and 1613 were draconian, removing
virtually all protection from the accused.[18]

A direct link between insecurity and ideology was evident in the
change of policy forced on Cologne when it became the base for
ultra-Catholic witch hunters expelled from their own territories by
the Swedish army. The municipal authorities in Cologne successfully resisted pressure from the Archbishop to hunt witches until
the city was occupied by forces of the exiled Archbishop of Mainz,
the Bishops of Bamberg, Würzburg and Speyer, and the Abbot of
Fulda. As a sign of their legitimacy they unleashed a major witch
hunt in the city that received them. The immense loss of life horri-
fied the Pope who sent two cardinals to stop the carnage. The
attack on Vice Governor Dietrich Flade of Treves followed the

accession of a new Prince-Archbishop who was obsessed with ideological purity. He expelled all heretics, exiled the Jews and turned
on the remaining deviants whom he labelled witches. In countries
where authority was less ideological in perspective and the elites
adopted a pragmatic approach to survival — the German petty
nobility, Cleves, the United Provinces and England — hunting
was less pronounced. The same was true of states who saw their
survival threatened by more obvious enemies. The Castilian elite
saw danger in the highly placed conversos, Venice in Islamic naval
power, and many Englishmen in the direct threat of Catholic
invasion. Scapegoats in the form of elderly rural women were not
necessary. Other states doubted the real effect of witchcraft, or
accepted the fallibility of human justice and preferred, as did
Geneva, to exile its witches.[19]

Some witch hunts occurred by default and the local elite were
often the victims. Absentee magistrates in Germany occasionally
appointed as their representatives men unfit both morally and pro-
fessionally for the role. The worst example occurred in Linheim,
jointly controlled by the Dean of Würzburg and Baron Von
Oynhausen. The two lords appointed a brutal mercenary, Geiss,
Chief Magistrate. He made four of his wartime cronies into
deputies and proceeded to rob the well-to-do of the city through
trumped-up charges of witchcraft. The lords refused to heed the
complaints of arbitrary slaughter and illegal prosecution that
emanated from the town, perhaps because they received their share
of the immense judicial profits. Their inaction also reflected the dis-
dain of feudal German nobility and ecclesiastics for the burgher.[20]

Correlation between type of regime and the degree of witch
hunting is difficult to establish beyond the axiom that large states
exercising superior jurisdiction, strong, secure and pragmatic, saw
little witch hunting. Those that were small, with superior jurisdiction, weak and ideologically based, experienced most. Insecure
regimes of all ilks, lacking more immediate and readily identifiable
causes of their anxiety, found agents of the Devil a very plausible
explanation.

A complicating factor for the state in dealing with diabolic
agents was that they had traditionally been the concern of the
church. Secular authorities gradually came to dominate the
prosecution of witches and one purpose of the *Malleus Maleficarum*
was to seek such aid. However, in the religious crisis the clergy
remained vitally concerned with the issue. Ecclesiastical judicial
power, while decreasing, was still effective in many areas and a

major vehicle for the exercise of authority. Although the leaders of the church were usually part of the same establishment that dominated the state, their aims and institutional structures led to a different emphasis. Despite lapses, the church was concerned to save souls, not burn heretics. The primary purpose of ecclesiastical justice was reconciliation, and its major weapon penance. In the sixteenth century, the inquisitorial method dominated in parts of Europe and with its assumption of guilt, convictions increased, as did the number of those relapsed to the secular arm for execution. Nevertheless, most ecclesiastical jurisdictions at the episcopal and lower levels showed great leniency towards accused witches.

Ecclesiastical power was never a monolith obsessed with the extermination of witches. Ecclesiastical power was widely dispersed. Even the Spanish Inquisition, that unique blend of secular and ecclesiastical jurisdiction, had no monopoly, nor overriding power in matters of witchcraft. Episcopal and secular courts successfully opposed its role in the Basque panics of 1610–14. In the early days the Bishop of Pamplona used his power to hinder the Inquisition in its prosecutions of witches. Later, when the Inquisition adopted a softer line after the internal victory of Salazar, the local secular courts kept the witch hunt going. The Inquisition's softer line reflected the moderation of a distant upper class superior power opposed to local interests, rather than an example of ecclesiastical moderation opposed to secular extremism. The local agents of the Inquisition were as much opposed to the soft line of their superiors as were the local mayors and regional secular courts. Yet the Inquisition with minor exceptions held this moderate line for almost a century. In 1526, it declared witchcraft beliefs an illusion and stemmed the panic reaction of the secular courts. In the first decade of the seventeenth century in the Basque areas of France the Bishop of Bayonne took a similar stand in defending his clergy and people against the fanaticism of a secular Royal Commissioner.[21]

The gradual decline of ecclesiastical jurisdiction in this matter and the growing subservience of the leading clergy to secular authority led to fewer but more effective witch hunts. The prosecution of witches remained a major issue in church–state relations in Scotland from the last decade of the sixteenth century well into the third quarter of the seventeenth. The first generation of Scottish religious reformers ignored witchcraft but, stimulated by the state in the early 1590s, a few fanatical clergy emerged. The regime utilised this professional support to convince the less enthusiastic members of the establishment rather than the populace. Neverthe-less, whenever the enthusiasm of the clergy over-reached itself, as occurred in 1597, the state acted quickly to stop witch hunting. The attempts of the church to keep hunts going against the will of the political elite invariably failed. Even among the Covenanters the clergy were kept in their place. This ultra-Presbyterian govern-ment of the late 1640s rejected the kirk's plans to tighten witchcraft control yet resolutely pursued individual cases of witchcraft to demonstrate the godliness of the regime. In Calvinist Scotland the clergy consistently missed out as leaders of the anti-witch crusade as the state acted directly for God without clerical intercession.[22]

It has been argued that the clergy, Catholic and Protestant, led the persecutions and condoned them in the name of Christianity. The latter was true, the former was not. The Jesuits entered Bavaria in 1541 and despite a major preaching and political effort to awaken establishment and populace to the dangers of witchcraft they had little impact for four decades. It was only when Duke William accepted their arguments that they had any success. In England, the Catholic bishops anxious to promote witch hunting unsuccessfully demanded a new Witchcraft Act from Queen Mary, and the Calvinist clergy immediately made a similar and unsuccessful demand on the accession of the new queen, Elizabeth. It was only when the queen's life was endangered a few years later that such an Act was forthcoming. The clergy were the propa-gandists but their message was usually regulated by the political elite. Without the support of that establishment the wailing of the clergy against witchcraft was to no avail.[23]

The clergy exercised their major influence through preaching and pastoral care and sometimes presented a viewpoint at variance with the political establishment and with each other. The Dominicans and Franciscans played a major role in evoking concern for witches. Their preaching in the Basque country stimu-lated the panic and made the moderating task of the Inquisition difficult. These mendicants attuned their message to the prejudices of the populace and played a major role in stimulating the anti-Semitic pogroms in Castile and in dehumanising the opposition in the French Wars of Religion which made possible the brutality and slaughter. The Jesuits, except those in Bavaria and Austria, were sceptical of the witch campaign and were a moderating influence on the secular princes. The steady preaching of the Genevan clergy brought about a more moral approach to life and found the cause of misfortune in personal misbehaviour rather than in the activities of diabolic agents. The Calvinist clergy in Scotland developed a concept of a spiritualised Devil which did not fit well with the physical monster of the *Malleus*. Their preaching concentrated on specific examples of immorality and they avoided excursions into popular demonology. The Scots clergy reserved their diabolic fears for their colleagues and the magistrates. It was not a topic for the popular pulpit.[24]

The lower clergy represented a cross-section of the populace whose views did not necessarily coincide with those of the dominant ecclesiastical or political elite. This was dangerous, and in some areas such as Würzburg the latter singled out clergy and accused them of witchcraft. Many clergy did reflect the animist beliefs of their congregations. Delumeau overestimated the effect of Christian preaching against traditional beliefs because many of these preachers continued to assert an animist-coloured Christianity. This pessimistic view of the ineffectiveness of post-Reformation, post-Tridentine clergy was shared alike by English Protestant Puritans and French Catholic Jansenists. The ambivalent role of the clergy with regard to witchcraft was illustrated in New England. One cleric was executed as a witch, another largely provoked the panic by his antagonistic behaviour towards his neighbours. Yet this same man was loathe to believe that witchcraft was involved. Another through his writings created the impression that New England was under threat from a diabolic conspiracy. In the end it was this man's doubts about the reliability of spectral evidence that helped bring the panic to an end. In England, the clergy did not as a group stand out from the popular views of their parishioners or the pragmatic stance taken by their local gentry. Nevertheless, some clergy were caught between the differing views of the elite and those of the populace. The independence of the ecclesiastical system, however, had been destroyed from on high, and ecclesiastical jurisdiction while it continued to function took cognisance of the views of the political elite. Long after the political establishment ceased to prosecute witchcraft sections of clergy clung to *Malleus* type beliefs. In England, Presbyterian cleric Richard Baxter published such views at the end of the seventeenth century and the Scottish clergy in 1773 publicly reaffirmed their belief in witchcraft. The mainstream clergy had long ceased to be anything but servants of the establishment and that establishment no longer accepted witch hunting as a means of survival.[25]

The witch hunt developed from the conjunction of two major

ingredients: popular reaction towards witchcraft and official action. At the village level, witchcraft was endemic and for most of the time accepted by the villagers without undue concern. At times the fear of witchcraft reached the level of a scare. When this witch scare reached obsessive proportions and came to dominate the life of the community a panic occurred. From the official side of the equation the political elite showed indifference to witchcraft and often to popular witch scares. Occasionally the elite took up the prosecution of a witch during such a scare. This prosecution became a hunt when the establishment believed that a threat existed and witches other than those before them had to be uncovered and punished. Such witch hunts created and maintained widespread panics that in turn justified the continuation of the hunt. Official action against witches was manifest in national panics, large regional panics, small localised prosecutions of from four to twelve persons, or in the prosecution of a single witch. All but the last could be labelled hunts.

The initial reasons for a local witch scare in a particular community usually had little to do with the reasons taken up by the magistrates and made central in the resultant panic. The populace was concerned with *malefice* and if the witch made good any losses she was believed to have occasioned she was seldom taken to court. The elite in parts of Europe saw the problem in a different light — apostacy had to be rooted out. Christian zeal for doctrinal purity made it easy for an isolated act of village magic to develop into a conspiracy intent on undermining Christian society.

Authorities usually took formal notice of such village activities when community harmony seemed disrupted. The Basque crisis gained official recognition when the local ecclesiastical authorities found that the usual methods of public confession and private reconciliation were not working. When a number of key witnesses to local deviance died officials suspected murder and a diabolical conspiracy. The local factor involved was the alleged power of witches over children and the disruptive effect of this on family and community life. Parent–child relations in the Basque foothills were clearly strained. Initially, the central authorities, through the regional branch of the Inquisition assisted by the secular regional courts, kept the populace at a high level of anxiety. This was maintained by a preaching crusade undertaken by the mendicant orders in 1610 which led to a glut of formal accusations. The sabbat became the critical issue in this as in most witch panics because the local witches who met there could be readily identified by any of their number who had been arrested.

Confession by the witch including the names of her associates was the object of the exercise. The witches of Rottenburg were the most fortunate. City officials discovered a truth drug. One draught of the magic potion caused the suspects to reveal all. In other German jurisdictions torture had to be used and had to be successful. As prosecution was based on the presumption of guilt, torture had constantly to reaffirm this guilt in the form of an acceptable confession. Every person who failed to confess under torture undermined this rationale — proof that innocent persons could be suspected and tortured.[26]

Witch hunts ended when the authorities stopped judicial action for one or more of five reasons. When accusations were made against highly placed officials and the establishment itself felt threatened, prosecution ceased. This occurred in many German principalities and in Salem. Secondly, hunts stopped when it was realised that witch hunting was destroying the community. The decimation of the female population, the withdrawal of students, the decline of trade, the withdrawal of finance and the opinion of the neighbouring principalities all had an impact on some German hunts. Hunting also ceased when outside forces dictated such action, as in Scotland in 1649–60 and in those parts of Germany under Swedish occupation. Fourthly, small scale panics — small usually because they lacked the automatic fuelling of spiralling accusations — usually ran their course and ceased when the specific problem confronting the community which had engendered official support came to an end. The ritual cleansing had been effected. The fifth factor that brought a witch hunt to an end was the death of a prime mover. The deaths of the witch hunting bishops of Bamberg and Würzburg and the accession of a new abbot at Fulda or a prince-archbishop in Cologne, Treves or Mainz ended prosecution overnight.[27]

The recourse to witch hunting itself ended for one or more of three reasons. The cumulative effect of destructive panics led many magistrates to question the logic of their judicial axioms; the elite lost confidence in the system. Elsewhere it slowed down and stopped because the magistrates, fearful of taking the initiative, increasingly adopted a literal and ultra-cautious approach to the law and its procedures; they were no longer willing to cut corners and refused to accept witchcraft as an exceptional crime. The Swiss magistrates limited torture to the strict interpretation of imperial law — three rounds on the strappado. This level of torture could be withstood by most women and 50 per cent of men. The same judges gave little credence to the evidence of children and were very careful about indicting persons whose only offence was to be named by an accused witch. They were predisposed to see such accusations as a peasant vendetta rather than a diabolic conspiracy. To protect themselves they rarely acted against witches unless there was a long history of attested *maleficium*.[28]

In France, according to Mandrou, the magistracy was struck by a crisis of conscience. A metaphysical frame of reference slipped from their minds and they looked for a natural explanation for the events brought before them. Belief in a natural explanation reflected the confidence of the magistracy, manifested especially in the *Parlement* of Paris. This sceptical approach to supernatural intervention was echoed in the public's disinclination to clamour for the persecution of the witch as their own world view had been changed by effective Christian preaching. Recent research suggests that the changing attitude in France was due less, if at all, to a crisis of conscience and a new world view but simply to a more rational and legal application of the law. The *Parlement* of Paris had always insisted on the full protection of the law for the accused and the *Malleus* approach slowly disappeared as the influence of the *Parlement* of Paris spread throughout France.

The precise nature of the law and its interpretation and implementation shaped witch hunting in the hundreds of jurisdictions across Europe.[29]

Notes

1. For the Christianisation of the populace see Jean Delumeau, *Catholicism between Luther and Voltaire; A New View of the Counter Reformation.* It is not necessary to agree with Delumeau's extremely negative view of the Christian impact on the medieval peasant to accept the basic changes wrought among the lower orders by Tridentine Catholicism; Christina Larner, *Enemies of God* pp. 25–6, 157–9, 194–6; Gustav Henningsen, *The Witches' Advocate* p. 15; Pennethorne Hughes, *Witchcraft* p. 164.

2. Christina Larner, 'Crimen Exceptum? The Crime of Witchcraft in Europe', Ch. 2 of B. Lenman, G. Parker and V. Gatrell (eds), *Crime and the Law: The Social History of Crime in Western Europe since 1500* p. 73; Larner, *Enemies of God* p. 58; Stuart Clark, 'King James' *Daemonologie*: Witchcraft and Kingship', Ch. 7 of S. Anglo (ed.), *The Damned Art: Essays in the Literature of Witchcraft* p. 177; Stuart Clark, 'Inversion, Misrule and the Meaning of Witchcraft', *Past and Present* 87 (May 1980) pp. 98–127.

3. Keith Thomas, *Religion and the Decline of Magic* pp. 670, 763; Sydney

Anglo, 'Evident Authority and Authoritative Evidence: *The Malleus Maleficarum*', Ch. 1 of Anglo, *op.cit.* p. 9.

4. Larner, *Enemies of God* pp. 1, 5, 53–8, 83, 89; Clark in Anglo, *op.cit.* p. 165.

5. Larner, *Enemies of God* pp. 15, 19, 23; Russell, *Witchcraft in the Middle Ages* p. 203; H. C. Erik Midelfort, *Witch Hunting in Southwestern Germany* p. 190.

6. Midelfort, *op.cit.* p. 65; E. William Monter, *Witchcraft in France and Switzerland* pp. 30–1, 61; Baroja, *op.cit.* p. 128; Thomas, *op.cit.* pp. 596–7; Ann Kibbey, 'Mutations of the Supernatural: Witchcraft, Remarkable Providences and the Power of Puritan Men', *American Quarterly* 34 (Summer 1982) pp. 125–48.

7. Midelfort, *op.cit.* p. 81; G. Henningsen, *The Witches Advocate* Chs. 10–13.

8. Rossell Hope Robbins, *The Encyclopedia of Witchcraft and Demonology* pp. 210, 318; Julio Caro Baroja, *The World of the Witches* p. 158.

9. For details of German 'atrocities' see Robbins, *op.cit.* under Bamberg, Cologne, Flade, Germany, Gwinner, Lemp, Schuler, Treves, and Würzburg, pp. 35–7, 99–100, 215–22, 238–9, 303–5, 449–51, 514–16, 555–7; Midelfort, *op.cit.* Chs. 5–6.

10. *Ibid.*

11. A. Soman, 'The Parlement of Paris and the Great Witch Hunt 1565–1640', *Sixteenth Century Journal* 9:2 (1978) pp. 31–44, especially p. 35; Gustav Henningsen, 'Witchcraft in Denmark', *Folklore* 93 (1982) pp. 131–7, especially p. 135; Robbins, *op.cit.* pp. 42–4; Paul Boyer and Stephen Nissenbaum, *Salem Possessed: The Social Origins of Witchcraft* pp. 40, 51, 68.

12. Robbins, *op.cit.* p. 42; Larner, *Enemies of God* p. 87.

13. Midelfort, *op.cit.* p. 75; Larner, *ibid.* p. 199; Robbins, *op.cit.* p. 221.

14. Henningsen, *op.cit.* p. 370–83; Robbins, *op.cit.* p. 301–3.

15. Robbins, *op.cit.* p. 165; Monter, *op.cit.* p. 77.

16. Thomas, *op.cit.* Ch. 14; Larner, *Enemies of God* Chs. 5–7; Robbins, *op.cit.* p. 156.

17. Midelfort, *op.cit.* Chs. 5–6; Robbins, *op.cit.* pp. 238–9, 289–93, 303–5.

18. Robbins, *op.cit.* pp. 32–3, 42–4.

19. Robbins, *op.cit.* pp. 100–1; Monter, *op.cit.* p. 66.

20. Robbins, *op.cit.* p. 450.

21. Robbins, *op.cit.* pp. 476, 41 and Henningsen, *op.cit.* p. 127.

22. Larner, *Enemies of God* pp. 56, 74, 85.

23. Robbins, *op.cit.* pp. 32, 156.

24. Henningsen, *op.cit.* Chs. 6 and 10; Monter, *op.cit.* pp. 58–66; Larner, *Enemies of God* p. 162.

25. Boyer and Nissenbaum, *op.cit.* p. 9; Robbins, *op.cit.* pp. 17, 456.

26. Midelfort, *op.cit.* pp. 91, 149.

27. Midelfort, *op.cit.* pp. 105, 158; Larner, *Enemies of God* pp. 60, 200.

28. Monter, *op.cit.* pp. 36, 87; H. C. Erik Midelfort, 'Witch Hunting

and the Domino Theory', Ch. 7 of James Obelkevich (ed.), *Religion and the People 800–1700* pp. 277–88.
   29. Monter, *op.cit.* pp. 61–2; 84–7.

9

The Law, Torture and Trial

The level of legal prosecutions for witchcraft rose in the fifteenth century, declined in the first half of the sixteenth, and reached a peak in the century after 1560, almost disappearing in the last three decades of the seventeenth. The latter period of increase reflected expanded judicial exertion more than the proliferation of diabolic activity. This judicial activity involved the delineation of the crime, and the codification of procedures as well as the escalation in prosecutions. Across Europe the level of prosecution varied considerably. The law was a weapon for social control and the establishment used it to define acceptable behaviour. The legal code made manifest the principle of inversion. The conventional world was protected by proscribing its opposite.[1]

This was true of a patriarchal society in its regulation of women. Two new crimes were created: witchcraft and infanticide, both associated with women and in which those females charged were held responsible for their alleged acts. The increase in the number of witch trials was in part a by-product of the criminalisation of women. Previously fathers and husbands were held legally responsible for women and continued to be so in most traditional crimes until well into the nineteenth century. Patriarchal society delineated its image of the ideal woman. The inverted model of this ideal was the witch. An independent and aggressive woman who failed to nurture her children and serve her husband had to be severely punished. As there were few outlets for female independence and aggression the male myth readily became the female reality. Sorcery was the vehicle through which some women could give vent to their frustrations. Feminist historians take this argument too far. Women *per se* were not the objective of the witch hunts. Witches were prosecuted by the law and feared by the populace as dangerous diabolic agents responsible for current misfortunes. This is not to deny that as many of them were women, partly the result of a stereotype emerging in a misogynistic culture, witch hunting played a role in sexual control. It reminded women that female security lay in conforming to the male ideal.[2]

The nature of this social control, in which gender-role conformity was part, and its reflection in judicial activity ranged across a spectrum from the repressive control of some continental jurisdictions to the more restrained approach of the English. The former was free from internal control, equipped with extraordinary powers to suppress deviance, and with a material interest (in the form of property confiscation) in convicting dissenters. The latter was accountable and restrained by other internal institutions, restricted by its own procedures and with little vested interest in the isolation and punishment of the deviant.[3]

This spectrum reflected the level to which far-reaching judicial changes had infiltrated the particular jurisdiction. This judicial revolution involved the replacement of private, interpersonal, accusatory and restorative justice by a public, bureaucratic, punitive and inquisitorial system. Responsibility for legal action moved from plaintiff or accuser to a public official. This often involved a change from an accusatory method of procedure, a system loaded in favour of the defendant, to an inquisitorial approach in which the defendant was placed in a difficult position; a situation made worse by the nullification of the law of talion. In medieval Europe criminal justice was largely left to the individual accuser, from arresting the culprit and finding the evidence to substantiating the case. If he failed he could suffer the penalty laid down for the crime he had unsuccessfully prosecuted. This 'talion' prevented frivolous accusations, especially in the cases of sorcery which were difficult to prove. In 1451, a man in Strasbourg was drowned when he was unable to prove his accusation of witchcraft against a woman. Three decades later the authors of the *Malleus* despaired of Coblenz as that town continued to use the accusatory procedures and apply the talion even in cases of witchcraft.[4]

The inquisitorial procedure, especially as it became institutionalised, first within the medieval Inquisition and then in a number of secular jurisdictions, completely changed the situation. Public officials took the initiative in gathering evidence — initially denunciations and depositions from witnesses whose identity remained concealed from the accused. The trial was conducted in secret, the accused kept ignorant of the charges for months, kept isolated from all human contact except for the investigating judge and denied counsel (or, where this was permitted, his role was to persuade the accused to confess). Torture was freely used to obtain such confessions and to discover accomplices — a process which kept the hunt going.

The purpose of the law was now retribution: the punishment of acts of wrongdoing rather than restoration, satisfying the losses of the victim. The initiative for action passed to the public official from the individual plaintiff, while the procedures adopted were inquisitorial rather than accusatory. How far such changes were implemented depended on how far legal system was centralised and the extent to which the central authorities saw fit to adopt them. This centralisation took four forms that were pertinent to the witch trials. Superior jurisdictions effectively controlled or vitiated inferior bodies; secular jurisdictions dominated ecclesiastical ones; new crimes were created under the jurisdiction of the dominant judicial body; and this jurisdiction was applied throughout the social order. In essence, the trend was toward a dominant centralised secular authority with its jurisdiction extended through usurping ecclesiastical crimes and creating new ones, and by applying its authority to the populace at large.

In England, major felonies were dealt with by the assizes rather than the quarter sessions; in France, the *Parlements* gradually dominated the lesser courts and the *Parlement* of Paris the lesser *Parlements*. In Castile, the initial policy of Henry IV to give jurisdiction to the local courts, as he did in 1466 in the case of witchcraft, was quickly reversed with the creation of the Inquisition. In Scotland, in 1597 the Privy Council obtained control over witchcraft prosecution. The state used the statute to bring under the control of its secular courts issues such as incest and adultery that had previously been the concern of the ecclesiastical authorities. Ecclesiastical courts were concerned with social harmony, ritually cleansing the offender and re-integrating him into Christian society. Even in the sixteenth and seventeenth centuries witches who confessed and were reconciled to the church often received a mild penance. Witchcraft was initially ecclesiastical and private. The secular courts were increasingly concerned to punish the offender and publicly proclaim her offence both as an ideological statement and as a deterrent. Secularisation of witch jurisdiction contributed to the increase in the level of prosecution.[5]

The state also used statute to create new crimes such as

134

infanticide and to redefine others such as witchcraft. After centuries of development, the church had finally accepted, in the pronouncements of its Renaissance popes at least, a concept of witchcraft as a diabolic conspiracy which was a blend of sorcery and apostacy. Secular states differed as to the precise composition of this blend. Witchcraft was defined differently from jurisdiction to jurisdiction. At one extreme witchcraft was defined as a thought-crime and persons were prosecuted because as witches by definition they had renounced their allegiance to God. They were tried as heretics. Until the witchcraft acts of the sixteenth century it was not a temporal offence to engage in magic *per se*. Many sorcerers had fallen foul of the temporal law for centuries but as poisoners, traitors, murderers or frauds. The Roman law reflected in much of Canon law and in many of the new legal codes, for example the Carolina, accepted the diabolic image of the witch. In Roman law jurisdictions the apostacy and the pact with the Devil remained the essence of the crime of witchcraft. In such jurisdictions the trend toward retribution and the use of the inquisitorial procedure went furthest.[6]

At the other extreme witchcraft consisted of individual acts of *maleficium*. In England, witches were tried as felons for anti-social behaviour. England was slow to adopt the many changes of the judicial revolution. It had little Roman law, no inquisition, and little unlimited royal authority. In most parts of Europe dominated legally by common and customary law, individual acts of *maleficium* remained the basic act of deviance and the accusatory trial procedures were retained. This system relied on trial by jury, a presumption of innocence on the part of the accused and a clear separation of prosecution and judgement. English magistrates took little initiative in investigation or prosecution and remained stubbornly independent and rarely a tool of ideological or moral interests, at least with regard to witches. The English witch could appeal to a higher authority and sue accusers for defamation. Such a system did not always live up to its ideals and there were ways for the establishment to bypass the legal protection offered to the defendant. The Privy Council acting in the Star Chamber could and did act in an inquisitorial manner under the king's absolute authority but limited itself to the powerful rivals of the Crown. The standard of proof required in practice in the English system was low compared to continental jurisdictions and to the ideals expressed by William Perkins. In most cases, the word of one witness if of higher social standing than the accused was accepted and defence counsel was not permitted until 1836. In the end, the English response to witch accusations rested on the common sense and disinterest of the magistrate.[7]

The law regarding witchcraft, which at the beginning of the sixteenth century was complex and confusing, remained diverse for the next two centuries. Ecclesiastical jurisdictions continued to treat all magic as a heresy but many showed great leniency if the culprit repented. Secular jurisdictions on the whole agreed that diabolic witchcraft which proved fatal warranted the death penalty. They reacted differently to a diabolic pact without evidence of harm, to harmful magic without a pact and to harmless magic itself. The decentralisation of justice left key aspects of law to the precedents or ordinances of local jurisdictions, or the enforcement of central laws to the policies or the whim of local officers. The requirement of the Constitutio Criminales Carolina 1535 that magistrates when in doubt should seek advice, and the use of Law faculties for this purpose added further variety to the situation. In practice most legal systems in Germany, Switzerland and France sought proof of both *maleficium* (harmful magic) and the diabolic pact. Saxony after 1572 was an exception, burning on the evidence of a pact alone. Whether by prescription (in Roman law areas) or by custom, local rules varied. The Danes in 1547 limited the type of testimony accepted, prohibited torture and later permitted appeals against conviction. The Scots did not require a confession before conviction, permitted defence counsel and subjected those who consulted witches to the penalties prescribed for the witches themselves. In Bavaria, property of the convicted was forfeit; in the Channel Islands torture was prohibited until after the death sentence had been imposed. The city authorities in Cologne permitted only their own officers to arrest for witchcraft, and punished through banishment.[8]

The Finns hanged males and burned women. In sixteenth century Sweden, witches were whipped and their clients fined. When penalties were increased six witnesses were necessary to substantiate sorcery but twelve compurgators could free an accused by simply swearing to his good name. In England, all three Acts (1542, 1563, 1604) imposed the death penalty for the conjuration of evil spirits and for *maleficium* that caused death but varied considerably on other aspects of witchcraft and sorcery. Henry VIII required the death penalty and forfeiture of property on those that tried to divine treasure, find lost property, cause or intend to cause physical harm, provoke unlawful love, or desecrate crosses. Elizabeth reduced these to one year's imprisonment while James I brought back the death penalty for bodily injury, the theft of corpses and all second offences.[9]

The legal system was concerned not only with a wider range of crimes but applied its sanctions further down the social scale. Prosecution for sorcery in the Middle Ages was directed against the court magician and powerful personalities consorting with him. The aberrent behaviour of illiterate elderly female peasants was of no concern to the law. In the sixteenth century the need of newly emerging regimes to enforce conformity throughout society expressed essentially in religious ideology became essential. The infliction of physical pain was also transformed during the 'judicial revolution'. Ordeal disappeared and judicial torture increased. The dominance of the ordeal in the early Middle Ages reflected the belief in immanent justice in which the case was submitted to the highest authority of all: God. The lower classes found themselves bound and immersed in water. If they sank they were innocent. Arms could be immersed in boiling water and the state of the scald marks after a few days would determine guilt or otherwise. The upper classes submitted themselves or their champions to ordeal by battle. Such trials slipped from prominence by the thirteenth century when a more direct appeal to God was seen as acceptable in the form of purgation. The accused simply swore his innocence and a specified number of compurgators swore that his oath could be accepted. This new development greatly assisted the defendent especially if he were wealthy enough to put together a group of reliable compurgators.[10]

The second quarter of the thirteenth century saw the re-emergence of judicial torture in urban Italy and Spain as authorities relied on human rather than divine agencies in their ruthless pursuit of criminals. The persons tortured in this period were not heretics but murderers. Torture was used to elicit the truth of their criminal offence when there was a strong presumption of guilt but little satisfactory evidence. In 1252 Pope Innocent IV permitted inquisitors to torture and to absolve each other from any abuse that might occur. He argued that as torture was applied to persons who broke the laws of man it was even more appropriate for those who broke the laws of God. Ironically the use of torture by ecclesiastical authorities was an attempt to rationalise the judicial procedure and to obtain firm evidence. It was ideally a sure means of arriving at the truth. The accused had to be freed from the power of the Devil and torture was believed to be effective in achieving this end. Torture had a quasi-religious function in bringing a suspect back into the realm of normal humanity, freed from his diabolic obsessions.[11]

Torture was used to obtain evidence, not as a punishment. In most countries the law required that the accused later affirm that the confession was offered freely and not given under duress — a process often abused. In Scotland, an often insensible victim had his confession mumbled to him by an inarticulate clerk and the sagging of the former's head was taken as an indication that such a confession was now offered freely. The restraints on torture applied with regard to age, sex and physical condition of the victim and the need to apply it always in a Christian and humane manner were often ignored. The Spanish Inquisition was exemplary in complying with such restrictions, the Bamberg authorities in ignoring them. The range of tortures available and the level of abuse involved resulted in acts of gargantuan inhumanity.[12]

The basic torture was the strappado, in which wrists were tied behind the back and the victim suspended by a rope tied to these wrists, and squassation, an extension of this, when weights were tied to the body and the rope jerked. The stretching, squeezing and cutting of flesh and the crushing of bones was achieved through thumbscrews, leg vices, the piercing of tongues, the removal of nails, fingers, thumbs and toes, the tightening of spiked bands around the head, prayer stools made of sharp spikes on which the victim was forced to kneel, the rack, eye gouging, rope burns on sensitive part of the body, constant flogging and the use of red hot pincers. Perhaps reflecting the sadism of the torturers was the use of scalding baths, the cutting of feet and the applica-tion of hot oil to the wound, pouring molten lead or hot oil into boots, soaking a victim's hair (pubic and otherwise) in alcohol and setting it alight, placing sulphur under the armpits and firing it, subjecting the accused to heated or spiked chairs and boxes, and probing the privy parts with sharp or heated needles and the anus with hot pokers. Less horrific but effective were starvation, deprivation of sleep, confinement in small dark holes, a salt diet and lack of water, a hair shirt steeped in vinegar, exposure while naked on cold stones, and constant exercise. A preview of the instruments of torture carefully explained and the stripping of the victim prior to actual torture were in themselves often sufficiently humiliating and fearful to produce a confession.[13]

An obvious manifestation of the 'judicial revolution' was the rapid growth of the legal profession. Lawyers increased in number, efficiency and power. The trained legal bureaucrat replaced the feudal magnate and the high ecclesiastic at the centre of power and as its major agent. As the law expanded it developed its own mysteries, code of ethics and monopolistic control of the judicial machine. The attitudes and work of the lawyer contributed to the spate of witch trials. It was the lawyer and not the theologian that carried out the trials. The former increasingly rejected the evidence of the latter and of the medical profession. Lawyers were convinced of the correctness of their proceedings. In Scotland, no lawyer openly expressed doubts about the legal system and witchcraft until the offence was abolished. Lesser magistrates and most lawyers in much of Germany and France rarely doubted the validity of their actions. They acted according to the law, they were the upholders of the law, they must not question.[14]

The lawyer had a vested interest in the legal system's approach to witchcraft in two ways. It was an aspect of a profession which gave him income, influence and power. Secondly it was a major vehicle in implementing an ideology or code of behaviour to which he subscribed on behalf of the political establishment to which he increasingly belonged as well as served. The lawyer played a decisive role in adjusting peasant complaints about isolated cases of *maleficium* into fully fledged proceedings against apostacy. In Scotland, the articles on which a witch was finally prosecuted bore little relationship to the bulk of charges under which she first came to the attention of the magistrates. Although lawyers and magistrates adapted the charges to meet the ideological and moral needs of the establishment they rarely initiated prosecutions in the face of peasant disinterest. There were cases where magistrates indulged in a personal vendetta and used their power to arrest their victim for witchcraft, as did Sir George Home with the aged healer Alexander Hamilton. In England, the lawyers showed no more or no less an interest in prosecuting witches than other groups in the community.[15]

Continental lawyers had an additional vested interest in witch trials which may have contributed substantially to their number and intensity: the legal right to confiscate the property of the witch. The higher social standing of many of the continental witches and the spread of the panic usually higher and higher up the socio-economic scale suggested that some magistrates were influenced by greed. The anxiety to discover accomplices within the wealthy victims' circle of friends ensured profitable confiscations. In Scotland, lawyers and magistrates made no profit other than their fees from witch trials. The Scottish system placed heavy financial burdens on the local authorities who initiated the prosecutions. The wealthy members of the parish footed the bill for the trial of local witches who, while not lacking property, had insufficient means to meet the cost of the trial. The financial benefits of witch trials in Scotland went indirectly to the central government, which was freed from the cost of the prosecution, and to a few minions employed to watch over the accused. The forfeiture of property common on the continent was severely limited in the English Act of 1563 which safeguarded the heir's inheritance and protected the widow's dower. In 1604 any claim on a witch's property was abolished. This reflected the advanced development of absolute and inalienable concepts of property in England rather than any greater humanity. This lack of material incentive, especially given the clamour for land by the establishment, explained in part the lack of zeal evident in England to prosecute witches and uncover their hordes of accomplices. Perhaps the Dissolution of the Monasteries pre-empted the need to free land for the greedy.[16]

The trends in legal procedures and attitudes discussed above were the result of general changes within which witchcraft was profoundly affected. There were a number of other aspects of the legal system that were directed more specifically to witchcraft itself. Prosecution of witchcraft was made easier by considering it as both *delictum mixti fori* and as a *crimen exceptum*. The latter enabled it to be considered by both ecclesiastical and secular courts and removed much of the jurisdictional conflict that occurred between these courts on less important matters. The latter made witchcraft unique in many jurisdictions.

Witchcraft was the most heinous of crimes aimed at the overthrow of Christian society. The legal processes were manifestations of the defence of Christendom. These were inadequate as they stood to deal with the problem. As Bodin argued, 'proof of such evil (is) so obscure and difficult that not one out of a million witches would be accused or punished if regular legal procedures were followed'. Judges must be concerned with the safety of society and ready in that cause to sacrifice individual rights. This ultimate need to protect Christian society justified the acceptance of evidence generally regarded as inadmissable — that obtained from accomplices, felons, excommunicants, heretics, children and through the use of torture. Witnesses were liable to torture if they equivocated or appeared unwilling to testify. The names of witnesses were withheld and witnesses and accused could be held in prison until the court believed it had sufficient evidence. These extraordinary means were required because witchcraft as a crime consisted not only of acts and statements but of thoughts. To get to the truth of this thought-crime the inquisitorial procedure backed by torture was essential. The evidence of witches against each other had to be accepted, as had that of other undesirables, because nice people, orthodox Christians, would know nothing of such a horrible crime and be in no position to provide evidence. This approach was not the legal norm. It ran counter to the trend for all other crimes. Modern standards of evidence and procedures were gradually gaining acceptance. For example, concern was shown that juries or judges had no material interest in the conviction or otherwise of a defendant, that the witnesses actually saw the crime committed, and that bribery and torture were eradicated.[17]

The exceptional procedural approach to witchcraft had popular support. The people at large as well as the lawyer regarded the trial of a witch as more important than those for theft, murder or sexual deviation. A feeling of insecurity developed especially if persons of previously good character were arrested. This was not because an innocent had been accused. Effective brain-washing precluded such an interpretation. It was fear that they or their kin may be next to fall under diabolic influence. Witchcraft had penetrated deeply into their society even to their own families. The trial of a witch was significant alike to authorities and populace. The witch was by definition an abnormal person. Her execution demonstrated group solidarity. In removing a deviant and reasserting the boundaries of normality the security of the virtuous was sustained. If witch trials became routine they lost their *raison d'être*.

The level of witch hunting depended on the degree to which jurisdictions accepted witchcraft as a *crimen exceptum* and adopted the appropriate measures. Prosecutions and convictions were less in Geneva because magistrates refused to accept the evidence of children and of witches, and they rejected guilt by association. In those parts of Germany which adhered strictly to the letter and spirit of the Carolina Code with regard to torture, extravagant witch hunts did not occur. The specified maximum three rounds of the strappado could be withstood by a third of men and probably half of the women subject to it and therefore a confession in such cases rarely emerged — a result which undermined the effectiveness and therefore the continuing use of the system.[18]

Even the extraordinary procedures adopted to deal with a *crimen exceptum* had their problems. As the crime of witchcraft became more spiritual in concept the essence of this redefined crime — the pact with the Devil — remained difficult to prove. The link between a particular misfortune and the *malefice* of the witch had also to be established. The blanket solution was the confession and the acceptance of hearsay evidence from dubious sources. In most jurisdictions the death penalty could not be imposed unless there was a confession; this confession had to be given freely and without duress. To get the initial confession torture was widely used. Ironically, the need for a confession made necessary the use of torture. The confession itself served two major purposes. The form of the confession which required the denunciation of accomplices was the major method of sustaining a hunt. The reading of the confession publicly at the execution, and the distribution of printed copies, reinforced the legitimacy of the trials and impressed on the popular mind the reality of witchcraft. This mind was so attuned to a conformist attitude that a witch's refusal to confess was proof of guilt. The Devil sustained her against all the pressures applied by the legal authorities. Without diabolic assistance she could not have withstood the torture applied. Bravery under torture was evidence that she had a pact with the Devil and he was fulfilling his part of the bargain. Confession without torture was also a sign of guilt. It was a diabolic device to confuse and mislead the Christian authorities.

Without a confession the pact was difficult to prove. The evidence was in the mind of the witch and witchcraft itself created an imaginary world of cause and effect in which the criteria of objective reality were inapplicable. Witchcraft was a belief system which protected itself from penetration unless a member of the world confessed. For this reason the presumption of guilt was assumed rather than proved. This 'evidence' consisted of the Devil's mark, reputation, familiars, mischief following a quarrel or curse, spectral evidence, guilt by association, denunciation by accomplices, the possession of magical objects and inability to recite the Lord's Prayer.

The acceptance of the belief that the Devil left a mark on the body of the witch as a sign of his agreement, gave pricking the appearance of a more objective method of proof. The mark was insensitive to pain. Therefore, the body of the suspect could be scrutinised for any strange mark and, if the victim exhibited no pain when this mark was pricked with a needle and the wound drew no blood, she was obviously guilty. The Scots developed the craft of pricking and Scots prickers were widely used in England in the 1640s until they were unmasked and prosecuted by the military regime. On the Restoration, this Cromwellian policy was endorsed and pricking was made illegal in Scotland in 1662. The system was less popular on the Continent, although in the Franche Comte in the middle of the seventeenth century Inquisitor Symard invariably tested the suspected witch 'with the needle'.[19]

In England, the belief that the Devil provided his witches with a special imp, a familiar to assist her in her wickedness, could provide proof of witchcraft. These familiars, in the form of known or unknown animals, needed to suckle at the teat of their witch. They would invariably seek her out for this purpose no matter where she was. If a suspect was locked in a closed room it was only a matter of time before a familiar would try to reach her. A fly finding its way through the cracks in an otherwise sealed room could be fatal for the person being watched.

The link with the Devil was difficult to establish. To prove *maleficium* and to relate the misfortune of one person with the malice of another was also difficult but this problem seemed to be solved by simple assumption. Magistrates either assumed or rejected the alleged connections on the basis of their common sense and prejudice rather than legal evidential criteria. In cases where the misfortune took the form of physical affliction the victims were often confronted with the alleged source of this pain and their reactions scrutinised. In Salem, the contortions and obvious discomfort of the female accusers in the presence of the accused were accepted as evidence of guilt. There, too, the claims of young girls that they had been tormented by the accused were accepted, despite evidence that at the time of the alleged experience the accused were identified as being elsewhere. This discrepancy was removed by accepting spectral evidence. This took two forms. The Devil created an image of the witch which was seen by many witnesses innocently drawing water at the village well while the real witch was tormenting her victims. Conversely, intangible spirits took the form of the witch, with her permission, and carried out these evil deeds.[20]

A major form of evidence considered by some jurisdictions and ignored by others was reputation. In those determined to uncover witches a person with a good reputation with her neighbours might be considered a witch because the Devil liked his agents to feign piety and goodwill. Yet in Scotland it was important for the prosecution to establish that the accused had a long history of ill-fame. Persons accused of witchcraft in Scotland usually had a reputation for scolding, sexual promiscuity and general bad neighbourliness. The reputation of being a witch, either black or white, was further evidence for the prosecution. In England, women were rarely prosecuted until they had developed quite a reputation built up over a number of years. Few contemporaries listened to the Gmund lawyer Leonhardt Kagen who strongly objected to the use of reputation as evidence because it amounted to little more than popular gossip.

The supply of persons with bad reputations was increased by the growing acceptance by the secular courts of the ecclesiastical view that all magic was black, and 'white' magic should be seen as dangerous and treated accordingly. Those claiming to heal received their power from the Devil and must be punished. As the assumed source of power, not its use, was the crime, hundreds of previously harmless sorcerers and dabblers in folk magic were suspect. The Scottish Witchcraft Act of 1563 adopted this new approach and considered those that consulted such persons worthy of death. Despite the Act there was no evidence in Scotland that healers were convicted on the assumed pact with the Devil alone and considerable *maleficia* had to be proved. In South-west Germany, the pact with the Devil *and maleficia* had to be established.[21]

Persons accused of witchcraft suffered from a legal paradox. The judicial authorities, under the influence of the prevailing ideology, became more convinced of the moral righteousness of their witch hunting and less inclined to look tolerantly on the accused. They became more rigorous and rigid in their approach to secure a conviction. Yet with regard to evidence they became lax, even to the point of permitting sloppy, if not illegal, interpretations of existing laws and practices. In such a situation a legal defence against witchcraft was almost impossible. The only role left to defence lawyers (in the few circumstances where they were permitted) was to persuade their clients to plead guilty. There was no point attacking the concept of witchcraft or its place in the criminal code. They could question the details of the evidence presented and try to undermine its credibility by depicting its source as an enemy of their client. This was often counter-productive as the prosecution assumed witches were odious to everybody and therefore all witnesses would be hostile. In practice, flight and suicide were the only ways of escaping the guilty verdict of the

144

courts. One in five indicted Scottish witches either fled or died before conviction.[22]

Nevertheless, even at the height of the witch craze, criticisms of legal procedures were being made and reforms introduced. The use of torture was restricted in many countries. In England it was never legal; in Hesse it was abolished in 1526; in Denmark, except for those sentenced to death, torture was abolished in 1547; and in Scotland in 1662. The confiscation of the property of the convicted was abolished in Bamberg in 1630 and as early as 1547 the Danes would not accept the evidence of accomplices. Lawyers such as Kagen disputed the use of common report as evidence. Salazar, the Spanish inquisitor in the second decade of the seventeenth century, compared the confessions of witches and tried to establish the exact location of their alleged sabbats, concluding that it was fantasy. He subjected those witches who flaunted their sexual adventures with the Devil to a medical examination which revealed that many were still virgins. Most evidence submitted to him was examined with objective scrutiny.[23]

Trial records are excellent for qualitative and impressionistic evidence. Due to their selective and incomplete nature any quantitative analysis must be treated cautiously. Such an analysis reflects a range of situations with regard to the execution rate. In selected years between 1560 and 1700, of those tried in the English county of Surrey at the assizes one in eleven was executed; in New England one-seventh; in Geneva one-fifth; in Essex one-quarter; in the Swiss territories of Zurich and Fribourg one-third; and in Lucerne just under one-half. In the southern provinces of the Spanish Netherlands, Scotland and the free city of Besançon (in the Franche Comte) well over half of those indicted were sentenced to death; in the Swiss jurisdictions of Neuchâtel nearly two-thirds; and in the Pays de Vaud over nine-tenths. The smaller German principalities such as Mergenthein, especially in the panic years of the 1620s and 1630s, also saw more than nine-tenths of the accused executed. These long-range averages conceal the dramatic changes that occurred from year to year. In Scotland in 1649–50, a total of 78 persons were indicted for witchcraft and 92 per cent were executed; 77 persons were indicted in 1652–7 and 10 per cent were executed; and in 1661–2 the number indicted was 76 persons of which 74 per cent were executed. The first period represents a desperate Covenanting regime trying to retain power amid widespread hostility, the second the rule of a sceptical English military regime, and the third an attempt of a restored establishment to settle old scores and reinforce its position. Execution rates did not necessarily reflect the rate of convictions. Many jurisdictions chose a variety of non-capital punishments. Geneva banished two-thirds of those tried for witchcraft, the southern Spanish Netherlands and Besançon one-third. One-fifth of those tried in Essex were imprisoned. Acquittal rates reflected the basic ideology of the jurisdiction. In Roman law countries, few of those tried were 'liberated': in Baden 6 per cent, Mergentheim 7 per cent, in Spanish Netherlands 8 per cent, in Besançon 12 per cent, in Geneva and Scotland 20 per cent. In customary law jurisdictions, more than half of those tried were freed — for example in northern Jutland and in Essex. The effect of 'ideology' on the level of acquittal was reflected in the Scottish situation. In 1649–50 only 4 per cent of accused were acquitted by hardline ultra-Presbyterians, whereas in 1652–7 the English military regime freed 87 per cent of those brought before it. The new Scottish establishment was fighting to legitimise its usurpation of power in the traditional way. The English army knew that they did the Lord's work. Their military success proved their legitimacy. They did not need to burn foreign women.[24]

Notes

1. Stuart Clark, 'Inversion, Misrule and the Meaning of Witchcraft', *Past and Present* 8 (May 1980) pp. 98–127, especially pp. 102, 104, 118–19, 125–7.

2. Christina Larner, 'Crimen Exceptum? The Crime of Witchcraft in Europe', Ch. 2 of B. Lenman, G. Parker and V. Gatrell (eds), *Crime and the Law: The Social History of Crime in Western Europe since 1500* pp. 49–75, especially p. 71.

3. Elliot P. Currie, 'Crimes without Criminals: Witchcraft and its Control in Renaissance Europe', in E. A. Tiryakian (ed.), *On the Margin of the Visible* pp. 191–209, especially pp. 192, 199.

4. Norman Cohn, *Europe's Inner Demons* pp. 160–3.

5. Christina Larner, *Enemies of God: The Witchhunt in Scotland* pp. 83–8; Alan Macfarlane, 'A Tudor Anthropologist: George Gifford's *Discourse and Dialogue*', in S. Anglo (ed.), *The Damned Art: Essays in the Literature of Witchcraft* p. 150; E. William Monter, *Witchcraft in France and Switzerland: The Borderlands Durings the Reformation* p. 25; A. Soman, 'The Parlement of Paris and the Great Witch Hunt 1565–1640', *Sixteenth Century Journal* 9:2 (1978) pp. 34–44; Currie, *op.cit.* p. 197.

6. H. C. Erik Midelfort, *Witch Hunting in Southwestern Germany 1562–1684* pp. 22–4.

7. Currie, *op.cit.* pp. 197–8; Alan Macfarlane, *Witchcraft in Tudor and Stuart England* Chs. 1–4; Midelfort, *op.cit.* pp. 22–4; Rossell Hope

Robbins, *The Encyclopaedia of Witchcraft and Demonology* pp. 158–9, 160–6.

8. Robbins, *op.cit*, pp. 215–17, 84–5; 42–3.

9. Robbins, *op.cit*. p. 208, pp. 199–201.

10. Charles M. Radding, 'Superstition to Science: Nature, Fortune and the Passing of the Medieval Ordeal', *American Historical Review* 84 (Oct. 1979) pp. 945–69.

11. Robbins, *op.cit*. pp. 498–510.

12. *Ibid*.

13. *Ibid*.

14. Monter, *op.cit*. pp. 35–6; Larner, *Enemies of God* pp. 176–8.

15. Larner, *ibid*. pp. 176–8; Keith Thomas, *Religion and the Decline of Magic* pp. 546–7.

16. Alan Anderson and Raymond Gordon, 'Witchcraft and the Status of Women — The Case of England', *British Journal of Sociology* 29 (June 1978) p. 176.

17. Larner, 'Crimen Exceptum?' *op.cit*. pp. 56–7; Monter, *op.cit*. p. 25; Midelfort, *op.cit*. pp. 18–19; Currie, *op.cit*. pp. 195–6; Gustav Henningsen, *The Witches' Advocate: Basque Witchcraft and the Spanish Inquisition (1609–1614)* pp. 65–6.

18. Monter, *op.cit*. p. 97.

19. Monter, *op.cit*. p. 164.

20. Paul Boyer and Stephen Nissenbaum, *Salem Possessed: The Social Origins of Witchcraft* pp. 10–21.

21. Currie, *op.cit*. p. 196; Larner, *Enemies of God* p. 9; Midelfort, *op.cit*. p. 23.

22. Larner, *Enemies of God* p. 177.

23. Midelfort, *op.cit*. p. 116.

24. Monter, *op.cit*. pp. 49, 66; Cohn, *op.cit*. p. 254.

10

Defamation, Deception and Corruption

Attitudes to witchcraft reflected the genuine fears and anxieties of individuals and communities. Some individuals, knowing the facts to be otherwise than they claimed, fraudulently manipulated these concerns for personal gain. This parasitic growth of fraud and deception was misinterpreted by the rationalists of the eighteenth century as the essence of witchcraft. To them, witchcraft did not exist as an objective phenomenon. Belief in it was a delusion, a nonsense, superstition and bunkum — a situation created deliberately by powerful sections of society from a mix of hysteria and ignorance. This rationalist interpretation was recently advanced by Rossell Hope Robbins, to whom witchcraft was an invention of the Inquisition. The Inquisition having crushed existing heresies was becoming redundant and created a new heresy with such a broad base that a never-ending supply of victims would keep the inquisitors employed. They created a frame of reference to make this new heretical witchcraft plausible — a successful development that rendered logical explanations of common events unacceptable against the assumptions of the new lore. Such an interpretation cannot be sustained. Heresies were not dying but proliferating, a situation recognised by the inquisitors in seeing beyond the plethora of evil groups to their diabolic source. The Dominican inquisitors played a major part in alerting society to this new concentrated effort of the Devil, as Trevor-Roper has shown. Yet this was no deception in the sense that the inquisitors deliberately misled society. They believed their analysis of the situation. They believed their own mythology. They deceived themselves. They may have been fanatics but they were not frauds.[1]

Marxists, such as Marvin Harris, also saw witchcraft as a vast hoax perpetrated on society in the interests of a dominant sector of that society:

> the witch mania . . . shifted responsibility for the crisis of late-medieval society from both Church and State to imaginary demons in human form. Pre-occupied with the fantastic activities of these demons, the distraught, alienated, pauperized masses blamed the rampant Devil instead of a corrupt clergy and rapacious nobility. Not only were the Church and State exonerated but they were made indispensable. The clergy and nobility emerged as the great protectors of mankind.

There is little evidence for this thesis. Firstly, while the result may have been the focusing of hatred on neighbours instead of the real oppressors, these oppressors were genuinely concerned that society as they knew it was under diabolic threat. Secondly, they were also aware of the socio-economic-cum-political threat of the populace. In England, at least, this was dealt with directly through a series of draconian labour and poor laws. The rapid increase in the number and power of the local gentry and especially the presence of one or more such families in most parishes by 1640 imposed efficient social control. Perhaps this explained in part the moderation of English witch hunting. It was not a vital element in establishment survival. Thirdly, while upper-class cynicism was not manifest in the basic concept of a diabolic plot it could be seen from time to time in the specific identification of diabolic agents — an identification that split the elite rather than misled the people. Segments of the establishment used the witch scare to rally the populace against opposing establishment factions and ideologies. The Devil did not exonerate all clergy and nobles. He served factional interests by pinpointing and highlighting the blame, often within the elite.[2]

The charge of witchcraft was a convenient and effective way for the French monarchy to remove economic and political rivals. The attacks on the Templars, Boniface VIII, Joan of Arc and Gilles de Rais fit this pattern. Witch accusations became part of medieval feuding and a major factor in the court factionalism of the fourteenth and fifteenth centuries. In fourteenth-century France it was also a weapon used against royal advisers and relatives of the crown to gain their property and power. Freed from the strong rule of Philip IV in 1314, a clique of aristocrats charged

Enguerrand de Marigny, the late king's chief adviser, with a series of crimes. When the new king showed loyalty to his father's servant and a disinclination to act, the plotters concocted a story that the Marigny family dabbled in witchcraft and through such means were threatening the life of the king. On the death of the Count of Artois, Philip IV awarded his possessions to the count's daughter, Mahaut, and not to his grandson Robert. When Mahaut's son-in-law became king unexpectedly (as Philip V), following the death of Louis X and his son in 1316, she was accused of witchcraft. Mahaut had used magic to kill the king and to reconcile her estranged daughter to her husband. Philip submitted these charges to the *Parlement* of Paris which cleared Mahaut and intimated that the source of the false rumours was Robert of Artois.

The dynastic struggle in fifteenth-century England saw the widespread use of witchcraft charges to denigrate or destroy political opponents. In 1399, Henry IV implied that his predecessor dabbled in, or was made demented by, sorcery. He presented parliament with scrolls allegedly containing instructions in magic seized from Richard II's chaplain. Henry IV was in turn accused of witchcraft in laying claim to both the French and English thrones by the Duke of Orleans; the charge elicited a direct response. 'It hath pleased him (God) to give us that which surely all the sorcerers and devils could not have known how or been able to give'. Henry V had his stepmother, the fiercely pro-French Joan of Navarre, deprived of her dowry and possessions and placed under house arrest on the grounds that she employed a Franciscan friar to kill him through occult means. On Henry's death his brother Humphrey, Duke of Gloucester, ruled in the name of his young nephew, Henry VI. In 1441, his former mistress, Eleanor Cobham, now his second wife, was accused of using witchcraft to kill the King in order that her husband might succeed to the throne. She was also charged with using magic to seduce Humphrey away from his first wife. The ecclesiastical court, stacked with her husband's enemies, declared her marriage to the Duke null and void on this ground and exiled her to the Isle of Man. Her husband's influence and power collapsed.[3]

Edward IV finally triumphed over the Earl of Warwick in 1469. A year later a supporter of the Duke alleged that the King's mother-in-law, the Duchess of Bedford, had used witchcraft to make Edward besotted with her daughter Elizabeth Woodville Grey whom he had married. Although dismissed at the time,

Richard III resurrected the charge to justify his claim to the throne ahead of Edward's heirs: 'the said pretensed marriage . . . was made by sorcery and witchcraft committed by the said Elizabeth and her mother Jacquette.' Henry VIII executed his potential rivals, the Duke of Buckingham in 1521 and Lord Hungerford in 1540, on the flimsy excuse that they dabbled in magic to discover the longevity of the King. The credulous political opponents of Oliver Cromwell noted that he began the siege of Drogheda (1649), won the Battles of Dunbar (1650) and Worcester (1651) and died (1658) during a storm — all on 3 September. This coincidence and the rise of such an insignificant squire to so powerful a position was proof that Cromwell had sold his soul to the Devil and been protected by the fiend. In Scotland, the monarchy with its tenuous hold on the country (the aristocracy having murdered or imprisoned each of their kings for centuries) used accusations of witchcraft and the support of the church to survive. James III accused his dangerous rival, the Earl of Mar; and James V successfully executed Janet Douglas, Lady Glamis, for attempting to end the life of the king through witchcraft. This tradition was revived in the late-sixteenth century when James VI of Scotland accused the Earl of Bothwell, the powerful leader of the ultra-Protestant faction, of an alliance with the Devil. The difficulty with these examples is to assess the motives of the accusers. Did they believe that their enemies were agents of the Devil or were they unscrupulously using 'the system' to eliminate rivals?[4]

In seventeenth-century Germany, accusers at the level of high politics were either fanatics or frauds. The accusation against the wives of opposition burgomasters in Offenburg was a master stroke whichever interpretation is accepted. A magistrate could not be judge in his own (and therefore his wife's) case and therefore they were excluded from the council although required to carry on their administrative functions. One councillor who sought to resign following the charges against his wife was refused permission, and subsequently told not to take the execution of his wife and daughter to heart.[5]

To accuse a woman of witchcraft was a good way of ruining her reputation and in a rural community most women were vulnerable. Defamation involving witchcraft took many forms. The direct slander was accompanied by a colourful range of adjectives including: 'wissen faced', 'horse good mother water', 'blared eyed', 'stinking rotten', 'poxy', 'jade queen'; and was usually linked with whoredom and theft. The tendency to link it more with theft than whoredom in the terminology of common abuse in parts of northern England might be a clue to significant regional differences. Nevertheless, 'common whore and witch' was a popular phrase in much of England. 'Arrant whore, thief and witch' covered the essentials. More common than aspersions on morality, such as incest or 'filthy behaviour', or religious deviance, including blasphemy or absence from church, was the link with 'a devilish tongue'. 'Railer, curser and scolder' was liberally used with 'witch' in the slander of the innocent. Other comments attempted to be a little less direct, implying, usually very broadly and heavily, the same message. One person was reported to have 'spoken bad speeches tending to witchcraft', another had 'glowing eyes', a third in an advanced state of pregnancy had 'the devil inside'.[6]

Such opprobrious speech was normally ignored by victim and authorities. For every nine cases of witchcraft and sorcery brought before the ecclesiastical courts of Essex 1560–80 there was one case of defamation involving witchcraft. The extent to which it was not, ignored the expensive and potentially dangerous court action instigated for defamation and was indicative of both the potential danger to the victim of such charges and the determination of women in particular to clear their reputation. In Durham, 79 per cent of defamation cases were brought by women and 39 per cent of these were against men. In many communities local opinion was mobilised to defend the slandered. In 1675 an unsavoury sixteen-year-old Yorkshire girl, Mary Moor, claimed that the respected Hinchcliffe family — Joseph, Susan and their daughter Anne — plotted to destroy a Martha Haigh by witchcraft. More than fifty of their neighbours signed a petition testifying to their good, and to their accuser's bad, reputation. Sadly, the damage caused by this spiteful and irresponsible claim could not be undone. The pressure created by the incident proved too much for the Hinchcliffes. Joseph hanged himself in the woods and his wife died of grief a short time later. People subject to similar slander often fled. To know why many innocent individuals libelled in this way chose to ignore it, yet others took the issue to court to clear their name, while some were unwilling or unable to cope and either fled or committed suicide, would reflect and require the detailed understanding of each individual's place in the community. Where this standing was high, local opinion and the authorities took firm action against the slanderer. In Paisley in 1692 six persons were heavily fined and made to stand in public bearing a placard noting that they had scandalised the good name of their neighbours. Conversely, where the standing of the victim was low and the rumour believed. the unjustly slandered was ostracised. She was refused work, her goods would not be bought nor items sold to her. If dependent on charity this was withdrawn and she was encouraged, often through violence to herself or property, to leave the village.[7]

Far more dangerous than name-calling was the deliberate deception practised by many children feigning possession which sent hundreds of persons to their death. The false claims that they were bewitched were often encouraged by parents and clergy. In Wasserburg in 1715 local schoolmaster Casper Schweiger was falsely accused by nine recalcitrant schoolboys. In Glen Luce, Galloway, a weaver's son, Thomas Campbell, was determined to continue his education in Glasgow and not be recalled permanently to follow his father's trade. He secretly imitated the activities of the poltergeist every time he was forced home by throwing stones, cutting threads, tearing clothes and lighting fires. Most locals suspected Tom and his siblings of deceit although the local cleric, more credulous than his parishioners, took Tom into his own home, an environment which the keen scholar enjoyed. Ann Gunter, a 14-year-old Berkshire girl suffered from fits, swellings, foaming at the mouth, temporary blindness and deafness, and exuded pins from her throat, breasts and fingers. She accused three women of bewitching her. The courts acquitted the three women but put Ann in the care of the Bishop of Salisbury who, with nineteen children of his own, had some experience of adolescents. The Bishop cleverly left some marked pins within reach of the girl and when these miraculously emerged from her body her deception was discovered. He sent her for further examination by interested parties including King James. She confessed that she had a nervous condition which her father encouraged her to exaggerate and that the details of her behaviour had been copied from a tract on the Warboy witches, even to naming the familiar of one of the women she accused by the same name as a familiar mentioned in the tract. The Attorney-General charged Ann and her father with conspiracy. In 1586, Catherine Wright of Derbyshire accused a woman of sending a demon to possess her but she quickly confessed that her visions and fits were faked to win kindness from her stepfather. William Somers, a Nottingham apprentice, alleged he was bewitched by thirteen women but under pressure admitted that his accusations were false and that his professed fits and subsequent exorcism by John Darrell were all faked. He had been taught by Darrell how to pose as a possessed person. Another adolescent, Thomas Darling, accused two old women of bewitching him and in their presence he went into convulsions. He later confessed it was all faked to get attention.[8]

English magistrates and bishops showed considerable perception in uncovering clerically-inspired adolescent fraud. William Perry in 1620 accused an elderly woman of bewitching him. The Bishop of Lichfield was convinced that the performance was inspired by Catholic priests anxious to demonstrate the truth of their faith. In the presence of Protestant clergy he convulsed; when visited by the Catholic priests, according to common report, he recovered. The passing of black urine was a Perry speciality. Morton and all his servants left the house, apart from the one left behind secretly to spy on the boy. When he thought he was alone Perry uncovered an ink pot from within his mattress and having urinated into the chamber pot added some ink. He inked a piece of cotton and concealed it under his foreskin in case he was forced to demonstrate this manifestation of his possession. The Bishop set his trap. The devil that supposedly possessed the boy sent him into fits every time St John I:1 was read. The Bishop pointed out to the boy that if it was really a devil and not a juvenile faking the performance the devil would be conversant in foreign languages and would respond to that verse read in any language. The bishop then read a number of verses in Greek out of sequence. The boy incorrectly responded to the first verse read and remained calm when John I:1 was recited. He admitted his hoax. Equally astute was Justice Bromley at the notorious Lancashire Assizes of 1612. A 14-year-old, Grace Sowerbutts, accused her grandmother and two other old women of bewitching her. She went on to recount how from a hiding place she saw these women cavorting with incubi and succubi. Bromley was a believer in witchcraft but the description was alien to his conception of how English witches behaved. He confronted the girl who broke down and confessed that she had been instructed by a Catholic priest to discredit and destroy the three women who had recently changed their religion from Catholic to Anglican. A recent arrival from the Continent, the priest was not familiar with English witch traditions and instructed her in line with the sex-oriented sabbat image of his own education.[9]

Another area of probable deception, although genine possession and hysteria were often involved, was in the accusation by young nuns of possession and sexual involvement with incubi through the agency of priests. Chaplains to convents, in a society in which female religious followers were still in part unwanted daughters rather than devout and spiritual women, were in a vulnerable position. Perhaps Fathers Louis Gaufridi (in 1611), Urbain Grandier (in 1634) and Thomas Boullé (in 1647) were victims of women — Sisters Madeleine Demandolx, Jeanne des Anges and Madeleine Bavent — who were not responsible for their actions. In 1731, however, Father Jean Baptiste Girard appeared to be more clearly the innocent victim of a conniving Catherine Cadière. She could not convince the priest that she was a saint. She failed to obtain the sexual intimacy she longed for. She confessed that Girard's presence made her feel wet and she sensed something like a finger moving about her privy parts.[10]

Many false accusations of witchcraft arose from face-saving excuses, which, once profered, had to be sustained for fear of even greater punishment. The Italian peasant discovered in a ducal wine cellar was still sober enough to explain his presence most plausibly. His wife had disappeared from their hovel after applying ointment to her body. He did the same and landed in the middle of a witches' meeting. His arrival dispersed the witches and he was attempting to find his bearings when discovered by the ducal guards. His wife was arrested and executed as a witch. An English vicar whose failing voice led to rumours of the pox accused one of his parishioners of bewitching his vocal cords. Children and servants who failed to complete an assigned chore explained their failure in terms of supernatural intervention. Edmund Robinson's neglect of his father's cattle and his fantastic explanation led to the prosecution of dozens of Lancashire witches. Milkmaids explained the absence of milk, the overturning of a full pail or the failure of cream to turn to butter as evidence of diabolic activity.[11]

Sometimes these lies attracted so much attention that the teller became a local celebrity which encouraged even greater lies and more fantastic stories. Edmund Robinson was taken from church to church to identify witches — which he did with abandon. The girls at Salem, inspired by their fame, became more and more theatrical in the presence of women they accused of witchcraft. William Perry, Thomas Darling and John Smith all revelled in their new-found importance and fabricated more stories and evidence. For the dependants of society — children, servants and women — the role of the witch-accuser brought considerable status. The system was ideal for the blackmailer. Robinson's father capitalised on his son's tour of village churches to identify witches by suggesting in advance of the visit to certain women that they might donate gifts and money to him. This would prevent his son making a mistake and naming them as witches. Other women who had healing powers were blackmailed into acting illegally for fear that closer investigation of their activities might prove fatal.[12]

Malice within a family arising from material loss was a major motive behind false accusations. When Thomas Methwold married (thereby potentially altering the fate of the family property) his three sisters, who opposed the match, framed him as a witch. When the 36 beneficiaries of the estate of Lady Mary Powell were thwarted by the successful transfer of her property to her estranged husband and his relatives, Thomas and Anne Levingstone, some of them plotted revenge. Four gentlemen and several of their friends and servants were involved. They offered a cunningwoman a large sum of money to swear that Anne had used sorcery to kill Lady Powell. When she refused, further pressure was applied but her husband intervened and the conspirators desisted. They looked around for a more pliant white witch. Once again they chose badly. A Whitechapel healer, Joan Peterson, refused to be a party to the plot. This time the conspirators decided to force her hand. Through the assistance of a friendly magistrate she was arrested for witchcraft, her home and body searched. With the discovery of a devil's mark she was brought to trial on the specific charge of poisoning Lady Powell in collusion with another, and of bewitching a Charles Wilson. She had only to implicate Anne Levingstone and all charges would be dropped. Despite dozens of perjured witnesses, four doctors deponed that Lady Powell, 80 years of age and long stricken with a host of illnesses, had died a normal death and Peterson was acquitted on the first charge. She was now a serious embarrassment, if not worse, to the conspirators. They had to ensure her conviction on the second charge.[13]

Wilson had been a client of Peterson but had not paid his bills. It was alleged that Peterson had threatened that if he did not pay he would become ill. A poor woman that Peterson had employed but had dismissed for theft gave perjured evidence against her. Court officials in the pay of the conspirators harassed those persons willing to give evidence on her behalf, or turned them away suggesting the trial was over. The original magistrate had threatened that if any persons gave evidence in favour of Peterson he would send them to prison. An agent of the conspirators stood outside the court offering money to anyone who would go inside and give evidence that Peterson was a black witch. When this was reported to the bench it was initially ignored. Ultimately, when those magistrates not in collusion with the conspirators prevailed and ordered the arrest of this agent, he could not be found. Peterson was found guilty and condemned to death. The conspirators were not finished. They approached her in prison and promised a reprieve if she implicated Levingstone. At the very end the chaplain officiating at the hanging pleaded with her to name Anne Levingstone as the murderer of Lady Powell. She refused and was hanged.[14]

The authorities were not unaware that witchcraft accusations were used to further private grudges. The Scottish Privy Council in 1597 revoked the commissions to prosecute witchcraft because these 'had been abused by individuals who had grudges' and new commissions were to be limited to prevent individuals settling old scores. The English judges in 1652 stopped a similar hunt in Scotland because they found 'so much malice'. Part of the deceit came from the accused. Many of these used counter-charges of slander to divert the course of justice. Some Basque witches accused the local witch hunter of perpetrating a hoax on the community. He wrote in his own defence: 'They declare without flinching that there are no witches, but that I fabricate them in my house: that everything I say in church is a lie and a fable and that I am not to be believed, that I get people to affirm things that do not exist at all by means of promises and threats, and they go on with a thousand shameless imputations'. Another area of deception in which old scores could be settled was by the accused or convicted witch herself. With all hope gone for her own acquittal and with authorities often anxious to discover her accomplices many an old woman must have succumbed to the temptation to name longtime enemies.[15]

Deception in accusation was often supported by deliberate falsification of evidence. A major ingredient in this mis-information was coercion, and this took many forms other than judicial torture. Some Basque witches lied to avoid the violence of their fellow villagers. Children were terrorised by their parents into false confessions. A naked nine-year-old was tied to a bed and thrashed by the local priest until he confessed to being a witch. These 'false' confessions forced from young children were necessary to save the family's property. An unconfessed child witch who went to the stake unrepentant alienated the family's estates. Judicial reaction to popular coercion varied. The Bishop of Pamplona proceeded against magistrates who accepted such evidence, and Inquisitor Salazar considered coercion sufficient grounds to stop further examination of an accused. On the other hand many Basque magistrates believed coercion was excusable in this situation where witches came between parents and their children.[16]

Lies were coerced from the innocent. Evidence was deliberately faked. A protuberance or hollow on the body that did not bleed when pricked with a sharp instrument was the Devil's mark — proof of a pact with Satan. Prickers with a rudimentary knowledge of anatomy and of confused sensations knew which parts of the body responded most readily to achieve the results they desired. Many did not risk exposure and used retractable needles and when long needles apparently driven deep into the body drew no blood, nor revealed even a pin-prick, the victim was clearly guilty. Basque officials anxious to produce the witches' magic ointment, forced a number of women to concoct a mixture from their peasant kitchens. At the trial the official chemists swore that the ointment contained substances unknown to medical science. At Loudun, a rare example of a contract between Devil and witch was offered in evidence, conveniently signed by the diabolic hierarchy — Satan, Beelzebub, Lucifer and Leviathan. Swimming a witch had been abolished in 1219 but James I had recommended it and the populace appeared to use it with the acquiescence of the authorities well into the eighteenth century. The witch had her left toe tied to her right thumb, right toe to left thumb and with a rope around her waist the ends of which were held by men on both banks of the stream. It was relatively easy, especially in a flowing river, to manipulate the ropes so that the woman would not sink. This then proclaimed her guilt. Occasionally, imprisoned victims were raped, blackmailed or brutalised into falsifying their evidence by lesser officials.[17]

Personal ambition and greed and a willingness often to ignore evidence that did not support their case governed the actions of some clergy and lawyers who saw in the discovery and persecution of witches a vehicle for promotion and recognition. The Basque witch scare in the Spanish Pyrénées was attributed to a French priest, de Hualde, anxious to gain preferment in Spain with the Inquisition. Sometimes a third party anxious for economic or political gain took advantage of the genuine zeal of Christian officials and falsely accused others. In many cases the fraud of one party required the gullible fanaticism of another to succeed.[18]

Greed encouraged many to abuse the system. Mathew Hopkins charged local authorities a fee for his services and he accumulated over £1000 in twelve months. The officials at Bamberg extracted

750,000 thaler from witch suspects in less than two years. Cornelius Loos had noted earlier that 'by cruel butchery innocent lives are taken and by a new alchemy gold and silver are coined from human blood'. In Germany and Scotland, the cost of the trial and the entertainment of official guests were paid for by the victim, including banquets for the court officials at each session and for town dignitaries at the execution itself. Fees were paid to scribes, guards, the torturers, the woman who shaved the victim, the men who went to fetch the torturer, for the tar, coal, peat, straw, wood and rope needed for the stake, and for each level of torture, as well as for the ultimate execution. The executioner at Cologne received most if he could tear the victim apart by using horses, or by beheading and tying the body to a wheel and placing the head on a pike. Quartering, strangling and burning, and burning alive were less lucrative. Cutting out the tongue completely was rewarded, as was nailing to the gallows an excised tongue or severed hand.[19]

Violence within the system varied. It was sometimes surpassed by the violence of the mob. Holmes suggested that the massacres of women at Naseby and Philiphaugh during the English Civil War were manifestations of the popular hatred of witches who, in Parliament's eyes, had been equated with Catholics. The camp followers of Charles and Montrose were not massacred because they were witches; they were massacred because they were seen as papist whores and Irish rabble, irrespective of their Scottish, English or Welsh origins. An extreme case of mob violence occurred at Pittenweem in 1705. A 16-year-old blacksmith's son, Patrick Morton, accused a woman of bewitching him when she had criticised his refusal to make some nails for her. The woman was tortured and implicated others. The Privy Council intervened and fined the accused but popular anger was so high that the released woman could not return home. Janet Cornfoot, a suspected accomplice, now became the prime object of the fears begun by Morton. She was tortured, flogged by the minister and removed from the jail and placed in the church steeple. She escaped and fled to a house of a friend. An enraged mob broke into the house, seized her and dragged her to the shore. She was tied to a rope fixed between the shore and a boat and pelted with stones. She was cut loose, beaten continually and placed on the rocks with an old door placed over her. This door was piled high with heavy stones, gradually crushing her to death. To be sure, a man with a horse and sled drove backwards and forwards over her several times. No official attempted to stop the lynching. No-one was prosecuted. The minister refused to bury the mutilated corpse. Patrick Morton was later exposed as an imposter.[20]

Pittenweem was only an extreme example of the physical danger that a person defamed as a witch might suffer. Casual unsubstantiated slanders were used by the more sadistic and brutal members of a community to have fun at the expense of the newly vulnerable neighbour. The gullible and fearful were easily led to participate. The conviction that to scratch a witch on the forehead would vitiate her powers led to vicious assaults by scratching, pricking and stabbing. A 94-year-old was subject to such an assault in 1604, and in 1664 Ann Warburton was set upon by three armed men determined to slice up her face. During this fracas her infant child was killed by the intruders. Popular violence took this form due to official indoctrination and, at the critical point, official inaction. Although the central authorities in most of Europe began to dismantle the apparatus of witch hunting from the last quarter of the seventeenth century to the mid-eighteenth, local magistrates continued to turn a blind eye to acts of popular violence directed towards women suspected of witchcraft — accusations often based upon the slanderous lies of a neighbour.[21]

Notes

1. Rossell Hope Robbins, 'The Heresy of Witchcraft', *South Atlantic Quarterly* 65 (Autumn 1966) pp. 532–43, and his *The Encyclopedia of Witchcraft and Demonology* pp. 9–10; H. R. Trevor-Roper, *The European Witch-Craze of the Sixteenth and Seventeenth Centuries and Other Essays* pp. 101–10.
2. Marvin Harris, *Cows, Pigs, Wars and Witches* p. 168.
3. William R. Jones, 'Political Uses of Sorcery in Medieval Europe', *The Historian* 34 (1971) pp. 670–87.
4. Jones, *ibid.*; H. A. Kelly, 'English Kings and the Fear of Sorcery', *Medieval Studies* 39 (1977) pp. 206–38; Ronald Holmes, *Witchcraft in British History* Chs. 3–4, 11–12.
5. H. C. Erik Midelfort, *Witch Hunting in Southwestern Germany* p. 128–30.
6. John P. Demos, *Entertaining Satan* pp. 246–7; Peter Rushton, 'Women, Witchcraft and Slander in Early Modern England: Cases from the Church Courts of Durham, 1560–1675', *Northern History* 18 (1982) p. 127; Alan Macfarlane, *Witchcraft in Tudor and Stuart England* pp. 277–301.
7. Macfarlane, *ibid.*; Rushton, *ibid.*; Christina Hole, *Witchcraft in England* pp. 94–5; Keith Thomas, *Religion and the Decline of Magic* p. 633.
8. Hole, *ibid.* Ch. 6 pp. 83–95; C. L'Estrange Ewen, 'A Noted Case of Witchcraft at North Moreton, Berks, in the Early 17th Century', *Berkshire*

Archaeological Journal 40 (1936) pp. 207 – 13; Rossell Hope Robbins, *The Encyclopedia of Witchcraft and Demonology* pp. 118 – 19, 224 – 6, 237 – 8; Ronald Holmes, *Witchcraft in British History* pp. 80 – 2, 114; Thomas, *ibid.* pp. 576 – 80.

9. Holmes, *ibid.* pp. 80 – 1, 114; Hole, *ibid.* pp. 52, 85; Robbins, *ibid.* pp. 48 – 9; Thomas, *ibid.* pp. 586 – 8.

10. Holmes, *ibid.* pp. 190 – 1, 205, 253; Robbins, *ibid.* pp. 385 – 7.

11. Robbins, *ibid.* pp. 381 – 2; Hole, *op.cit.* pp. 20, 44, 85 – 8, 106 – 7, 156 – 8; Thomas, *op.cit.* pp. 544, 645 – 6, 689.

12. Robbins, *ibid.* pp. 48 – 9, 61 – 6, 301 – 3, 381 – 2, 429 – 49.

13. C. L'Estrange Ewen (ed.), *Witch Hunting and Witch Trials* Appendix III pp. 270 – 81.

14. *Ibid.*

15. *Ibid.*

16. Gustav Henningsen, *The Witches' Advocate: Basque Witchcraft and the Spanish Inquisition (1609 – 1614)* pp. 139 – 42, 217 – 18.

17. Henningsen, *ibid.* p. 220; Holmes, *op.cit.* pp. 25, 111, 136 – 7, 181, 185; Hole, *op.cit.* pp. 72 – 9, 171 – 4.

18. Henningsen, *ibid.* pp. 130 – 6.

19. Robbins, *Encyclopedia of Witchcraft and Demonology* pp. 16, 111 – 16, 249 – 53; Holmes, *op.cit.* Ch. 10 pp. 131 – 43, 175 – 7.

20. Holmes, *ibid.* Ch. 9 pp. 118 – 30, 190 – 1; Robbins, *ibid.* pp. 385 – 7.

21. Thomas, *op.cit.* p. 633.

11

Motivation and the Village Community: I, The Witch

People labelled as witches received this designation from within a village community. Certain attributes predisposed individuals to such an accusation. This stereotype of the witch suspect broke down in periods of panic, changed over time and place, rarely applied in total to anybody and in a few cases was completely irrelevant. Above all, it has been wrongly drawn. Nevertheless, villagers who were dependent, deviant, different and whose traits were durable were most vulnerable to community suspicion. Women were likely to be suspected more because of the aspects and implications of these characteristics than because they were innocent victims of an irrational misogyny. The emphasis on dependence was misplaced. It was a major precondition for accusation in normal periods, usually a necessary prerequisite, but never sufficient on its own. The key elements in dependence were age, isolation, poverty and gender. The old, lonely, poor woman was the traditional victim. Monter emphasised gender, and Thomas poverty. Both were wrong: age was the critical element in this complex of factors.[1]

The age of the vast majority of witches (usually taken from the time of their formal accusation) is unknown. Contemporary literature referred to the witches as old and the few sample studies available, based on very small numbers, do in large measure support such a claim. In four Swiss jurisdictions (Basle, Fribourg, Geneva and Neuchâtel) the median age was 60, and in the Nord 55. The proportion under 50 ranged from 10 per cent in Basle to 33 per cent in Neuchâtel. At the Essex Assizes in 1645, 13 per cent of the accused were between 40 and 49, 20 per cent between 50 and 59, 47 per cent between 60 and 69, none between 70 and 79, and 20 per cent between 80 and 89. The first four Basque witches arrested by the Inquisition in 1609 were aged 80, 70, 36 and 22. Overall, in Europe (including England) persons accused of witchcraft were between 50 and 70. In the New England colonies they were a decade younger, between 40 and 60. There, at least 50 per cent were under 50. This emphasis on age should be kept in perspective as there were still thousands of younger women accused in normal circumstances — one in nine New England witches were under 30. Secondly, this age stereotype broke down in periods of panic. In the Salem hunt one in five of the accused was under 20, almost two-fifths under 40. In the Würzburg trials of 1627–9, a quarter of the victims were children. In the six periods into which these trials have been divided, the proportion of children rose from none in the first to 61 per cent in the fourth, then fell to 41 per cent in the fifth and to 7 per cent in the last.[2]

Age in large measure influenced both gender balance and isolation. Amongst the poor of Norwich in 1570 there were twelve times as many unmarried or widowed women over 61 as there were men. If age and marital status were the basic criteria and the Norwich example typical, witch suspects would be lonely women. In addition, there was a decline with age in the ability to earn a living. As women received a third to a half of a male wage the onset of poverty and the need for community help were more likely. Age often brought senility which affected personality and behaviour patterns which were at odds with community norms. Recent research has suggested that the beginnings of unacceptable behaviour exaggerated by senility had their beginnings during menopause — a gender-specific condition. Reginald Scot noticed in the late-sixteenth century that some women came under village suspicion after 'the stopping of their monthly melancholic flux or issue of blood'. Middle and advanced age was a key factor in the gender, isolation, poverty and unacceptable behaviour of suspect villagers.[3]

The isolation and poverty of some women appeared to depend on marital status. This status was in itself a major element in a woman's ability to avoid group suspicion. Patriarchal society expected all women to be under the discipline of father or husband. There was an increase in the proportion and absolute numbers of never-married women. The medieval norm of one in twenty gave way in Sweden in the seventeenth century to one in three. In the Swiss borderlands, one in ten of rural and one in five of urban women remained single. This trend fuelled misogynistic fears and such women invited suspicion. The traditional view that widows and spinsters were most commonly accused of witchcraft, far out of proportion to their numbers in society, cannot be sustained for spinsters were represented among the accused in proportion to their numbers in population. Spinsters accounted for 6 per cent of the accused in Basle; 10 per cent in Montbéliard, in three witch-prone villages of Essex, and in New England; 16 per cent at the Essex Assizes of 1645, 21 to 22 per cent in Geneva and Toul and 34 per cent in Sweden.[4]

The number of spinsters increased but such a status was not a major factor in the village labelling of a neighbour as a witch. Neither was it for the widow, although she was over-represented among the accused. Widows constituted 55 per cent of these at Toul, 40–50 per cent in Essex and Montbéliard, around 33 per cent in Geneva and Basle, and an atypical 10 per cent in New England. When widows are compared with married women no clear pattern emerges. In Toul there were five widows to every two married women accused, and in New England and Scotland one widow to every one married woman. Elsewhere, married women outnumbered widows: Geneva 9:7, Montbéliard 5:4, in Sweden 4:3, in Basle 2:1 and in New England 8:1. This New England pattern provides a significant clue to the precise role of the widow. It reflected the mores of a frontier society in which women were scarce and widows invariably remarried. It also mirrored the younger age of the New England witch. These women were suspected, and in the highly disciplined Puritan communities formally accused, before the deaths of their husbands. Monter was correct when he suggested that the 'superabundance of widows among accused witches might merely reflect their relatively old age'. Advancing age increased the chances of outliving their husbands and thereby becoming more vulnerable to successful village accusations.[5]

In 70 English villages averaged over more than two centuries, one-fifth of householders were widowed and gender differentiation was most marked. In these villages widows outnumbered widowers by more than two to one. In specific villages the proportion of the widowed was higher, up to a third, and predominance of women even greater. In Coventry in 1523 widows outnumbered widowers nine to one, and in Lichfield in 1695 by three to one. This disparity increased with age, as the Norwich figure of twelve to one for persons 61 and over indicated. This was due in part to the earlier death of the male but more so to the remarriage of old men.

Of men over 60 years old 88 per cent were married; of women only 25 per cent. Two-thirds of these men had wives more than ten years younger than themselves, compared to only one-eighth of men 60 and under. One-third of wives over 60 had husbands a decade or more younger than themselves. Yet the assumption that the widow was poor and isolated ignored the economic security and protection offered through custom and the manorial courts. Most widows were householders who rarely lived alone. The majority had children living with them and only a few lived as lodgers or in institutions. Widowhood was not significant in provoking suspicion. This would have arisen years earlier during the lifetime of her husband. In a patriarchal society, even at the lower end of the social scale, a husband could exert considerable influence in containing rumour. With his death this protection disappeared and village labelling could proceed unhindered. Widowhood simply made formal accusation easier. The wealthy but unpopular Katherine Harrison of Connecticut was brought to trial within two years of her husband's death, 'a distressed widow . . . meeting with overbearing exercises'.[6]

Poverty was an alleged attribute of the witch suspect and regional variations were significant and in dispute. Keith Thomas saw the English witch as a dependent, a person in receipt of charity. He believed that witch labelling was a manifestation of conflict between the poor and the very poor in a society 'which no longer held a clear view as to how or by whom its dependent members should be maintained.' Alan Macfarlane placed the typical witch slightly higher up the social scale. It was not the poorest in the village who were automatically suspected but the 'moderately poor', such as the woman who felt she ought to get poor relief but was refused. The famous Hatfield Peverel witches, Elizabeth and Agnes Francis, were wives of a yeoman and weaver respectively. In Boreham the accused witch, Margaret Poole, was the wife of another successful yeoman and none of the ten persons in receipt of charity in that village in the late-sixteenth century was accused of witchcraft. Of the husbands of witches accused before the Essex Assizes 1560 – 1680 two-thirds were labourers or husbandmen and just under a quarter were artisans. The remaining few were yeomen. In Essex there was no link between local destitution, bad harvests, famine or general agricultural dislocation and suspicion of witchcraft. The burden of supporting the community's dependants in times of acute economic crisis and personal economic difficulties was not critical in inciting suspicion.[7]

In Geneva in 1571-2, half of the fathers or husbands of the *engraisseurs* (the plague-spreading witches) were labourers and the remainder artisans and fishermen. However, in the rural communities of the Jura both vagabonds and wealthy peasants were accused, although, again, most witches were drawn from the settled moderate poor. Larner claimed that Scottish witches were socially and economically a little higher than the English — a wife or widow of a tenant farmer 'fairly near the bottom of the social structure'. Paupers, itinerant labourers and vagabonds were outside the system and rarely accused. Those accused were the wives and widows struggling to stay on the bottom rung of a feudal society. Larner described as typical a woman with a tenancy and enough land and livestock to subsist yet who failed occasionally to pay her rent, was short on grazing, stole corn and ran out of food. She periodically failed to cope and depended to some extent on the goodwill of the community. On the other hand, McLachlan and Swales argued that they had 'no reason to believe that most of those suspected of witchcraft were particularly poor.' Given the lack of knowledge on social stratification in early modern Scotland it has been impossible to claim a tendency for any particular stratum to be more susceptible to witch accusation than another. If most Scots were poor and most witches were poor, poverty itself could not account for a community's suspicion. New England lacked the rich and poor of the Old World yet it quickly developed a social and economic hierarchy. John Demos divided a number of communities into three equal parts according to social rank: high, middle and low. The upper third provided only 12 per cent of witches, the middle third 20 per cent, and the lower third 60 per cent. The remaining 8 per cent were socially mobile. Some suspected witches such as Elizabeth Garlick were married to men at the bottom of the economic scale, others like Mary Parsons to men at the top. Despite the modifications and cautions witches were drawn predominantly from the poorer classes, probably in excess of their proportion in the population in general. Yet poverty to the point of dependency was not a critical factor in the labelling of a villager as a witch.[8]

It was not dependency but deviance which set certain individuals apart from others. Sexual immorality and criminality, despite the definition of the witch as sexual pervert and the ultimate criminal, were not major attributes of the witch suspect although they were by no means absent. Few persons labelled as witches in England had criminal reputations. Macfarlane found no link between witches and theft, murder, Sabbat-breaking and non-attendance at church. Yet one in five witches described in the Essex pamphlets was guilty of deviant behaviour; seven of the nine committed sexual offences, one quarrelled excessively with her husband and another said her prayers in Latin. Conversely, of 36 sexual offences committed in Boreham village in the later part of the sixteenth century 35 had no connection with witch suspects. Ursley Kemp and the other St Osyth witches had illegitimate children but few witch suspects were in this position and thousands of women with such children never came under suspicion. Macfarlane concluded that witches 'were not usually accused of other offences'. Thomas would go further, seeing little criminality or immorality in the past record of the accused witch. She was in most cases morally right and it was her accusers who had something to hide. In New England one in three witch suspects had committed other offences. Of these, two in five were guilty of forms of assaultive speech, one in five of theft, one in eight of lying, one in eight of physical assault or resisting authority and one in ten of sexual offences. The initial suspects at Salem had been righteous women for decades but could not conceal unacceptable sexual experiences in their youth. Yet this was a contributory rather than a decisive factor.[9]

Scottish and European villagers were more inclined to suspect the deviant. Delcambre considered that in Lorraine 'a fairly large number' were thieves, swindlers, sexual perverts, rapists, fornicators and poisoners. In the Jura region sexual offenders and thieves were prominent. In Neuchâtel, a well-known thief who attended an odd assembly outside the town was arrested for witchcraft and began a small panic as she named other participants in the meeting. Near Lausanne a woman who committed incest and adultery with her aunt's husband, and another who had two illegitimate children, were suspect. In morally austere Scotland, women with a background of sexual deviance were more likely to be accused of witchcraft. Among those arrested during the panic of 1661–2 was Helen Cass, who had been sexually promiscuous with the English soldiers as early as 1655, and Helen Concker, who admitted to fornication just prior to her arrest. Although the evidence is thin, Midelfort's conclusion regarding south-western Germany may have wider application. When panic situations arose the stereotype of the suspect in which deviance played a minor role broke down. In this situation the deviant became a plausible substitute.[10]

Deviance as defined by the political establishment was not a major factor in witchcraft accusations for two reasons. The overt deviants — murderers, robbers and heretics — were dealt with directly for the offences committed. Such persons put themselves outside their village community. Secondly, deviance as defined by central authorities may not have been seen as such by the village community. Illicit sexual activity was an acceptable part of rural life and not a cause for suspicion. Perhaps this became more important as Catholic and Protestant reformers gradually changed village attitudes. Theft raised a similar problem. It was endemic in English parishes and in some areas appeared to be an acceptable by-employment. In such a society theft would not be seen as significant deviance. Conversely, in the New England colonies it was. In essence, if your behaviour conformed to the mores of your neighbours or of a considerable sub-group of them you did not provoke suspicion.[11]

It was divergence from such norms even in areas that might appear trivial that was far more important. The effect of physical appearance has been played down by modern historians although contemporaries were clearly made suspicious by abnormalities and deformities. They were warned to 'beware of all persons that have default of members naturally, as of foot, hand, eye or other member; one that is crippled; and especially of a man that hath not beard'. A bearded woman was a prime suspect. A squint, squeaky voice, limp, hare lip, club foot, retarded speech or contorted face increased concern. Macfarlane did not believe that people were selected as potential witches because of their looks but appearance confirmed attributes one expected to find in a witch. A witch was expected to be 'bent to a hoop', 'having her chin and her knees meeting'.[12]

Eccentric behaviour was more significant than abnormal appearance. Major eccentricities and madness were not an issue. These were seen for what they were and treated accordingly. It was the slight divergence of behaviour from the local norm that invited suspicion — the wealthy woman in a religious community who never tried to join the church, or one servant in a household who was able to spin so much linen yarn that she must have had 'some unlawful help'. Others were too friendly with animals, raising thoughts of familiars; dug at the ground with their staff in an unusual manner; inspected new premises 'in the wrong direction' when such anti-clockwise movement was known to indicate evil intent. A woman witnessed a witch trial and was so affected that she experienced fits. This was not unusual in children but rare in a mature woman. People talked. Why was such a 'respectable' woman affected in this way? Another seemed too intent on obtaining the services of a young girl. The behaviour of relatives could adversely affect community opinion, such as the grandson who ate ashes and threw rocks at all and sundry, and a husband who refused to take his share of local administration.[13]

To be of a different race or religion was not a major factor. In over a hundred suspects in New England one was Dutch, two had Catholic backgrounds and another was of Huguenot descent. Half a dozen were Anglicans; most were Puritan and English. Towards the end of the seventeenth century this concentration probably over-represented their numbers in the population. Where significant numbers of racial minorities existed it was more influential. Geneva suffered an influx of Savoyards and Frenchmen. The former were over-represented among the *engraisseurs* of 1571. As these were conceived as mobile plague-carrying witches the concentration on migrants was not surprising. In the rural areas of the Jura, Savoyards were often suspect and increased this racial concern by naming compatriots as their accomplices. In the Pyrénées Spanish Basques often named French women as suspected witches, to the point that a contemporary priest, Lope Martinez de Isasti, called on the Inquisition to purge the region of 'foreigners from France'. In Essex not one of the accused witches was a Catholic, although there may have been some religious input into accusations in Lancashire where those who changed their religion were suspect.[14]

Two aspects of difference were very important: an undue interest in the occult and social mobility. The overt healer, cunningman or charmer was openly persecuted in parts of Scotland and Europe, or ignored as in England. They constituted a fee-receiving profession usually of higher status than a witch suspect. The known occupations of 23 leading English cunningmen were 6 medical practitioners, 3 clergy, 2 schoolmasters, 2 astrologers, 1 churchwarden, 1 gentleman, 2 yeomen, 2 labourers, 1 miller, 1 comber and 1 shoemaker. There was little link between such people and the witch suspect, although the early Essex witches Margery Skelton (1572) and Ursley Kempe (1582) had prior reputations as cunningwomen. Of 41 identified Essex cunningfolk only 4 were later accused of witchcraft. No more than 6 of the 400 persons accused of black witchcraft had reputations as white witches. It was the display of such ability or interest where it was not expected which provoked suspicion. In New England magic was anathema and its overt practice condemned by the authorities. Neighbourly assistance with specially prepared soups and drinks for the ill was potentially very dangerous, especially if death should result. The ability to predict the future, or possession of unauthorised and inexplicable knowledge of others' secrets was upsetting. A husband who commented on his wife's intuitive powers in always finding the key to the door wherever he hid it started a rumour that was later used against her. Jokers such as Elizabeth Seager stirred her listeners. She told a credulous group who suspected her of witchcraft that she had asked Satan to tell them she was not witch — who better to call as a witness. Talking about witchcraft itself aroused suspicion. Persons who named witches and described their activities with 'excessive detail' worried the New England villager.[15]

In stable early-modern European villages in which everybody had a designated place rapid success or failure was remarkable. In the newly created hierarchical and corporate towns of New England the old traditions were quickly established. As most settlers received considerable amounts of land the loss of this within a lifetime reflected poorly on the parties concerned, not only socially but morally. In 1647, Eunice Cole's husband was ranked 51st among the 60 householders of Hampton. Six years later he was last among 72. Several other women who became suspects had experienced a similar and dramatic decline in their fortunes. Yet success beyond the norm could also incite talk. In Salem, Boyer and Nissenbaum suggested that the successful were so successful that they could not be accused directly and antagonism toward them was projected onto others. Mary Verens, the Putnams' entrepreneurial stepmother remained untouched — women with similar experiences but less power were accused. In other villages neighbours were not so hesitant. Joseph Parsons developed an extensive business empire embracing fur trading, tavern keeping, wine sales, land dealing, general trade and the ownership of warehouses and a wharf at Boston. Parsons brooked little opposition. He forcibly resisted the attempts of the authorities to confiscate some of his property and scandalised his Puritan neighbours by his lascivious attitude towards women. His wife shared this success and scandal but added her own extraordinary achievements in a female society pre-eminently directed to childbearing. Mary Parsons bore children over 25 years, had 12 pregnancies, was delivered of 14 babies and raised 9 of them to maturity. The community refused to bestow the title of Mrs on Goody Parsons and suspected her of witchcraft. James Wakeley, another successful businessman, invited suspicion and fled to Rhode Island rather than face constant rumour. Even in the late-eighteenth century exceptional economic success in the eyes of rural New England implied 'diabolic' assistance.[16]

Elements of dependence, deviance and difference contributed to the labelling of a neighbour as a witch but none of these was critical. The two most important traits that predisposed villagers to suspect one of their number was a divisive and defiant personality. A sceptical Essex vicar, John Gaule, believed that every old woman with 'a scolding tongue' was considered a witch. Cautious churchwardens refused to confirm that a certain woman was a witch but they admitted that she was 'devilish of her tongue'. This tongue was exercised in an angry, threatening context. A Somerset woman became frightened by a neighbour who 'hath divers times since given threatening language to this informant'. A Scots woman caught red-handed with a sheaf of corn bid the Devil pick out the eyes of her discoverer. In Puritan New England anger was itself a sign of weakness and its very existence disturbed many villagers. David Wheeler of Newbury wanted to talk at length with a witch suspect 'concerning her being angry with me'. This anger arose from discontent and envy and was expressed maliciously. Eunice Cole, an elderly widow, became threatening when the town authorities refused her wood but gave some to a healthy young man. Mary Johnson rationalised her behaviour on the grounds that she was tempted to serve the Devil through discontent and envy.

These women were sometimes needy; they were invariably greedy. Deodat Lawson, one-time Salem cleric, isolated the problem. He warned his readers that Satan gained a foothold if people gave way to sinful and unruly passions 'such as envy, malice, or hatred of our neighbours and brethren'. His senior colleague, Cotton Mather, wrote of slanderings, back-biting and animosities. Agnes Brown, an English witch, was 'ever noted to be of an ill nature and wicked disposition, spiteful and malicious and many years before she died both hated and feared among her neighbours'. The malicious impact of a simple phrase 'I shall remember you when you little think on it' or the more direct use of a powder 'to rot their guts in their bellies; the leaves (dill) . . . to make their teeth fall out of their heads and the paring of nails to make them drunk and mad' capture the venom. A debt forcibly repayed was accompanied by a simple malediction: 'It shall be but as wild fire in your house and as a moth in your clothes'.[17]

Such personalities thrived on conflict and appeared to seek out quarrels. Domestic quarrels were seen as a major manifestation of conflicting personalities and as a reason for treating with suspicion members of a household in disharmony. A wife went out at night. Her husband locked her in the cellar to stop her wanderings. She pretended to be distracted by the experience and railed at her husband. On another occasion she tried to stop her husband beating one of their children for losing a shoe, claiming she had already done so. A free-for-all developed with the result that she was beaten by her husband. Quarrelsome personalities could turn any interpersonal contact into conflict. Major arguments occurred over either the provision or non-provision of services or the rejection of social overtures. Essex women who were accused of witchcraft at the 1582 assizes were initially angered by the refusal of help when they needed it — a dole for a sick husband, a piece of pork, some milk, mutton, a cheese or a pig. Others were cross at being cheated — a food dole was of poor quality, the price of malt was too high, the payment for goods supplied too low and money borrowed was demanded back unexpectedly. Violence done to their persons or property angered others. Swine were beaten and pitchforked, cattle and geese were driven off a neighbours' land and hurt in the process. The lack of consideration by neighbours infuriated some. Green places in front of a house were muddied, boughs they placed over muddy spots were removed. False accusations of sexual immorality and theft and the refusal of villagers to allow them to nurse children made others angry.[18]

In such a mood these women became deliberate sowers of discord through mischief, gossip and lying. Accusations of witchcraft and the spreading of malicious rumours set neighbour against neighbour. Glastonbury women tried to isolate Elizabeth Castles because she was 'apt to speak of things which concerned her not'. The lie devastated social harmony. Ann Hibbens, a notorious liar especially where money was concerned, was excommunicated by the Boston church. Years later she was accused of witchcraft. A common pattern was when one party told a second party that a third party had done or would do something which on enquiry was found to be untrue. Servants in large households were particularly destructive in this regard.[19]

The spoken word created fear. Although many comments were made on the spur of the moment with little evil intent the recipients often dwelt on what was said, and read into them a range of threats. The informal threat was viewed as a variant of the formal curse. The curse was a powerful weapon used by the church and the poor. As late as 1628 following the theft of church silver the Bishop of Barcelona cursed the surrounding countryside and that season the crops failed. Reformers changed the emphasis. The curse was not an automatic display of God's wrath, it was a prayer, a petition for divine assistance. Although English legislators in the seventeenth century tried to eradicate the curse the Anglican church still cursed among others those 'that removeth away the mark of his neighbour's land'. During the English Civil War rival religious groups counter-cursed. The Presbyterian church in Scotland encouraged witch victims to curse their tormentors. The key aspect of cursing was the popular belief that an unjustified curse would rebound on its utterer but the more justified it was the more likely it was to be effective.

Curses of the poor, especially the beggar's curse, enjoyed a long currency and continued to frighten the more respectable classes; Keith Thomas put it succinctly: 'The idea that God would avenge all injuries, and that moral retribution was to be found in this world no less than the next, was the justification for the curses and maledictions which were such an enduring feature of sixteenth and seventeenth century village life'. Hundreds of villagers never linked to witchcraft cursed formally, and viciously. The onset of a painful and horrible illness was a popular curse: the rotting-off of the tongue, the pox, piles and the plague. Fire was the other vehicle — burn the victim and his family alive. Whether Joanna Powell's curse was effective is not known. A witness recalled that she cursed 'in Welsh language, kneeling down upon her bare knees and holding up her hands, but otherwise the words he could not understand'. The use of the curse by a quarrelsome angry woman deeply concerned her neighbours and made them suspicious of her. As contemporary Thomas Cooper wrote, 'when a bad-tongued woman shall curse a party and death shall shortly follow this is a shrewd token that she is a witch'. An Elizabethan noted that habit of the poor in 'cursing when they are not served as themselves desire'.[20]

The ability of certain people to divide the community through their quarrelsome scolding personality, through their envy, malice, anger, gossip and lying predisposed them to be labelled as witches. There was another vital element in this labelling process. Divisive people who were also defiant and lacked deference were prime suspects. To be aggressive, assertive and intrusive caused the ultimate communal disharmony. A Puritan New Englander 'hunched' the congregation with her elbow as they entered the meeting house and abused them as hell-hounds and whoremasterly rogues. A woman about to be excommunicated by a church court told them in no uncertain terms what she thought of them. Another reviled a neighbour for producing shoddy yarn and ill-treating animals. It was this intrusive nature of certain personalities that annoyed. They 'thrust into the parlour', 'rushed in' and, although 'forewarned not to come', they 'asked very inquisitively'. They pushed themselves into private family matters. The behaviour pattern of an English woman, Margaret Legate, typified the problem. 'Soon after this Legate came to this informants house upon he threatened if she came there any more he would throw her into the river he being a miller, yet after this she came to his house and although he reviled her yet she came into his house and sat upon his bed and he forced her out of his house . . .' The courts ordered such a woman not 'to go in an offensive way to folks' houses in a railing manner, as it seems she hath done, but . . . keep her place and meddle with her business.[21]

A woman's failure to keep her place was critical in witch labelling. Lack of deference to those who provided charity and to those in authority was the critical attribute. When refused community aid a New Hampshire woman did not slink away, she abused the local officers. On another occasion, with her husband's aid, she resisted their attempt to distrain several of her pigs. She bit the constable, knocked him down and recovered the swine. Burning warrants and attacking local officials was par for the course. Those higher up the social scale expressed their aggression in legal action. Mary Parsons delighted in acting against the authorities and the community. Her cow was detained. She sued and won. The community diverted water past her property to the town mill. She took her neighbours and local officials to court and again won. Women in dangerous situations continued to defy the community. Anna Marsh was kept awake and watched for several days as a witch suspect. She told her watchers, 'those that had thus used her she would be revenged of them'. Almost as she spoke the unattended young child of one of her gaolers rolled into the fire. When the local minister rebuked Janet McMurdock for not wearing her best clothes to her execution she was not contrite: 'what she wore was good enough for the hangman and her own children would get her plaid'. Such women may have been needy and greedy but they were never grateful.[22]

To be formally accused of witchcraft most women exhibited these traits over a long period. The patience of the village and the durability of unacceptable behaviour patterns were characteristic. In the Essex panic of 1645, of the fourteen witches who confessed, nine had been suspect for over fifteen years and the remaining five admitted to less than six months. The latter are characteristics of panic situations. In other normal samples suspicions existed from seven to thirty years but there were many exceptions. The evidence against Elizabeth Castle in Glastonbury was based on experiences from two to six years previously. Many factors were relevant in this context. The length of residence in the village concerned was important as women appeared to take considerable time to build up a reputation. This reputation was assisted by two popular beliefs — that the power of witches increased over time and that witchcraft was hereditary. Mother and daughter suspects were common. The extension of suspicion from mother to child often took time to become effective. In New England, Jane Walford was charged in 1656 and 1669, her daughter Hannah Jones in 1682. The latter's major accuser affirmed that 'Goody Jones and all her generation . . . were accounted witches'. Hannah was obviously fed up with his campaign: 'If he told her of her mother, she would throw stones at his head'. There were a number of accusations in which mother and daughter (and, in a few cases, grandmother as well) were charged simultaneously. This family link served to extend the longevity of reputation. Yet only one in ten Essex cases involved blood relatives.[23]

Certain persons were more likely to be suspected as witches by their village neighbours than others. Age, gender, poverty, immorality and criminality were contributing factors and any activity slightly different to the norm, no matter how trivial was conducive to unfavourable comment. However, it was the combination of divisive and defiant behaviour over time that was critical.

The second stage in this labelling process was the acceptance or recognition of the role of witch by the accused. Why did women believe themselves to be witches and why did others believe such women became witches? Dependants were impotent to change their position by ordinary means. A belief that they could use supernatural power transformed their position in society. They readily accepted the label as a manifestation of their enhanced place in the eyes of their contemporaries. Ego enhancement readily

175

explains the admission of witchcraft by thousands of women who never saw a torture chamber, an ego-enhancement based on their new-found power. This power was accepted or used to improve existing conditions. A witch's fantasy world was a mirror of the unsatisfactory aspects of contemporary domestic life. Immediate rewards for becoming a witch were to gain improved economic conditions and a more satisfactory sex life. In both south-west Germany and England the Devil offered a little money or goods and a vague promise that a new recruit would not starve. There is no Faustian promise of fortune. A slight amelioration from grinding poverty was all that a politically practical Devil needed to offer. An unhappy marriage or sex life was overcome in the fantasies of continual seduction. The Devil offered sympathy to distressed and frustrated women — a frustration created in part by the patriarchical anti-sexual ethic of Christianity. The reiterated comment that sex with the Devil was painful (although not painful enough to prevent further compliance) may reflect an attempt to conceal enjoyment of such forbidden fruit, especially as confessed to male inquisitors who could not accept such a hedonistic premise.[24]

Witchcraft offered much more to women than improved economic conditions and sexual contentment. It provided on a general level a sense of adventure and excitement, the lure of living dangerously. To be part of a supernatural conspiracy with its sense of power, titillating fear and secret knowledge were attractions difficult to reject. It has been argued that becoming a witch was part of an attempt to humanise the supernatural (an approachable Devil) and to lessen the intolerable majesty of God so fervently preached by Reformation and Counter-Reformation cleric alike, and that this act transferred the basic fear of death to fear of the Devil. The latter fear unlike the former was subject to mollification. In essence, the acceptance of the Devil was the ego's attempt to rationalise a personal eschatology rather than the work of the Freudian id. Yet again the magico-religious sexual release provided by this new real or fantasy world compared with the rigorous austerity of Christianity was appealing. Religious despair pushed people to seek unorthodox methods of salvation. The emphasis placed on the Devil by the contemporary church made Satan a major ingredient in the consciousness of troubled souls. Devil-worship was a common temptation for those in a state of religious depression immediately prior to Puritan conversion experiences. In essence, becoming a witch was, or was seen to be, a major cure for impotence, creating a sense of superiority within and community respect without — a respect or fear that ensued better material treatment.[25]

This respect was often a gloss for fear, and this fear stemmed from the second major category of motivation of the witch, vengeance. Many witches were seen by others, and saw themselves, as embittered misanthropes who revealed nothing but malice and hatred towards their neighbours. To Thomas the main desire of a witch was not personal amelioration but vengeance against her enemies. The dependent poor and lonely had no weapons of revenge against their superiors except arson and witchcraft. Ill-treated by their fellows, witches hated their neighbours and it was the vibrations of this evident malignity which gave their threats plausibility. In village communities the neurotic belief that harm can be done by willing it became institutionalised as witchcraft developed as a socialised channel for aggressive impulses for all parties, especially for women. Men had several channels for aggression, women had none. Men murdered, women resorted to the Devil. Pervading this vengeance motive within witchcraft was the assumption that the witch had a case. She had been ill-treated by her neighbours and her response if not morally acceptable was at least understandable.

Others allowed no such justification. The witch was primarily a destructive deviant rather than an abused dependant. Her acts were gratuitous displays of malevolence. These were frustrated, twisted persons, often women disappointed in love, who hated the world and embarked on a deliberate campaign of corruption. They consciously rejected Christianity and served the Devil in overturning the accepted values of society. Basque and Swiss villages located their witches among women who were not the innocent victims of another's projections. There, witches were people who had a long history of deliberately corrupting the values of society.[26]

In conclusion, women were labelled witches and accepted this for a variety of reasons. A most perceptive assessment was made by Arthur Wilson, gentleman steward of the powerful Earl of Warwick. Commenting on the Chelmsford trials in 1645 Wilson wrote:

> I . . . could see nothing in the evidence which did persuade me to think them other than poor, melancholy, envious, mischievous, ill-disposed, ill dieted, atrabilus constitutions; whose fancies . . . make the imagination ready to take any impression; whereby their anger and envy might vent itself

into such expressions, as the hearers . . . might find cause to believe, they were such people as they blazon'd themselves to be. And they themselves, by the strength of fancy, may think they bring such things to pass, which, many times, unhappily they wish for and rejoice in, when done, or of the malevolent humor which is in them: which passes with them as if they had really acted it. And, if there be an opinion in the people that such a body is a witch their own fears . . . resulting from such dreadful apprehensions, do make every shadow, an apparition; and every rat or cat, an imp or spirit.

These victims and accusers warrant attention.[27]

Notes

1. E. William Monter, *Witchcraft in France and Switzerland: The Borderlands During the Reformation* p. 124; Keith Thomas *Religion and the Decline of Magic* p. 633.
2. Monter, *ibid.* p. 122; Gustav Henningsen, *The Witches' Advocate: Basque Witchcraft and the Spanish Inquisition* p. 52; Alan D. Macfarlane, *Witchcraft in Tudor and Stuart England* p. 161; John P. Demos, *Entertaining Satan: Witchcraft and the Culture of Early New England* p. 65; H. C. Erik Midelfort, *Witch Hunting in Southwestern Germany 1562–1684: The Social and Intellectual Foundations* p. 182.
3. Ralph A. Houlbrooke, *The English Family 1450–1700* p. 213; Reginald Scot quoted in Macfarlane, *op.cit.* p. 163.
4. Monter, *op.cit.* p. 121; Midelfort, *op.cit.* p. 185; Macfarlane, *ibid.* p. 164; Demos, *op.cit.* p. 72.
5. Monter, *ibid.* p. 122.
6. Houlbrooke, *op.cit.* pp. 208, 213; Demos, *ibid.* pp. 360–1.
7. Thomas, *op.cit.* p. 673; Macfarlane, *op.cit.* pp. 149–52.
8. Monter, *op.cit.* pp. 115–18; Christina Larner, *Enemies of God: The Witchhunt in Scotland* pp. 89–90, 124; Hugh V. McLachlan and J. K. Swales, 'Stereotypes and Scottish Witchcraft', *Contemporary Review* 234 (1979), p. 89; McLachlan and Swales, 'Witchcraft and Anti-Feminism', *Scottish Journal of Sociology* 4 (May 1980) pp. 150–1; Demos, *op.cit.* pp. 85, 244.
9. Macfarlane, *op.cit.* p. 159; Alan D. Macfarlane, 'Witchcraft in Tudor and Stuart Essex', Ch. 4 of M. Douglas (ed.), *Witchcraft Confessions and Accusations* p. 88; Thomas, *op.cit.* pp. 659, 674; Demos, *op.cit.* p. 78.
10. Monter, *op.cit.* pp. 135–7; B. P. Levack, 'The Great Scottish Witch Hunt of 1661–1662', *Journal of British Studies* 20 (1980), p. 101; Midelfort, *op.cit.* p. 187.
11. G. R. Quaife, *Wanton Wenches and Wayward Wives* p. 245; Demos, *op.cit.* p. 78.
12. 'The Compost of Ptolomeus', quoted in Thomas, *op.cit.*

pp. 677–8; Macfarlane, *Witchcraft in Tudor and Stuart England* p. 158; K. M. Briggs, *Pale Hecate's Team* pp. 83, 85.

13. Demos, *op.cit.* pp. 73, 91, 134–5, 148–9, 171, 235, 257, 356; Larner, p. 123.

14. Demos, *ibid.* p. 71; Monter, *op.cit.* pp. 94–6, 45; Julio Caro Baroja, *The World of the Witches* pp. 191–2, 198; Macfarlane, *Witchcraft in Tudor and Stuart England* p. 186.

15. Larner, *op.cit.* p. 142; Macfarlane, *ibid.* pp. 127–8; Demos, *op.cit.* pp. 81, 134, 82, 141, 253, 356, 89, 90, 320, 331.

16. Demos, *ibid.* pp. 261, 272–3, 335, 353–4.

17. Macfarlane, *ibid.* pp. 158–9; Quaife, *op.cit.* p. 35; Larner, *op.cit.* p. 123; Demos, *ibid.* pp. 176–8, 345, 89; Briggs, *op.cit.* pp. 22–4.

18. Demos, *ibid.* pp. 255–7; Macfarlane, *ibid.* p. 173.

19. Demos, *ibid.* pp. 77, 89–90, 253, 356; Quaife, *op.cit.* p. 35.

20. Thomas, *op.cit.* pp. 600–11; Larner, *op.cit.* p. 143.

21. Demos, *ibid.* pp. 91–2, 175, 178–9, 257, 273; C. L'Estrange Ewen, *Witch Hunting and Witch Trials* p. 295.

22. Demos, *ibid.* pp. 262, 321; Ewen, *ibid.* p. 295; Larner, *op.cit.* p. 125.

23. Macfarlane, *Witchcraft in Tudor and Stuart England* p. 162; Ewen, *ibid.* pp. 291–313; Quaife, *op.cit.* pp. 32–5; Macfarlane, *ibid.* p. 170; Demos, *ibid.* p. 70.

24. Midelfort, *op.cit.* p. 192; Thomas, *op.cit.* p. 621; Midelfort, *op.cit.* p. 126.

25. Larner, *op.cit.* p. 96; Jeffrey Burton Russell, *Witchcraft in the Middle Ages* pp. 275–7; Thomas, *op.cit.* pp. 622, 674.

26. Thomas, *op.cit.* pp. 623–4; Russell, *ibid.* p. 276; Larner, *op.cit.* p. 96; Thomas, *ibid.* p. 628; Henningsen, *op.cit.* pp. 158–9; Monter, *op.cit.* pp. 136–8; Russell, *ibid.* p. 276.

27. Arthur Wilson quoted in Briggs, *op.cit.* p. 12.

12

Motivation and the Village Community: II, Victims and Accusers

Ordinary villagers throughout Europe believed that some of their neighbours were witches. This belief was a manifestation of a specific concept of misfortune. Misfortune could be attributed to God, the Devil, a neighbour or oneself. Christianity accommodated all four: Reformation and Counter-Reformation theologians emphasised God and self, popular religion preferred Devil and neighbour. To the reformers, God initiated misfortune to test his servants or to warn or punish sinners. This view was not a comfortable explanation in the social matrix of the early-modern village. Although God alone knew the real reasons for such affliction neighbours were very inquisitive. They looked on misfortune not with sympathy but with dangerous speculation as to the underlying causes of God's visitation. Rumours concerning the nature of this guilty secret destroyed the self-esteem of the victim of misfortune and pushed him to the margins of acceptability. This dangerous position could be avoided if misfortune was interpreted as diabolic malice. As Reginald Scot observed of Elizabethan England, 'None can with patience endure the hand and correction of God. For if any adversity . . . happen . . . they exclaim upon witches'.[1]

This explanation transferred the suspicion of guilt from the unfortunate to another. The villagers were no longer concerned to discover why their neighbour suffered misfortune but were obsessed to uncover who had caused it. The accuser was sometimes involved in a complex process of coping with guilt. The Christian punitive view of misfortune was adapted rather than ignored. Misfortune stimulated a search by the victim for an unworthy act that warranted diabolic malice. The guilt stemming from this provocative act was assuaged by accusing the provoked person of witchcraft. Keith Thomas located the trigger for this guilt reversal in the ambivalent attitude of village communities towards the poor, in the conflict between resentment and obligation. The accuser had refused a person he later labelled a witch a request for assistance. Boyer and Nissenbaum found it in the seduction of some members of corporate Puritan communities by economic individualism and their subsequent lack of success. The Salem accusers 'felt deeply the lure of the forces . . . they feared and despised'. They lashed out against those who succeeded because these successful people 'reminded them how far they . . . had already been seduced from their traditional moorings.' In Salem the accusers projected upon others 'the unacknowledged impulses which lay within themselves', eagerly sought a public confession and readily granted absolution. Not a single confessing witch at Salem was hanged. The basic values of society had been challenged but at the last moment reaffirmed. The guilt-reversion model of Thomas and the guilt-projection one of Boyer and Nissenbaum are psychologically dubious, at the best simplistic. The historical foundation of the Thomas thesis — guilt stemming from the resentment–obligation approach to the poor — is invalid. Calvinists and most English Protestants quickly developed a rationale for not helping the poor. The religious conscience of the day was not troubled by refusing charity to the undeserving.[2]

Much more clearly evident in the motivation of accusers was the need to protect and enhance the ego. The act of accusation reversed village attitudes and attracted to the accuser popular support and sympathy instead of suspicion. In some cases it went further than the re-integration of the latter into the village consensus. Accusers sometimes became leaders of village opinion and in a few cases the centre of regional attention. Ego enhancement occasionally developed into exhibitionism. This was especially true of children, adolescents and women in the highly disciplined adult male communities of early modern Europe. The Burton Boy and his ilk in England, the girls at Salem and the demonic nuns in Loudun, normally dependent and powerless, through their witch accusations exercised real power.[3]

Private misfortune, witch accusations and basic ideology were inextricably linked in most societies. Accusations reduced the stress caused by the perceived threat to basic values. Change itself was a disaster for a community indoctrinated with concepts of an unchanging cosmos. Traditional beliefs provided security. When these were threatened and the key values of society undermined the individual was forced to construct a meaningful view of the world that would reduce stress and provide security. In such circumstances most individuals modified their world view to reaffirm the ideology under threat. They cemented traditional values by defining all destabilising forces as diabolic. Boyer and Nissenbaum suggested that the main issue at Salem was the perceived threat to Puritan ideology. They concluded that 'the fundamental issue was not who was to control the village, but what its essential character was to be'. Private misfortune created the anxiety and in coping with this the elements conducive to such misfortune were conceived by the individual victim as a threat to the basic values of society. Concern developed from the individual outwards. Persecution and prosecution depended on the extent to which the village community and the political authorities accepted in each specific case the correlation between private misfortune and ideological threat. The extent of the threat to basic values conceived in diabolic terms was intensified by the reaction of a few who failed to cope with this threat and in various stages of psychological imbalance were considered 'possessed'. A still smaller number reacted to the crisis by seeking a new security when they embraced a system which was the inverse of Christianity, after their religion's failure to protect them. These exceptions joined, or thought they had joined, the diabolic conspiracy.[4]

To accuse another of witchcraft enabled action to be taken against the perceived source of personal misfortune. God could not be dealt with, the witch neighbour could. Major elements in this positive accusation were aggression, anger and hostility. This tension manifested itself in spiritual terms in a society in which the spiritual world was very real and all-embracing. Witchcraft accusations became an institutionalised and acceptable channel for the expression of aggressive impulses. These impulses were directed towards those who were bad neighbours. The witch and her accuser lived in a state of concealed and eventually overt hostility. It was usually a relationship in which normal avenues of solution, such as the law and open violence, were unavailable. Therefore, to be plausible accusations of witchcraft had to involve those persons not in a social or economic position to use these more direct methods of revenge. Men, whatever their status, and younger women could resort to violence. The most plausible user of a diabolic power would be poor elderly women. This process was reciprocal. There was a danger that aggressive impulses would not be satisfied if witch accusations were directed against people in a position to hit back, or against whom such accusations appeared dubious. Witchcraft accusations occurred most often when other aggression-satisfying mechanisms failed, essentially due to the inability of those normal mechanisms to give emotional satisfaction. Witch accusations were rarely a transference of direct aggression into an area considered less emotional and less socially disruptive despite theories of guilt-projection at Salem. Neither was it an outlet only for those people with aggressive tendencies. There was real anger expressed by most accusers and victims. John Carr attacked the alleged New England witch John Godfrey and 'ran his fist' into Godfrey's breast and drove him 'against the chimney stock'. A possessed Elizabeth Kelley demanded that witch suspect Goody Ayers be scalded on a great furnace and beheaded with a broad axe. Governing this rage and hostility was an even deeper motive — fear.[5]

This simple explanation of witch accusation has been lost in the misconceptions of a witch as a scapegoat. Scapegoating, as defined as the deliberate selection of an innocent party to be blamed for a crime, is irrelevant in this context. Where it did occur it was deliberate deception and some instances of this have been discussed. Such blatant conscious redirection of blame was rare in the village community. Boyer and Nissenbaum suggest that in some situations the fears of accusers were projected onto other persons away from the real source of these fears. In Salem Village the Putnam family condemned to declining social status and relative poverty through the activities of a powerful stepmother sought a surrogate scapegoat. They subconsciously chose a woman who had not only some characteristics of their stepmother but whose life reflected the economic insecurity they now faced. They accused Sarah Good whose plunge into poverty reflected the precarious nature of economic security so easily shattered by the death or remarriage of a parent. Sarah represented the ultimate fate of the Putnams, a fate created by a wicked stepmother, Mary Verens, who was too powerful to be attacked directly. This is a plausible but almost unprovable hypothesis.[6]

In most cases scapegoating was more direct, although not central, or did not occur at all. In the great majority of accusations villagers were genuinely frightened and believed the accused responsible for their problems. In a strict sense these people were not scapegoats but the real source of anxiety. However, in the earlier stages of the labelling process a form of scapegoating often

183

occurred. As a result of gossip, particular women, for reasons discussed in the last chapter, were blamed for specific events, often
trivial. The initial attribution may have resulted from a lie, unsub-
stantial rumour or deliberate exaggeration. Over the course of
years it became easier and more plausible to believe the accused
guilty of a vast range of crimes. Cumulative scapegoating over
diverse issues developed into a genuine fear of this person as a real
threat. Life, limb and property were now at stake.[7]

Guilt, hostility and fear, and the need for ego-enhancement and
security, in times of crisis were more likely to be manifested in
witch accusations in certain situations and among particular types
of people. The precise source of the accusation and the relationship
between accuser and accused is controversial but two basic positions have been advanced. Accusations arise within the family and
are directed against relatives. They arise within sub-groups in the
village and are directed against a close neighbour for a variety of
reasons or against an unacceptable category of villager. The key
links between accuser and accused are alleged to be kin, geographical proximity or socio-economic conflict at the base of society.

The role of the family in both witchcraft activity and accusations
varied. Baroja believed that the Basques saw witchcraft activity as
a family affair with secrets passed down from generation to generation. Sceptical judges at Ceberio confronted with 24 witches, all
from the same family, concluded that the local witch cult was little
more than a family crime syndicate. Castenega, a contemporary
commentator, warned family members to whom had been handed
down, along with old clothing, the art of malevolent magic, as
these people were not aware of the dangers involved. De Lancre in
his investigation on the French side of the border considered that
the large number of priests uncovered as witches was explained by
their having come from families of witches. In Scotland, a witch's
daughter was assumed to have learned her mother's art.
Henningsen, looking at the same material as Baroja, agreed that
the Basques believed that witchcraft was hereditary but that this
belief limited such knowledge to a sub-set of the family and in fact
had no objective reality.[8]

The husband of an accused witch was sometimes ignorant of his
wife's activity. Thousands of husbands testified that they were
unaware that their wives were engaged in witchcraft. There are too
many unverifiable assumptions required to quantify this situation.
The wife may have been completely innocent, therefore there had
been nothing, in fact, to conceal from her husband. On the other

hand she may have been guilty and the husband knew of her activities but was lying to save his own life. This approach often failed. A significant proportion of men accused of witchcraft were husbands of suspected witches. Their wife was a witch therefore they were guilty by association. In reality there were very few husband and wife witch partnerships; they existed in the minds of the accusers not in the real world. Many husbands, such as John Proctor at Salem, certainly tried to save their accused wives and as a result suffered prosecution themselves. In a patriarchal society the role of the husband was a vital factor in village persecution. Many a New England witch escaped prosecution, despite village complaints, as long as her husband lived. A powerful husband stilled popular action. As an unprotected widow the woman became vulnerable. At the other extreme, some husbands in Scotland played a leading role in the accusation of their wives. The range of charges against Agnes Williamson originated from her husband and his drinking companions, and those against Elspeth Thomson from her spouse and his family. Although these Scottish examples suggest that witch accusations may have been a manifestation of marriage breakdown and an attempt to remove the spouse there is little other evidence to support such a thesis.[9]

Mothers, mothers-in-law and stepmothers were susceptible to witchcraft activity and accusation due to the tension created by the unfortunate marriages of their children. The son of Barbara Rufin married against her will. She tried to poison him, and he accused her of witchcraft. In-law tension often manifested itself in this way because suitable means of alleviating or channelling such unacceptable yet not uncommon family hostility did not exist in most communities. The stepmother was an even more obvious object of attack. In Salem, Thomas Putnam's quarrel with his stepmother and stepbrother was basic. Ann Putnam was unable to vent her antagonism on her own mother whose death, or her mother-in-law whose remarriage, deprived the Putnam children of their inheritance. The wicked stepmother was often seen as the cause of misfortune, as a manifestation of evil, as a witch. The vulnerability of menopausal women to delusions of witchcraft, as victims, accusers and witches, was known to contemporaries. The depression associated with menopause was seen as the aspect which triggered such developments. Demos probes much deeper. Such women were preoccupied with illness and injury and with the morbidity and mortality of children. In New England, with its high birth-rate and supportive cultural and ideological imperatives, child-bearing was an essential element in a woman's identity. The sudden cessation of what gave her life meaning and the need to chart anew the future, created fears that could easily be made manifest in feelings of diabolic assault.[10]

Family tensions were evident also in the large number of young men and adolescent women who saw themselves as victims of witchcraft. Young men anxious to free themselves from parental, especially maternal, dependence were antagonistic towards women of their mother's generation. They inexplicably refused to co-operate in the simple aspects of everyday living. When misfortune struck these able younger men it was perceived as instigated by an older woman. Younger women had an even harder bond to break and a more difficult task to establish their identity. In freeing themselves from the authority of their mothers, basic feelings of love and dependence were sometimes transformed into hostility and aggression — an aggression often directed against women of their mother's generation. At Salem the original accusers were women under 20, their victims women over 40. All young people were not equally vulnerable to diabolic assault. Clearly an individual's lack of psychological development increased the possibility. John Demos provided a case study in the 'possession' of Elizabeth Knapp. Knapp was in many ways a typical victim – accuser except that her attempts to accuse two women as her tormentors failed. Demos suggested that as a first child, quickly supplanted by a young brother who then died, her upbringing as an only child (rare in New England), the adultery of her father, the criminal activities of her uncle, the religious deviance of one grandfather and the incompetence of the other, and the possible instability of her mother inhibited 'normal' development. Her father's rapid rehabilitation in a new town and subsequent acceptance as a pillar of the establishment and her early relocation in a foster household complicated the situation. Demos concluded that Elizabeth missed 'those forms of parenting . . . most essential to inner development'.[11] Nevertheless, the research of Demos and Thomas suggested that in Old and New England although the family was basic in developing susceptible personalities it was not itself a major conduit of witchcraft activity and accusations. Problems often developed within the family but the object of the accusation was usually not a relative. In the Basque lands, the Franche Comte and in Scotland the role of the family was greater. A quantitative answer awaits a more thorough understanding of family life throughout early modern Europe.

Perhaps the development of the family in England beyond that of the traditional peasant family as postulated by Alan Macfarlane provides an explanation. Where the family was still central to social and economic life it remained central to witchcraft, where it had ceased to perform such a function it gave way to other elements in the rural community.[12]

All the same, the interaction of family and community was a basic element of village life. A crucial element in both and in witchcraft accusations were children. In the Salem hunts the accusers were girls under 20 and the accused women over 40. Demos suggested that this reflected a hatred of the mother by an adolescent girl which would normally be expressed within the family. Where cultural imperatives prevented this, female juvenile aggressive impulses were projected by these girls onto socially marginal women who had some of the characteristics of their mothers. This thesis rests on a psychological model rather than historical evidence. One hint that the problems of adolescence, whether mother-hatred or not, lay at the base of the Salem accusations was the endeavour of subsequent Salem clergy to institutionalise the village young and give them a sense of identity as a group within a school. The rarity of young persons among those accused of witchcraft, except in periods of panic, was also advanced in general support for the 'generational conflict' thesis. Children were not normally accused of witchcraft because it took decades to develop the necessary reputation.[13]

However children played a major role in Basque witchcraft as accuser–witches. Basque children were placed under tremendous pressure by their parents, priests and neighbours. Basque villagers were in a state of panic over their inability to prevent the seduction of their children by their witch neighbours. Witches enticed children to the nocturnal sabbat and initiated them into their evil cult. To prevent this, children were kept awake all night. On one occasion, thirty to forty children were sent by their parents to the local rectory for their protection. This was not successful and local priests asked the Inquisition to condone the murder of witches who took local children to the sabbat. Even when children were observed peacefully asleep at home when they were allegedly at the sabbat this was interpreted as a diabolic illusion. The Devil had put an image of the child in bed while the real person was at the sabbat. The evidence for these sabbats and the enticement of children to them came in large measure from young children. The incredible stories told by 9-year-olds were tributes to bizarre imaginations based on dreams and information transferred deliberately or subconsciously by parents, priests and inquisitors. Baroja used a late-nineteenth-century psychological model of the mythomane to explain such behaviour. The mythomane was a liar — vain, malicious, with precocious sexual appetites and very suggestible. In children such behaviour was not pathological; fantasy was real. The naming of witches, that is of those women allegedly seen at the sabbat, was a major function of the child. Tremendous pressure was placed on the child by their own parents to confess to being a witch themselves and by parents and priests to name their adult seducers. Inquisitor Salazar found that most children were victims of this pressure and made up stories that the adults wanted to hear. Confession of their own guilt was essential due to Basque hereditary laws which enabled the property and estates of unconfessed witches to be confiscated. A child witch destroyed a family's security.[14]

In south-western Germany the prominence of children was a new and increasing feature of seventeenth-century trials — again as witches and accusers. This increase coincided with a greater public concern towards children which included the publication of anti-child tracts and treatises. The key element in this type of publication was the new emphasis that the sins of the children rather than those of their parents was the provocation for the diabolic assault. A deeper understanding of the role of children and of the attitudes of Reformation and Counter Reformation teaching in this area is necessary before an authoritative stance can be taken. Whatever the cause, the effect of greater juvenile participation increased the intensity of the trials. Adults, unless broken by torture or suffering from specific psychological problems, were reluctant to confess in detail. Vagueness was a useful defence and to name others as fellow witches was fraught with danger. Children had no such inhibitions — a developmental trait of childhood encouraged in the majority of German jurisdictions by the law. Some argued that children could be fully fledged witches but most believed that even if they followed their elders and indulged in abominable crimes as children they could not be accused as witches. Children could thus confess to the most outrageous perversions and were able to name adult accomplices with impunity. This increased a child's power in the adult community and made him the centre of attention. Parents often encouraged this form of activity to the point of deception, as occurred in England.[15]

The reformers, Catholic and Protestant, seeing the confessions of children as the beginning of many witch panics, were convinced that Satan had taken over the youth of the day. This they interpreted as a result of the breakdown of parental authority. The new concern of parents with children and the increased desire to bend them to the parental will created anxieties for the younger generation which may have expressed themselves in a conscious or subconscious desire to be revenged against their harsh discipline. To bring a flogging adult patriarch to his knees through an accusation of witchcraft was indeed juvenile vengeance. Such power depended on the readiness of adults to accept the evidence of children either informally or legally. In the Jura the magistrates treated children's confessions as fantasy and no child was indicted for witchcraft in Geneva or the Protestant jurisdictions of the area and only a few in the Catholic areas. The magistrates rarely accepted the evidence of children against adults unless it was substantiated by other adults. Until the history of childhood is better understood this vital element in witchcraft accusation remains ill-defined and its impact unknown.[16]

Children linked family and neighbours in the web of witch accusations. The subject of most accusations was a neighbour rather than a relative. The issues that isolated a neighbour and subjected her to suspicion were discussed in the last chapter. In essence, an unpleasant person who lived within the community and was the source of discord was accused. Some historians have located the source of antagonism in the social structure rather than the specific personality of an individual. In Basque coastal villages the lifestyle of the ocean-going fishermen underlay many accusations. The men were absent for most of the year and returned comparatively wealthy — for a short time. Having rapidly spent their wealth in hedonistic pursuits, with or without their families, they returned to sea. The families of spendthrift, licentious fishermen were left unprotected and dependent on goodwill, becoming a burden on the hard-working, barely surviving and austere farming community. In addition, the alleged breakdown of morality and marriages that accompanied such a situation rendered the wives of fishermen especially vulnerable to both the practice of witchcraft and attendant accusations.[17]

The socially mobile — up or down — were often suspect but this debate has been bedevilled by the plausible yet unacceptable thesis of Keith Thomas that the object of attack was the dependant — the recipient of charity. He argued that the accused was almost at the bottom of the socio-economic ladder and the accuser only slightly better off. Witchcraft accusations arose from the hostility and aggression of villagers who could find no legitimate avenue for settling the problem. These persons were too poor to use the law and too weak and old to use force. Hostility was created by the emergence of economic individualism which clashed with the traditional virtues of communal charity towards the less fortunate. These socio-economic changes helped destroy the institutions which had cared for the poor, the sick and the old, and at the same time increased the number of poor dependants that needed assistance. The village community had to cope with a growing number of dependants when its value-system concerning charity was changing. A dependant, usually an elderly woman, sought help from a neighbour, often a small essential such as cheese, milk, some fire or a household implement. The neighbour refused such aid but felt guilty about this response. The old woman wandered away muttering abuse. Later, often years later, misfortune struck the uncharitable neighbour who saw his difficulties as the righteous revenge of the poor person who had been refused help. Thomas believed that it was a sense of guilt that gave intensity to this exercise: an exercise in guilt-reversal. The greedy accused the needy.[18]

This thesis has little merit. The socio-economic changes that Thomas considered occurred in the sixteenth and seventeenth century are now thought by Macfarlane to have taken place centuries earlier. There was certainly no dramatic economic change to alter relationships within the English village. The model of guilt-reversal as indicated earlier is psychologically dubious and historically invalid. Calvinists and most English Protestants soon had a rationale for not helping the poor. The religious conscience of the day was not troubled by refusing charity to the undeserving poor. Thirdly, the average villager had no need to feel guilty. They had helped the deserving and not so deserving poor for years until pushed beyond the limit by the unreasonable demands of the habitual parasite. Social harmony was disrupted by undue demands not by acts of uncharity. Villages tolerated demanding dependants for decades. Fourthly, the New England and Scottish evidence suggests that witches were to be found among troublesome neighbours rather than specifically among those dependent on charity.[19]

The overwhelming majority of witches were accused from within their village by neighbours but only occasionally by family. Strangers were sometimes accused in circumstances where they threatened social harmony although this was more common in urban areas. During the panic created by an outbreak of the plague in Geneva, newly arrived French migrants were accused of its introduction — and of witchcraft. When struck with misfortune, towns on major trade routes found a sense of community and a source of their troubles in blaming individual strangers or groups of outsiders. In German towns outsiders were regularly accused but in village communities, which saw few strangers, the bad neighbour was the object of attention. In times of panic village accusations did expand beyond the parish border along four avenues: geographical proximity (the next village), association (someone seen with a witch from another village), family ties and exhibiting similar traits to someone accused elsewhere.[20]

The reaction of a village community to the presence of a witch varied considerably. The basic need of the individual victim of misfortune and the disrupted community was protection from diabolic assault and the restoration of harmony. The traditional approach was to attempt a reconciliation of the hostile parties. In the Basque villages witches were persuaded to confess their role in the problems confronting their neighbours. They were pardoned by the parties involved and a general reconciliation took place. A second defence was a employ counter-magic. A third approach was an 'armed' truce. Alleged witches operated for decades — and in many places for life — without formal action being brought against them. They could be blamed for the misfortunes of the community thereby providing a permanent scapegoat. One aspect of this reaction was clearly fear. A witch was feared and action against her could be counter-productive. It was better to suffer her presence than to provoke her. In some communities violence was more common. Basque communities, convinced that witches seduced their children, murdered accused women, tortured them by half garrotting them and dragged them through town. They were ducked in icy ponds or subjected to beatings, slashings and scratchings. This popular violence was also directed against the property of the witch. Katherine Harrison, a reasonably wealthy suspect in New England, had her cattle mutilated and killed and her crops prematurely harvested.[21]

In much of the Spanish Netherlands peasants preferred to deal with the problem of witch accusations within the context of private vengeance rather than seek recourse to the law. A taverner seeking the payment of outstanding debts was beaten to death by two brothers who had recently lost three horses. A Bruges diviner had given the latter clues as to the identity of their persecutor. A Hainault peasant employed two bullies to obtain a confession from a woman he suspected of witchcraft. This interrogation, brutally physical, ended in the suspect's death. In this system of private justice the accused as well as the accuser resorted to physical violence. A priest who suggested that one of his parishioners should avoid the company of a woman he considered a witch was killed by the person he was trying to warn. Antoine Tournier, accused of witchcraft publicly in church, slew his accuser. Another accuser who abused a neighbour as having the eyes of a sorcerer received a fatal blow from a hoe in return. Two drinking companions quarrelled and one was asked to urinate in the cinders to prove he was not a witch. He refused and in the resultant fight one of them was stabbed to death. The charge that all women in a particular village were witches led to the fatal attack on the accuser by a local whose mother, unbeknown to the accuser, had come from that village. In some cases such murderers were pardoned and in most received little more than temporary exile.[22] Another response to witchcraft was mockery. Confident in their Christian faith or sceptical of a particular incident as an example of diabolic malevolence some villagers viewed their witches as senile, unpleasant and befuddled troublemakers. They became the butt of village humour and the object of general mockers. Children teased them and they were the victims of the village pranksters. The inherent danger of this approach lay in the thin line between fun and fear. Should misfortune strike, village attitudes, especially of the pranksters and mockers, could change rapidly.[23]

When a formal accusation was made and the authorities brought in the situation altered. Once legal processes were begun the ultimate reaction depended on the outcome of the trial. If the accused was convicted and executed the village reflected mixed emotions. The execution of the witch, of a familiar neighbour, who had been part of the community for years was in itself a major event. On the other hand there was great relief. The long-standing cause of village problems had been removed. However, tension could remain in cases where doubt existed as to the guilt of the accused. This could create village feuds and continue to be a source of disharmony for generations. Secondly, the removal of a convenient scapegoat could be counter productive — the village now had to look elsewhere to explain its problems. Not only was the witch removed but usually her husband and sometimes her children left the village. In many cases the witch and her family left their village even after acquittal. This occurred frequently in New England where movement was an accepted norm of the frontier community. In Europe it appears less common and only in the most extreme cases of village hostility would a witch leave her home. Nevertheless, the voluntary removal of the witch and her family from a community on acquittal was probably the most satisfying solution. The village achieved the removal of their problem without the trauma of execution. Some jurisdictions in Europe, including Geneva, adopted banishment as the major weapon against witchcraft — the convicted witch was exiled. However, the surprising feature of the New England experience was that the majority of witches acquitted by the courts returned to their communities. Demos believed that apart from the difficulties of moving in terms of property, acceptance in another village and general fears of the unknown, the accused and accusers were drawn back together. The witch had notoriety and therefore status in her village and the community still had someone to blame for their misfortunes.[24]

The effect of witchcraft accusations on a village community differed. In most cases it powerfully reinforced the norms and mores of society. Crime drew a community closer by defining in a practical and dramatic way those who were outside its fold. Witchcraft in a theologically oriented society defined the good and delineated people who were not only bad neighbours but enemies of God and the godly state. This gave greater strength to the sanctions that the community sought to impose and greater legitimacy to the agents of their implementation. Larner saw this enforcement of community norms at the level of moral and political conformity to national ideological values. In Scotland these were the values of the Calvinist state. Thomas believed it operated at a such lower level of village harmony, inhibiting bad temper, scolding and other forms of vicious behaviour, and it encouraged assistance to the needy. Lack of charity might provoke witchly vengeance. In essence, material misfortune resulted from breaches of moral behaviour; the fear of witches, and of accusations of witchcraft, upheld the norms of village life and clearly delineated the level of deviance tolerated by society.[25]

In upholding traditional norms, witch beliefs and accusations may have acted as a severe check on innovation and reform. In technical fields witch beliefs lessened the need to find the real causes of plant and animal disease, and protected the status of the medical profession. Blame for undiagnosed illness and the failure of treatment could be attributed to witchcraft. Witch beliefs may have hindered economic change and the emergence of dynamic peasant leadership. The enterprising peasant could have this success attributed to diabolic help. The fear of emerging above the ruck and inviting an accusation of witchcraft led many potential village entrepreneurs to abort that potential. Such pressures were manipulated in many parts of Europe to impose ideological and political conformity and undoubtedly constituted a weapon at a number of levels in society for social control. The normative function of witch accusations nevertheless could have a therapeutic effect on the local community, including the witch. Festering issues were brought to the surface and, depending on the results of persecution and prosecution, harmony could be re-established and the community reunited. Thomas claimed that the conservative impact of witch beliefs was not so evident in England as these beliefs were adapted by the entrepreneurs and village leaders to free themselves from traditional restraints, especially in the provision of charity for the dependants of the community — a thesis already considered untenable.[26]

There were dangerous and pathological effects of witch accusations especially in the large-scale panics so common in south-western Germany. Tension increased and fear dominated. Accusations spread through society implicating the natural leadership and even the witch hunters themselves. In such situations significant numbers of inhabitants were executed and order collapsed. The scars of such hunts took generations to heal. Yet even within a small English village an isolated accusation might develop into a long-term disaster. In trying to impose community norms and sanctions against a mild deviant an accusation might further isolate the accused. This sense of isolation and bitterness against the community might engender genuine attempts to seek revenge. Such accusations created witches and led old women to believe that they had powers to effect vengeance. In doing so they raised the level of hatred and bitterness within the community, creating a permanent catalyst for disharmony.[27]

Nevertheless, at the level of the village community witch accusations were on the whole conservative, normative and beneficial. When these accusations got out of hand and the good order of the community was threatened such accusations became destructive. In normal years witch beliefs and accusations acted as a panacea and safety valve for communities in their attempts to maintain good order and good neighbourliness in a changing demographic and ideological environment. These beliefs even gave many of the accused a new lease of life, bringing colour and power to a few elderly, isolated and often dependent women.

Village communities increasingly came under the influence of the elite, either through the enforcement of central jurisdictions or through the effective use of the pulpit. The level of interaction between academic fears of the Devil and traditional peasant concern with *maleficium* varied. Some villages appear to be uninfluenced by elite fantasies. Others, such as those in Scotland, appear to have incorporated the views of the political and ecclesiastical establishment. It appears that the Devil assumed an increasingly important role in the witch beliefs of the peasant. Larner believed that Scottish witchcraft and witch hunting were phenomena imposed on the powerless by the powerful. Yet even in Scotland the porosity of peasant beliefs should not be too readily accepted. Popular accusations almost entirely originated in terms of *malefice*, or only include the activities of the Devil as one of many charges. The courts adjusted the evidence to magnify if not create a role for diabolism to meet the demands of the Witchcraft Act.[28]

The porosity of the village to elite opinion and its effects have been emphasised recently by Robert Muchembled. He adapted Keith Wrightson's division of peasant communities into those that were 'open' to such elite influences and those that were 'closed' and saw this impact as an essential element in the witch hunt. Witch hunting was prevalent in villages that adopted elitist satanic sabbatical views and which had recourse to legal tribunals to solve their internal problems. The closed villages solved their own problems, including that of sorcery within the context of private vengeance, and little witch hunting occurred. The effort by the authorities to impose law and order on the peasant community was part of the campaign to destroy popular culture and in this they were assisted by the wealthier segments of 'open' peasant communities. These communities were disrupted by economic and demographic changes in which the minority became richer and the majority very much poorer. The minority saw that by supporting the central authorities and by using external tribunals to isolate and punish witches (usually drawn from the poorer majority) they could maintain their newly established position as the village elite. In the Spanish Netherlands the traditional particularist peasant village had to be subverted in this manner — successfully in Flanders and Hainault, and otherwise in Artois. In New England the legal and ideological framework of the elite existed before the

195

village. What the Counter Reformation and Calvinist states strove to achieve in Europe — peasant conformity to their ideology — Puritan Massachusetts and Connecticut enforced from the beginning.[29]

The concept of diabolic malice through the agency of a troublesome neighbour was a more comfortable and actionable explanation of misfortune than divine retribution. The witch victim and accuser may have been guilt-ridden, under stress, needing ego-enhancement and unable to give legitimate expression to anger, aggression and hostility, but the particular aspects and causes of this varied from individual to individual. These symptoms, except in rare cases, were not pathological, nor were their accusations crude attempts at scapegoating. Most victims and accusers genuinely feared their witch. Although the psychological conditions leading to such fear may have developed within the family the object of this fear was usually the close neighbour. Young men, adolescent girls, children and menopausal women appeared most vulnerable to such fears. Socio-economic deprivation and differentiation were key factors in the sociology of accusations. Accusers were generally better off economically than the accused although there were many exceptions. Beyond this generalisation and the widespread suspicion of the socially mobile, few theses have more than regional application. Village fears were projected on the bad neighbour rather than the dependant. Witches once labelled were reconciled, killed, feared, respected, mocked or ignored within the peasant community or increasingly handed over to the legal authorities for formal trial. The response to such judicial decisions also varied. Although the effect on a village of such accusations could on occasions be inhibiting, divisive and destabilising, in the majority of cases they were conservative, normative and beneficial. Excesses were usually stimulated from without the village by an over-zealous petty official. Peasant villages were increasingly subjected to elitist attitudes and where these were accepted by the more notable members of the community the intensity of village conflict was more often reflected in the witch hunt.

Notes

1. Alan Macfarlane, 'Witchcraft in Tudor and Stuart Essex', Ch. 4 of M. Douglas (ed.), *Witchcraft Confessions and Accusations* p. 88; Keith Thomas, *Religion and the Decline of Magic* p. 648.

2. Thomas, *ibid.* pp. 659, 665, 673; Paul Boyer and Stephen Nissenbaum, *Salem Possessed: The Social Origins of Witchcraft* pp. 107, 180, 212–15.

3. John P. Demos, *Entertaining Satan* pp. 118, 151, 160, 202; for psychological basis see notes and references Demos, *ibid.* pp. 440–4.

4. Christina Larner, *Enemies of God: The Witchhunt in Scotland* pp. 134–40; Boyer and Nissenbaum, *op.cit.* pp. 180, 103, 109.

5. Boyer and Nissenbaum, *ibid.* p. 208; Demos, *op.cit.* pp. 187–8; Thomas, *op.cit.* pp. 669.

6. Boyer and Nissembaum, *op.cit.* pp. 143–9.

7. Wolf Bleek, 'Witchcraft, Gossip and Death: A Social Drama', *Man* 11 (1976) pp. 526–41; Leonard Berkowitz, 'Anti-Semitism and the Displacement of Aggression', *Journal of Abnormal and Social Psychology* 59 (1959) pp. 182–7; Leonard Berkowitz and James Green, 'The Stimulus Qualities of the Scapegoat', *Journal of Abnormal and Social Psychology* 64 (1962) pp. 293–301, especially pp. 293–4.

8. Julio Caro Baroja, *The World of the Witches* pp. 47. 153, 151; Gustav Henningsen, *The Witches' Advocate: Basque Witchcraft and the Spanish Inquisition (1609–1614)* pp. 11, 150.

9. Boyer and Nissenbaum, *op.cit.* pp. 200–2; Larner, *op.cit.* pp. 128–9, 34, 96, 150; Demos, *op.cit.* pp. 358–9; L. G. Baldwin, 'Witchcraft in East Lothian', Ph.D thesis (work in progress), University of New England.

10. H. C. Erik Midelfort, *Witch Hunting in Southwestern Germany 1652–1684* pp. 1–2; Larner, *op.cit.* pp. 99, 128; Boyer and Nissenbaum, *op.cit.* p. 149; Demos, *op.cit.* p. 155.

11. Demos, *op.cit.* pp. 125ff, 156–8.

12. Demos, *op.cit.* pp. 22–35, 61–2, 67, 70–1, 74–5, 254–5, 257, 271, 284; Boyer and Nissenbaum, *op.cit.* 'Ch. 6; Alan D. Macfarlane, *Witchcraft in Tudor and Stuart England* p. 169–70; E. William Monter, *Witchcraft in France and Switzerland: The Borderlands During the Reformation* p. 119.

13. John P. Demos, 'Underlying Themes in the Witchcraft of Seventeenth Century New England', *American Historical Review*, 75 (1970) pp. 1311–26; Boyer and Nissenbaum, *op.cit.* p. 220; Midelfort, *op.cit.* p. 5.

14. Henningsen, *op.cit.* p. 139; Baroja, *op.cit.* p. 163, 195, 251–2.

15. Midelfort, *op.cit.* p. 141.

16. Monter, *op.cit.* p. 126.

17. Baroja, *op.cit.* pp. 159, 134–5, 140.

18. Thomas, *op.cit.* pp. 670–1, 698, 652, 658–62, 669, 673, 677;

19. Alan D. Macfarlane, *The Origins of English Individualism*, Blackwell, London, 1978, pp. 59–60; Stanislav Andreski, 'The Syphilitic Shock', *Encounter* 58–5 (May 1982) p. 9.

20. Midelfort, *op.cit.* p. 95; Monter, *op.cit.* pp. 177–8.

21. Christina Larner, *Witchcraft and Religion: The Politics of Popular Belief* Part II, Ch. 3.

22. Robert Muchembled, 'L'Autre Côté Du Miroir: Mythes Sataniques et Réalités Culturelles Aux XVIe et XVIIe Siècles', *Annales ESC* 40–2 (mars-avril 1985) pp. 288–306, especially pp. 292–4.

23. David Nichols, 'The Devil in Renaissance France' *History Today*

30 (Nov. 1980) pp. 25–30; Baroja, *op.cit.* pp. 217–18.
24. Demos, *Entertaining Satan* pp. 300–2.
25. Thomas, *op.cit.* pp. 634, 674–6; Midelfort, *op.cit.* p. 195.
26. Thomas, *op.cit.* pp. 643, 650.
27. Midelfort, *op.cit.* p. 93; Thomas, *ibid.* p. 674.
28. Larner, *Enemies of God* p. 88–9.
29. Muchembled, *op.cit.*, especially pp. 301–3.

13
Dreams, Drugs and Madness: Conclusion

Dreams have played a major, if varied, role in most societies. Western Christendom linked dreams, especially unpleasant ones, with deviant sex and diabolic activity. Until the thirteenth century the detailed subject matter of such dreams remained restricted to the world of illusion. The subsequent acceptance of these fantasies as objective facts in the waking world was the significant imput into the lore of witchcraft, a lore widely accepted as objective reality by the sixteenth century.[1]

The aetiology, the role and meaning of the dream are subjects of controversy and dispute. The Freudian position that dreams are a key to the unconscious — an area ruled by instinct in which sex and fear dominate — fits neatly an interpretation of the deviant fantasies of the witch as the manifestation of the sexual repression of emotionally unstable and highly suggestible victims of the austerity of early modern Christianity. The Jungian view that the dream attempts to compensate, to meet needs and to balance a personality helps explain the 'evil' dreams of 'good' people. The more perfect a person is during the day, often denying aspects of their personality, the more the dream attempts to compensate by night. This balancing is achieved in terms of deep inherited cultural values which may not reflect those of a current norm, such as austere Christianity. It was often the respectable married woman who was besieged by the incubus. This situation probably shocked and disoriented the dreamer, contributed to a personal crisis and validated the cultural imperatives of a powerful diabolic assault on society. If the Devil seduces a godly wife in her own bed his powers are almost irresistible.

In the village community, anxiety dreams, in which fear of

failure or conflict with neighbours loom large, invariably depict the threatening force in terms of these well-known friends and acquaintances. These threats are exaggerated and take fantastic forms in which the friend of waking hours is the menacing fiend of the dream. The inability to separate the dream from waking reality is the critical factor in the accumulation of witch lore. This inability to distinguish is due to both individual disfunctioning and cultural conditioning. Young children, in particular, cannot readily separate the two realms on suddenly awakening. If this situation is badly handled the wolf at the window and the devil sitting on the end of the bed will become increasingly real and the ability to distinguish the dream from waking consciousness retarded. Many societies, especially the Amerindian, accepted the dream world as the real world and acted accordingly. Villages were moved and wars planned on the evidence of the dreamer. Many saw dreams as predictive of events that would transpire in the waking world. However, this predictive nature of dreams, an aspect of the paranormal and part of the trade of the cunningman, played only a minor role in the alleged activities of the diabolic witch.

Sleep was viewed traditionally as either a dangerous period in which life was just maintained or, conversely, as a period of renewal. The former attitude dominated peasant life in the sixteenth century when behaviour during sleep was closely monitored for signs of danger. Any unusual behaviour during sleep, when the forces of evil were at their strongest, could be interpreted as a sign of diabolic assault. Recent research into the nature of sleep throws a little light on the confusion of dreams and waking reality. Sleep consists of sequences of levels involving two distinct categories: REM (rapid eye movement), which appears to relate to sorting ideas and emotions; and non-REM sequences, which involve physical renewal. REM sleep occupies one-quarter of the sleeping period and is the state from which, if the subject is awakened, dreams are remembered. This sleep state is very similar to waking but with some specific manifestations: muscle paralysis (the feeling that you cannot move), high blood pressure, uneven breathing, penile erection and wet dreams. On awaking from such a sleep remembered dreams are rich in hallucinatory images. It is sometimes difficult to remember whether such images are recalled from the dream or are a manifestation of a disfunctioning common to the borders of sleep and wakefulness. In this state, internal fantasies are externalised in a vivid form but are usually perceived as such. The sick, the aged, and children experience greater difficulties in separating the fantasy and objective reality.

Such dreaming is influenced not only by the psychological state of the person concerned but by the substances consumed before sleep. These do not need to be heavy drugs. Protein-rich foods, such as eggs, meat and cheese, contain the amino acid trytaphon which speeds up the onset of the REM period and remembered dreams. The old belief that cheese eaten before retiring leads to nightmares does have a scientific base. The ingredients in the witches' ointment produced waking delusions followed by a deep sleep in which dreams on awakening became confused with objective reality. Drugs played a major role in creating the witch world of early modern Europe, both in their deliberate use by the witch and in their unintentional ingestion by the populace. Contemporaries accepted a close link between witchcraft and drugs. Throughout much of Europe the witch was synonymous with the poisoner, and De Lancre divided witches into the blasphemous heretics who accepted diabolic leadership and those simply given over to drugs.[2]

The belief that witches flew to the sabbat was seen as a drug-induced illusion by a significant minority of contemporaries. Johannes Nider in the early-fifteenth century recorded the case of a woman who 'believed herself to be transported through the air during the night' when in fact 'rubbing ointment on herself . . . she lay her head back and immediately fell asleep' and did not move. Early in the sixteenth century Spina wrote of women deluded 'in such a way as they imagine they are carried a long distance while they remain immobile at home'. Recent research has verified such claims. Natural hallucinogens were found in Jimsom weed, deadly nightshade, henbane, belladonna and mandrake in the form of alkaloids such as atropine, hyoscyamine and scopolamine. Atropine in a plaster form had been used for centuries and was highly absorbable even through unbroken skin. When applied as 'witches' ointment' to the more susceptible skin of the vaginal region, often broken by lice bites and scores, the effect was immediate — sleep dominated by illusions of flight and sexual fantasies. The poisonous skin of the toad also used by the witch contained numerous drugs including digitalis and the powerful hallucinogen bufotenin, which produced a specific hallucination — flight.[3]

Shapeshifting (the ability to change into animals) was another significant feature of witch belief explicable in terms of drugs.

Specific drugs can induce people into believing they are animals. The reported characteristics of the werewolf — dry throat, difficulty in swallowing, great thirst, impaired vision, a tendency to stagger and a sensation of growing feathers or hair — were manifestations of atropine poisoning. Although most reported sabbats were illusions, many meetings of drug-affected persons took place. At such meetings according to Guazzo 'the eyes of those who attend such assemblies are not sure and clear of sight . . . like those blinded by drunkenness'. Belladonna was a major ingredient used at such meetings which created hallucinations, made the partakers highly suggestible, dilated their pupils and created a personality mix of excitability and docility. The witches' ointment was depicted for centuries as either a myth or a hoax. Alleged witches created an innocent blend to fool authorities insistent on the production of such evidence. Conversely, the authorities perpetrated the hoax to denigrate further the reputation of the witch by emphasising the loathsome ingredients — the fat of an unbaptised child and the blood of the bat. Recent research suggests a very different scenario. The witches' ointment was real and effective. The dozen or so recipes reflected a knowledge of the effects of specific herbs and their interchangeability depending on supply and purpose. Every element had a purpose. This was no placebo. The witches knew what they were doing.[4]

The base was usually fat or oil which specifically increased the absorption of the ingredients into the body. The addition of soot had a key chemical role. As charcoal it would free the active agents in the mixture and thereby speed up the effect. The extreme toxicity of the elements used was recognised and balancing agents were added to modify such consequences. Mandrake was balanced with belladonna, belladonna with digitalis. The prime purpose of the ointment was to create hallucinations and the key elements responsible for this were the alkaloids scopolamine, hyoscyamine and atropine which were found in differing proportions in most of the Solanaceae family — belladonna, mandrake, henbane and thorn apple. It is suggested that some drugs created specific hallucinatory experiences; scopolamine created the impression that the body is sprouting fur, feathers or scales, while hyoscyamine gave the impression of flight. Others see these specific forms resulting from the blend of drugs. Aconite creates an irregular heartbeat and belladonna delirium. Together they create an exaggerated sense of falling or flying. The expectation of the user is probably more important than the specific impact of the drug but the

202

sensations of flying and growing fur or feathers has been the experience of modern investigators. Investigation has also shown that after the cessation of the primary effects of drugs such as those present in thorn apple the subject matter of the hallucination continues to appear real and is remembered as an objective experience. In addition to the active hallucinatory elements in the ointment there were ingredients designed to protect the user. Wild celery would produce a deep and refreshing sleep after the excitement of the hallucination, while cinquefoil, parsley or smallage purified the blood. Hallucinogens are cumulative and the constant purification prevented the poisoning of the system and serious toxic consequences. All this indicates that the witches' ointments were sophisticated mixtures designed for specific purposes with great care taken to protect the user. Quantities never appear in surviving contemporary recipes. These recipes came from the authorites and not the users. The establishment, faced with what they conceived as a dangerous drug cult, concealed details to weaken the cult's appeal and prevent the spread of such dangerous knowledge. On the other hand the members of any such group, or more probably the individual involved, committed such information to memory which was passed down from generation to generation. The real secret of the ointment lay in the precise quantity of each ingredient required to suit the physiological and pyschological needs of each particular client. The so-called witches' ointment may have had little to do with a diabolic cult but it was an effective element in the lifestyle of the early modern drug addict.

Perhaps less acceptable to some scientists is the argument that the accidental ingestion of drugs by the populace explains some aspects of the witch phenomenon. Linnda Caporeal argued that the witch hunt at Salem resulted from accidental ergot poisoning. Ergot is a fungus hosted by cereals, especially rye, containing lysergic acid amide with 10 per cent of the potency of its artificial cousin LSD (lysergic acid diethylamide). Ergot poisoning took two forms: gangrenous (the holy fire of the Middle Ages), and convulsive. The convulsive form manifested various symptoms: convulsions, hallucinations, sensations of tingling, choking and biting. In New England, rye was planted in April and the new crop became available for eating in early December, although harvested in August. The very cold and wet conditions of 1691 were most suited to the development of ergot, the drought of 1692 the opposite. The Salem girls began to show strange symptoms in December 1691 and these stopped suddenly twelve months later.

203

Those afflicted obtained their rye from a common source in the wetter and more ergot-susceptible areas of the parish. Joseph Bayley and his wife visited the house of the Putnams. Putnam's wife and daughter were both afflicted and played a major role in the witch crisis. Bayley ate a hearty breakfast and on his way home began hallucinating, convinced that he was knocked from his horse and had seen a witch approaching. His wife, who had eaten little at the Putnams', saw nothing except a disoriented husband and an approaching cow.[5]

This plausible thesis has been challenged by Nicholas Spanos and Jack Gottlieb. To them the characteristics of convulsive ergotism and the features exhibited by the afflicted girls were dissimilar. Convulsive ergotism should not occur in regions such as Salem with sufficient vitamin A. If ergotism occurred in well-nourished New England it would be of the gangrenous type. Convulsive ergotism strikes the younger children first and usually ultimately affects the whole household. Neither of these conditions occurred in Salem. Isoergine (lysergic acid amine) was not a powerful enough drug to produce the hallucinations described. In testing 80 witnesses for evidence of the sixteen symptoms of convulsive ergotism, 59 had none, 15 had one or two, and 6 had three or four — hardly convincing evidence of a community struck down with ergot poisoning. A recent defence of the ergot theory has suggested that the symptoms of convulsive ergotism vary according to other factors involved, that the court records do not report the real condition of the afflicted girls or the witnesses (recording only those aspects considered relevant to the prosecution of the case) and that the highly suggestible nature of LSA victims is the critical fact rather than its specific potency. Above all, to explain the strange behaviour of the afflicted girls as role-playing in response to special cues (as Spanos and Gottlieb suggest in opposition to the ergot-ingestion theory) does not explain the animal victims of 1692 which died from eating wild rye.[6]

The fantasy world of witch lore developed from dreams and drugs and from the occasional ravings of deranged individuals. However, the thesis that 'hysteria could explain many and perhaps most of the phenomena of witchcraft' and that witches were mentally ill cannot be sustained. The psychiatric interpretation of witchcraft emerged through the nineteenth century and culminated in the works of Gregory Zilboorg. Zilboorg believed that the *Malleus Maleficarum* could serve as a textbook in clinical psychiatry. There was a major increase in mental disorders in the fifteenth century and the church chose to define the victims of these disorders as witches. Those accused of witchcraft were the mentally disturbed in that they confessed to impossible behaviour (flying and shapeshifting) and exhibited specific characteristics (local analgesia and insensitivity to pain). The highly suggestible reactions of the witch and predominance of women amongst them, taken with the other factors, suggested that hysteria was the common problem.[7]

The psychological concepts underpinning such a hypothesis are meaningless. The range of characteristics attributed to the basic condition, hysteria, have no common aetiology. Many of these conditions can be explained by organic disorders rather than mental illness. For example, insensitivity of the skin could arise from poor peripheral circulation, arthritis, a partial stroke, vitamin B deficiencies or syphilis rather than 'hysteria'. The evidence in the case studies used by the proponents of the hysteria thesis often resulted from torture or was based on popular gossip and can rarely be used as a scientific description of personality traits. The evidence seems to point in the opposite direction. The vast majority of alleged witches appeared normal. Of course individual witches exhibited personality traits that evoked attention but these characteristics reflected the range of normality rather than any stereotyped serious mental aberration. When Weyer and his contemporaries accused some witches of melancholia rather than diabolic loyalties they were describing temporary victims of menopausal depression not permanently deranged depressives. In 1589 the *Parlement* of Paris freed 14 convicted witches on medical advice. The term melancholia used in that context appeared to cover aspects of behaviour now associated with menopause and senility.[8]

Definitions of madness were subjective and culturally defined. The early-modern physician following Paracelsus was aware of the idiot, the lunatic, the temporary victim of drink or drugs and the demoniac. The treatment of the mentally ill had a long history and was not affected by the witch phenomenon. None of the 20 cases of insanity uncovered by Macfarlane in Essex was in any way associated with witchcraft. Contemporaries did distinguish carefully between the demoniac and the witch, between the involuntary victim of diabolic possession and the rational willing partner of the Devil. It was the confusion of these two by nineteenth-century French psychologists and Freud's equation of sixteenth- and seventeenth-century demonological theory of hysteria that gave rise to this false thesis linking witches with insanity. Diabolical possession was a form of insanity but witch and demoniac were clearly separate things — the victims of the witch or her master, the Devil, might be mad; the witch herself was not.[9]

The fantasies which became part of witch lore — flight to the sabbat, transformation into animals and sexual acrobatics in which a single devil could perform vaginal, anal and oral sex simultaneously — were believed by the 'participants' who readily confessed to their neighbours and less readily to the authorities. Their deluded perception of reality had been formed by the effects of drugs and by an inability to separate dreams from waking objectivity. These conditions were often intensified by sleep-deprivation. In order to elicit a confession, suspects were kept awake for days, during which the accused became victim to a range of hallucinatory experiences. Most suspects could function normally for three or four days but then succumbed progressively through three stages of disorientation. Initially, the victim began to see things which she knew were not there; secondly, these misperceptions were accepted as real; and, thirdly, such perceptions took a horrific and terrifying form. The onset of these developments occurred sooner and the effect was more severe in the sick and aged. Sleep deprivation as an aid to confession served to increase the role of hallucinations in moulding and enforcing the popular and elite image of the witch and her acitivities.[10]

In conclusion, it remains to step back from the detail, to ignore the modifications and exceptions, the variations and the doubts, and to emphasise the essential nature of the witch and to explain the pre-eminence she achieved in the world view of her contemporaries from the late-fifteenth to the mid-seventeenth century. Few people practised any form of diabolic witchcraft. Many more persons *thought* they engaged in such activity, a fantasy derived from the general intellectual environment or by accepting as true specific accusations made against them. The dramatic increase in the witch phenomenon in this period resulted from the conviction by the political elite, and increasingly by the populace, that diabolic witchcraft existed, that peasant women were the satanic agents and that this situation posed a threat to Christian government and individual fortunes. Consequently certain types of people were redefined as diabolic witches. The witch in early modern Europe was not a diabolist in fact, and rarely in fantasy. She was a bad neighbour perceived as a diabolic threat by some fellow villagers and some political authorities. The nature of this diabolical perception ranged from viewing the Devil as an informal participant in the witch's individual *maleficium*, through emphasising that the witch and Devil had compacted together to render evil, to the extreme 'sabbatical' position that the witch met regularly with her fellows and with the Devil in a highly organised hierarchical cult.

The detailed nature of the witch phenomenon depended on the witch image of the particular elite, and the extent to which it was presented to, and accepted by, the populace. This phenomenon expanded in early modern Europe as a result of the political elite's concern to influence and control popular opinion and to this end impose its witch image. This concern varied in intensity across Europe and stemmed from the need of some regimes, in a society divided by religious conflict especially as manifest in Reformation and Counter Reformation, to legitimise its authority and to coerce its populace to adhere to the new politico-religious ideology of the state. This ideology, Protestant and Catholic, imposed an austere code of behaviour which was both a test of political loyalty and a rejection of traditional popular culture. Popular culture was undermined by these authorities through redefining as diabolic its key elements: peasant magic, public festivals such as May Day, and types of sexual behaviour. For the state to accept the long-standing view of elements within the church that all magic involved a pact with the Devil, created potential agents of Satan in every village in Europe. The increased power of the central authority which made it able to interfere effectively in the provinces, the changes in the judicial system which increased the likelihood of convictions, as well as the communications revolution of preaching, printing and effective pastoral care, combined to impress the elitist image of the diabolic witch on the peasantry.

In its most simple form this elite message struck a responsive chord in village communities as individuals strove in a constantly changing environment to maintain their identity and livelihood. To attribute misfortune to the *maleficium* of a bad neighbour was a satisfying and actionable response to personal difficulties. The element of diabolism in such an approach was often minimal and usually remained so when the matter was dealt with from within the village. When referred to superior authorities, peasant *maleficium* was most often redefined in terms of diabolism and the accused was prosecuted accordingly. The acceptance of this diabolic image and use of the central authority to deal with the problem increased dramatically in those villages in which the peasant notables, now differentiated economically and culturally from their fellow villagers, aligned themselves with these outside views and solutions.

Herein lies the real nature of the witch in early modern Europe. She was the bad neighbour but the definition of the bad neighbour varied. In much of Western Europe the bad neighbour emerged from the village consensus as a person who through her personality, often intensified by her economic condition and age, created disharmony. In other villages, in which the elitist image had penetrated more effectively and in which peasant notables had effective power, the bad neighbour was defined by this oligarchy as one who did not conform to the new ways, as one who continued to wallow in traditional popular culture.

The early modern witch was not guilty of diabolism. She was in the view of the village consensus an unpleasant person guilty of social disruption, or through the eyes of the village notables an embarrassing example of cultural intransigence. In both cases she was a nonconformist who had to be neutralised, either for the sake of village harmony or ideological conformity. She was the creation of either the godly zeal of the political and religious elite and their peasant allies or the furious rage of her discomforted and ill-fortuned neighbours.

Notes

1. Dreams are a major aspect of psychological research. The following open a complex and controversial topic: Edwin Diamond, *The Science of Dreams*; Christopher Evans, *Landscapes of the Night: How and Why We Dream*; Ann Faraday, *Dream Power*; J. A. Hadfield, *Dreams and Nightmares*; Nathaniel Kleitman, *Sleep and Wakefulness*; S. G. Lee and A. R. Mayer (ed.) *Dreams and Dreaming*. An excellent popular yet responsible discussion of a major aspect of witchcraft and dreams is Sandra Shulman, *Nightmare: The World of Terrifying Dreams*.
2. The positive use of drugs by witches is well covered by Michael J. Harner, 'The Role of Hallucinogenic Plants in European Witchcraft', Ch. 8 of M. J. Harner (ed.) *Hallucinogens and Shamanism*; Bernard Barnett, 'Drugs of the Devil', *New Scientist* 27 (22 July 1965) pp. 222–5; A. Allen, 'Toads: The Biochemistry of the Witches Cauldron', *History Today* 29 (April 1979), pp. 265–8; reference to De Lancre see Bernard Barnett, *op.cit.*, p. 222.
3. For Nider and Spina see Harner, *op.cit.*, pp. 131–2.
4. For Guazzo see Barnett, *op.cit.*, p. 224. Much of this discussion is based on Sally Hickey, *An Alternative View of Witchcraft: Hallucinogens and the*

16th and 17th Century English Witches unpublished Litt. B. thesis, University of New England.

5. The accidental ingestion of drugs especially ergot, see Frank J. Bove, *The Story of Ergot*, and G. Barger, *Ergot and Ergotism*. For the Salem hunt see Linnda R. Caporael, 'Ergotism: The Satan Loosed in Salem?', *Science* 192 (2 April 1976) pp. 21–6.

6. N. P. Spanos and Jack Gottlieb, 'Ergotism and the Salem Village Witch Trials', *Science*, 194 (24 Dec. 76) pp. 1390–4; and for a not too successful reply in defence of Caporael see M. K. Matossian, 'Ergot and the Salem Witchcraft Affair', *American Scientist*, 70 (1982) pp. 355–7.

7. The equation of witches with the mentally ill and the attempt to explain the witchcraft phenomenon essentially in terms of hysteria, see G. Zilboorg, *The Medical Man and the Witch During the Renaissance* p. 73; G. Zilboorg and G. Henry, *A History of Medical Psychiatry* p. 155; R. E. L. Masters, *Eros and Evil: The Sexual Psychopathology of Witchcraft* pp. 144–63; R. E. Hemphill, 'Historical Witchcraft and Psychiatric Illness in Western Europe', *Proceedings of Royal Society of Medicine*, 59 (1966) pp. 891–904, and many general histories of psychiatry published during the sixties and earlier, such as F. Alexander and S. T. Selesnick, *The History of Psychiatry* pp. 96–7.

8. The debunking of the hysteria thesis is seen in N. P. Spanos, 'Witchcraft in Histories of Psychiatry: A Critical Analysis and an Alternative Conceptualisation' *Psychological Bulletin*, 85 (1978) pp. 417–36; and Thomas Schoeneman, 'The Role of Mental Illness in the European Witch Hunts of the Sixteenth and Seventeenth Centuries: An Assessment' *Journal of the History of Behavioral Sciences*, 13 (1977) pp. 337–51. Other relevant works are George Rosen, 'The Mentally Ill and the Community in Western and Central Europe during the Late Middle Ages and the Renaissance' *Journal of the History of Medicine and Allied Sciences* 19 (1964) pp. 377–88 and H. C. Erik Midelfort, 'Madness and the Problem of Psychological History in the Sixteenth Century' *Sixteenth Century Journal* 12 (1981) pp. 5–12 and the very controversial Thomas S. Szasz, *The Myth of Mental Illness*.

9. Alan D. Macfarlane, *Witchcraft in Tudor and Stuart England*, pp. 226–7; For discussion of hysteria and the early psychologists see Szasz, Chs. 1, 4, 10.

10. For sleep deprivation see Christopher Evans *op.cit.* pp. 136–54.

Select Bibliography

Books

Alexander, F. and S. T. Selesnick, *The History of Psychiatry* (Harper and Row, New York, 1966).

Allegro, John, *Lost Gods* (Michael Joseph, London, 1977).

Anglo, Sydney (ed.), *The Damned Art: Essays in the Literature of Witchcraft* (Routledge and Kegan Paul, London, 1977).

Baker, Roger, *Binding the Devil: Exorcism Past and Present* (Hawthorn Books, NY, 1974).

Barger, George, *Ergot and Ergotism* (Gurney and Jackson, London, 1931).

Baroja, Julio Caro, *The World of the Witches* (Weidenfeld and Nicholson, London, 1964).

Bernheimer, Richard, *Wild Men in the Middle Ages: A Study in Art, Sentiment and Demonology* (Harvard University Press, Cambridge, 1952).

Bove, Frank J., *The Story of Ergot* (Karger, Basle, 1970).

Boyer, Paul and Stephen Nissenbaum, *Salem Possessed: The Social Origins of Witchcraft* (Harvard University Press, Cambridge, 1974).

Briggs, K. M., *Pale Hecate's Team* (Routledge and Kegan Paul, London, 1962).

Bromberg, Walter, *Man Above Humanity. A History of Psychotherapy* (Lippincott, Philadelphia, 1954).

Burke, Peter, *Popular Culture in Early Modern Europe* (Temple Smith, London, 1978).

Burr, G. L. (ed.), *Narratives of Witchcraft Cases 1648–1706* (Barnes and Noble, NY, 1914/1959).

Cohn, Norman, *The Pursuit of the Millenium* (Mercury Books, London, 1962).

—— *Europe's Inner Demons* (Paladin/Granada, Frogmore, 1976).

Crow, W. B., *A History of Magic: Witchcraft and Occultism* (Abacus/Sphere, London, 1972).

Davies, R. Trevor, *Four Centuries of Witch Beliefs* (Methuen, London, 1947).

Deacon, Richard, *Matthew Hopkins: Witch Finder General* (Muller, London, 1976).

Delumeau, Jean, *Catholicism between Luther and Voltaire: A New View of the Counter Reformation* (Burns and Oates, London, 1977).

Demos, John P., *Entertaining Satan: Witchcraft and the Culture of Early New England* (Oxford University Press, NY, 1982).

Diamond, Edwin, *The Science of Dreams* (Eyre and Spottiswoode, London, 1962).

Douglas, M. (ed.), *Witchcraft Confessions and Accusations* (Tavistock, London, 1970).

Dworkin, Andrea, *Woman Hating* (Dutton, NY, 1974).

Ehrenreich, Barbara and Deidre English, *Witches, Midwives and Nurses:*

Select Bibliography

A History of Women Healers (Feminist Press, NY, 1973).

Eliade, Mircea, *Occultism, Witchcraft, and Cultural Fashions: Essays in Comparative Religions* (University of Chicago Press, Chicago, 1976).

Evans, Christopher, *Landscapes of the Night: How and Why We Dream* (Hodder and Stoughton, London, 1985).

Ewen, C. L'Estrange, *Witch Hunting and Witch Trials* (Kegan Paul, London, 1929).

Faraday, Ann, *Dream Power* (Hodder and Stoughton, London, 1972).

Firth, Raymond W. (ed.), *Man and Culture: An Evaluation of the Work of Bronislaw Malinowski* (Routledge, London, 1957).

Forbes, Thomas R., *The Midwife and the Witch* (Yale University Press, New Haven, 1966).

Frazer, Sir James, *The Golden Bough: A Study in Magic and Religion* (Macmillan, London, 1922/57).

Gardner, G. B., *The Meaning of Witchcraft* (Aquarian Press, London, 1959).

Gibson, Walter B., *Witchcraft* (Grosset and Dunlap, New York, 1973).

Gifford, George, *Discourse of the Subtil Practises of Devilles* London, 1589 (Theatrum Orbis Terrarum, Amsterdam, 1977).

Ginzburg, Carlo (trans. J. and A. Tedeschi), *The Night Battles: Witchcraft and Agrarian Cults in the Sixteenth and Seventeenth Centuries* (Routledge and Kegan Paul, London, 1983).

Gooch, Stan, *The Paranormal* (Harper Colophon, New York, 1980).

Goode, William J., *Religion and the Primitives* (Free Press, Glencoe, 1951).

Graham, H., *Eternal Eve*, (London, 1952).

Hadfield, J. A., *Dreams and Nightmares* (Penguin, London, 1954).

Haining, Peter (ed.), *The Witchcraft Papers: Contemporary Records of the Witchcraft Hysteria in Essex 1560 – 1700* (Hale, London, 1974).

Hansen, C., *Witchcraft at Salem* (Mentor, New York, 1969).

Harner, Michael J. (ed.), *Hallucinogens and Shamanism* (Oxford University Press, NY, 1973).

Harris, Marvin, *Cows, Pigs, Wars and Witches: The Riddles of Culture* (Fontana/Collins, Glasgow, 1977).

Harrison, Michael, *The Roots of Witchcraft* (Muller, London, 1973).

Hays, H. R., *The Dangerous Sex: The Myth of Feminine Evil* (Methuen, London, 1966).

Henningsen, Gustav, *The Witches' Advocate: Basque Witchcraft and the Spanish Inquisition (1609 – 1619)* (University of Nevada Press, Reno, 1980).

Hole, Christina, *Witchcraft in England* (Book Club Associates, London, 1977).

——— *A Dictionary of British Folk Customs* (Paladin/Granada, London, 1978).

Holmes, R. *Witchcraft in British History* (Muller, London, 1974).

Houlbrooke, Ralph A., *The English Family 1450 – 1700* (Longmans, London, 1984).

Hughes, Pennethorne, *Witchcraft* (Pelican, Harmondsworth, 1952).

Huxley, Aldous, *The Devils of Loudun* (Harper, New York, 1952).

Jahoda, Gustav, *The Psychology of Superstition* (Pelican, Harmondsworth, 1970).

Jammer, Max, *Concepts of Force* (Harvard University Press, Cambridge, 1957).

Keitman, Nathaniel, *Sleep and Wakefulness* (University of Chicago Press, Chicago, 1963).

Kelly, Henry Ansgar, *Towards the Death of Satan: The Growth and Decline of Christian Demonology* (Geoffrey Chapman, London, 1968).

—— *The Devil, Demonology and Witchcraft* (Doubleday, NY, 1974).

Kieckhefer, Richard, *European Witch Trials: Their Foundations in Popular and Learned Culture 1300–1500* (Routledge, London, 1976).

Kiev, Ari (ed.), *Magic, Faith and Healing: Studies in Primitive Psychiatry Today* (The Free Press, London, 1964).

Kingdom, Robert M. (ed.), *Transition and Revolution: Problems and Issues of European Renaissance and Reformation History* (Burgess Pub. Co., Minneapolis, 1974).

Kittredge, George L., *Witchcraft in Old and New England* (Russel and Russel, NY, 1929/56).

Kors, Alan C. and Edward Peters, *Witchcraft in Europe 1100–1700* (Dent, London, 1973).

Kramer, Heinrich and James Sprenger, (trans. Montague Summers), *The Malleus Maleficarum* (Dover, NY, 1971).

Ladurie, Emmanuel Le Roy, *The Peasants of Languedoc* (University of Illinois Press, Urbana, 1974).

Lambert, M., *Medieval Heresy: Popular Movements from Bogomil to Hus* (Arnold, London, 1977).

Langdon-Brown, Sir Walter, *From Witchcraft to Chemotherapy* (Cambridge University Press, Cambridge, 1941).

Larner, Christina, *Enemies of God: The Witchhunt in Scotland* (Chatto and Windus, London, 1981).

—— *Witchcraft and Religion: The Politics of Popular Belief* (Basil Blackwell, London, 1984).

Lee, S. G. and A. R. Mayer (eds), *Dreams and Dreaming* (Penguin, London, 1973).

Lenman, B., G. Parker and V. Gatrell (eds), *Crime and the Law: The Social History of Crime in Western Europe since 1500* (Europe Publications, London, 1980).

Lerner, Robert E., *The Heresy of the Free Spirit in the Later Middle Ages* (University of California Press, Berkeley, 1972).

Levine, Robert A. (ed.), *Culture and Personality: Contemporary Readings* (Aldine Pub. Co., Chicago, 1974).

Levi-Strauss, Claude, *The Savage Mind* (Weidenfeld, London, 1962).

—— *Structural Anthropology* (Basic Books, New York, 1963).

Loomis, C. Grant, *White Magic: An Introduction to the Folklore of Christian Legend* (Medieval Academy of America, Cambridge Mass., 1948).

McCall, Andrew, *The Medieval Underworld* (Book Club Associates, London, 1979).

Macfarlane, Alan D., *Witchcraft in Tudor and Stuart England* (Harper, NY, 1970).

—— *The Origins of English Individualism* (Blackwell, Oxford, 1978).

Maclean, Ian, *The Renaissance Notion of Women: A Study in the Fortunes of Scholasticism and Medical Science in European Intellectual Life* (CUP, Cambridge, 1980).

Mair, Lucy, *Witchcraft* (Weidenfeld, London, 1969).

Maple, Eric, *The Dark World of Witches* (Hale, London, 1962).
—— *The Domain of Devils* (Hale, London, 1966).
Martello, Leo Louis, *Witchcraft: The Old Religion* (University Books, Secaucus, New Jersey, 1973).
Marwick, Max, *Witchcraft and Sorcery* (Penguin, Harmondsworth, 1970).
Masters, R. E. L. *Eros and Evil: The Sexual Psychopathology of Witchcraft* (Matrix House, NY, 1966).
Mauss, Marcel, *A General Theory of Magic* (Routledge and Kegan Paul, London, 1972).
Michelet, Jules (trans. A. Allinson), *Satanism and Witchcraft* (Citadel Press, NY, 1963).
Midelfort, H. C. Erik, *Witch Hunting in Southwestern Germany 1562 – 1684: The Social and Intellectual Foundations* (Stanford University Press, Stanford, 1972).
Moeller, C., *Satan* (Sheed and Ward, London, 1951).
Monter, E. William (ed.), *European Witchcraft* (Wiley, New York, 1969).
—— *Witchcraft in France and Switzerland: The Borderlands During the Reformation* (Cornell University Press, Ithaca, 1976).
Morewedge, R. T. (ed.), *The Role of Women in the Middle Ages* (State University of New York Press, Albany, 1975).
Mount, Ferdinand, *The Subversive Family: The Alternative History of Love and Marriage* (Unwin, London, 1983).
Munday, J. T., *Witchcraft in Central Africa and Europe* (Lutterworth Press, London, 1956).
Murray, Margaret A., *The God of the Witches* (Faber, London, 1952).
—— *The Divine King in England* (Faber, London, 1954).
—— *The Witch Cult in Western Europe* (Clarendon, Oxford, 1962).
Nauman, St Elmo (ed.), *Exorcism Through the Ages* (Philosophical Library, New York, 1974).
Newall, Venetia, *The Witch Figure* (Routledge and Kegan Paul, London, 1973).
—— *The Encyclopedia of Witchcraft and Magic* (Dial Press, New York, 1974).
Norbeck, Edward, *Religion in Primitive Society* (Harper, NY, 1961).
Notestein, W., *A History of Witchcraft in England* (Crowell, NY, 1911).
Obelkevich, James (ed.), *Religion and the People 800 – 1700* (University of North Carolina Press, Chapel Hill, 1978).
Odier, Charles, *Anxiety and Magic Thinking* (International Universities Press, NY, 1956).
Oesterreich, T. K., *Possession: Demoniacal and Other Among Primitive Races in Antiquity, the Middle Ages and Modern Times* (University Books, Secaucus, New Jersey, 1966).
Paine, Lauran, *Witches in Fact and Fantasy* (New English Library, London, 1976).
Parrinder, Geoffrey, *Witchcraft: European and African* (Faber, London, 1963).
Peters, Edward, *The Magician, the Witch and the Law* (University of Pennsylvania Press, Philadelphia, 1978).
Pratt, Antoinette Mari, *The Attitude of the Catholic Church Towards Witchcraft*

and Allied Practices of Sorcery and Magic (National Capital Press, Washington, 1915).

Quaife, G. R., *Wanton Wenches and Wayward Wives* (Croom Helm, London, 1979).

Ravensdale, Tom and James Morgan, *The Psychology of Witchcraft* (Bartholomew, Edinburgh, 1974).

Reiter, Rayna, R. (ed.), *Toward an Anthropology of Women* (Monthly Review Press, NY, 1975).

Riencourt, Amaury de, *Sex and Power in History* (David McKay, NY, 1974).

Robbins, Rossell Hope, *The Encyclopedia of Witchcraft and Demonology* (Bonanza Books, NY, 1981).

Rogers, Katherine, *The Troublesome Helpmate: A History of Misogyny in Literature* (University of Washington Press, Seattle, 1966).

Rosaldo, M. Z. and L. Lamphere (eds), *Women, Culture and Society* (Stanford University Press, Stanford, 1974).

Rose, Elliot, *Razor for a Goat: A Discussion of Certain Problems in the History of Witchcraft and Diabolism* (University of Toronto Press, Toronto, 1962).

Rosebury, Theodor, *Microbes and Morals: A Study of Venereal Disease* (Paladin/Granada, Frogmore, 1975).

Rosen, Barbara (ed.), *Witchcraft* (Taplinger, New York, 1972) and (Arnold, London, 1969).

Rowse, A. L., *The Case Books of Simon Forman: Sex and Society in Shakespeare's Age* (Pan Books, London, 1976).

Russell, Jeffrey Burton, *Witchcraft in the Middle Ages* (Cornell University Press, Ithaca, 1972), also (Citadel Press, Secaucus, New Jersey, 1972).

—— *A History of Witchcraft: Sorcerers, Heretics and Pagans* (Thames, London, 1980).

Scot, Reginald, *Discoverie of Witchcraft* London, 1584 (Theatrum Orbis Terrarum. Amsterdam, 1971).

Shulman, Sandra, *Nightmare: The World of Terrifying Dreams* (Macmillan. NY, 1979).

Shuttle, Penelope and Peter Redgrove, *The Wise Wound: Menstruation and Everywoman* (Victor Gollancz, London, 1978).

Simons, G. L., *The Witchcraft World* (Barnes and Noble, NY, 1974).

Summers, Montague, *The Geography of Witchcraft*, (Kegan Paul, London, 1927).

—— *The Werewolf* (Kegan Paul, London, 1933).

—— *Witchcraft and Black Magic* (Rider, London, 1946).

—— *The History of Witchcraft and Demonology* (Routledge and Kegan Paul, London, 1973).

Swanson, Guy, *The Birth of the Gods: The Origin of Primitive Beliefs* (University of Michigan Press, Ann Arbor, 1960).

—— *Religion and Regime: A Sociological Account of the Reformation* (University of Michigan Press, Ann Arbor, 1967).

Szasz, Thomas S., *The Myth of Mental Illness* (Paladin/Granada, Frogmore, 1973).

—— *The Manufacture of Madness* (Paladin/Granada, Frogmore, 1973).

Tenenbaum, Joseph, *The Riddle of Woman: A Study in the Social Psychology of Sex* (Bodley Head, London, 1936).

Select Bibliography

Thomas, Keith, *Religion and the Decline of Magic* (Penguin, Harmondsworth, 1971).
—— *Man and the Natural World: Changing Attitudes in England 1500–1800* (Penguin, Harmondsworth, 1984).
Tiryakian, E. A. (ed.), *On the Margin of the Visible: Sociology, the Esoteric and the Occult* (Wiley, NY, 1974).
Trachtenberg, Joshua, *The Devil and the Jews: The Medieval Conception of the Jew and its Relation to Modern Anti-Semitism* (Meridian Books, Cleveland, 1961).
Trevor-Roper, H. R., *The European Witch-Craze of the Sixteenth and Seventeenth Centuries and Other Essays* (Harper, NY, 1969).
Walker, Nigel, *Crime and Insanity in England: The Historical Perspective* Vol. 1 (Edinburgh University Press, Edinburgh, 1968).
Weisser, Michael R., *Crime and Punishment in Early Modern Europe* (Harvester Press, Sussex, 1979).
White, Andrew Dickson, *A History of Warfare of Science with Theology* (Dover, NY, 1960).
Williams, Charles, *Witchcraft* (Meridian, Cleveland, 1959).
Williams, Selma R. and Pamela J. Williams, *Riding the Nightmare: Women and Witchcraft* (Atheneum, NY, 1978).
Zacharias, G. (trans. Christine Trollope), *The Satanic Cult* (Allen and Unwin, London, 1980).
Zilboorg, G., *The Medical Man and the Witch During the Renaissance* (Johns Hopkins Press, Baltimore, 1935).
—— and G. Henry, *A History of Medical Psychiatry* (Norton, NY, 1941).

Articles

Allen, A., 'Toads: The Biochemistry of the Witches Cauldron', *History Today* 29 (April 1979), pp. 265–8.
Anderson, Alan B. and Raymond Gordon, 'A Study in the Sociology of Religious Persecution: The First Quakers', *Journal of Religious History* 9 (1976–7). pp. 247–62.
—— 'Witchcraft and the Status of Women — The Case of England', *British Journal of Sociology* 29 (June 1978), pp. 171–84.
—— 'The Uniqueness of English Witchcraft: A Matter of Numbers', *British Journal of Sociology* 30 (1979), pp. 359–61.
Anderson, Robert D., 'The History of Witchcraft: A Review with Psychiatric Comments', *American Journal of Psychiatry* 126 (1970), pp. 1727–35.
Andreski, Stanislav, 'The Syphilitic Shock: A New Explanation of the Witch Burnings', *Encounter* 58–5 (May 1982), pp. 7–26.
Balfe, Judith H., 'Comment on Clarke Garrett's, *Women and Witches*', *Signs: Journal of Women in Culture and Society* 4 (1978), pp. 201–2.
Barnett, Bernard, 'Drugs of the Devil', *New Scientist* 27 (22 July 1965), pp. 222–5.

—— 'Witchcraft, Psychopathology and Hallucinations', *British Journal of Psychiatry* 111 (1965), pp. 439–45.

Ben-Yehuda, Nachman, 'Problems Inherent in Socio-Historical Approaches to the European Witch Craze', *Journal for the Scientific Study of Religion* 20 (1981), pp. 326–38.

Berkowitz, Leonard, 'Anti-Semitism and the Displacement of Aggression' *Journal of Abnormal and Social Psychology* 59 (1959), pp. 182–7.

—— and James Green, 'The Stimulus Qualities of the Scapegoat', *Journal of Abnormal and Social Psychology* 64 (1962), pp. 293–301.

Bernard, Paul, 'Heresy in Fourteenth Century Austria', *Medievalia et Humanista* 10 (1956), pp. 50–63.

Bleek, Wolf, 'Witchcraft, Gossip and Death: A Social Drama', *Man* 11 (1976), pp. 526–41.

Brann, Noel L., 'The Conflict Between Reason and Magic in Seventeenth Century England: A Case Study of the Vaughan-More Debate', *The Huntington Library Quarterly* 43 (1980), pp. 103–26.

—— 'The Proto-Protestant Assault upon Church Magic: The Errores Bohemanorum According to Abbot Trithemius (1462–1516)'. *Journal of Religious History* 12 (1982), pp. 9–22.

Briggs, K. M., 'Some Seventeenth Century Books of Magic', *Folklore*, 64 (1953), pp. 445–62.

Brucker, Gene H., 'Sorcery in Early Renaissance Florence', *Studies in the Renaissance* X (1963), pp. 7–24.

Bullough, Vern, 'Heresy, Witchcraft and Sexuality', *Journal of Homosexuality* 1 (1974), pp. 183–202.

Burstein, Sona R., 'Demonology and Medicine in the Sixteenth and Seventeenth Centuries', *Folklore* 67 (1956), pp. 16–33.

—— 'Folklore, Rumour and Prejudice', *Folklore* 70 (1959), pp. 361–81.

Butler, Jon, 'Magic, Astrology and the Early American Religious Heritage', *American Historical Review* 84 (1979), pp. 317–46.

Campbell, Mary Ann, 'Labeling and Oppression: Witchcraft in Medieval Europe', *Mid-American Review of Sociology* 3 (1979), pp. 55–82.

Caporael, Linnda R., 'Ergotism: The Satan Loosed in Salem?', *Science* 192 (2 April 1976), pp. 21–6.

Caulfield, Ernest, 'Pediatric Aspects of the Salem Witchcraft Tragedy', *American Journal of Diseases of Children* 65 (1943), pp. 788–802.

Chodoff, P., 'The Diagnosis of Hysteria: An Overview', *American Journal of Psychiatry* 131 (1974), pp. 1073–8.

Clark, Stuart, 'Inversion, Misrule and the Meaning of Witchcraft', *Past and Present* 87 (1980), pp. 98–127.

—— and P. T. Morgan, 'Religion and Magic in Elizabethan Wales: Robert Holland's, *Dialogue on Witchcraft*', *Journal of Ecclesiastical History* 27 (1976), pp. 31–46.

Cohn, Norman, 'Myths and Hoaxes of European Demonology I: Was There Ever a Society of Witches?', *Encounter* 43 (Dec. 1974), pp. 26–41.

—— 'Myths and Hoaxes of European Demonology 2: Three Forgeries', *Encounter* 44 (Jan. 1975), pp. 11–24.

Conklin, George N., 'Alkaloids and the Witches Sabbat', *American Journal of Pharmacy and the Sciences* 130 (1958), pp. 171–4.

Connor, John W., 'The Social and Psychological Reality of European Witchcraft Beliefs', *Psychiatry* 38 (1975), pp. 366–80.

Davidson, Thomas, 'Animal Charm Cures and Amulets', *The Amateur Historian* 3 (1957/58), pp. 237–48.

Demos, John P., 'Underlying Themes in the Witchcraft of Seventeenth Century New England', *American Historical Review* 75 (1970), pp. 1311–26.

—— 'John Godfrey and his Neighbors: Witchcraft and the Social Web in Colonial Massachusetts', *William and Mary Quarterly* 33 (1976), pp. 242–65.

Diethelm, O., 'The Medical Teaching of Demonology in the Seventeenth and Eighteenth Centuries', *Journal of the History of Behavioral Sciences* 7 (1970), pp. 3–15.

Dworkin, Andrea, 'What Were the Witches Really Brewing?', *MS* 2 (April 1974), pp. 52–5, 89–90.

Ehnmark, Erland, 'Religion and Magic — Frazer, Soderblom and Hagerstrom', *Ethnos* 21 (1956), pp. 1–10.

Estes, Leland, 'The Medical Origins of the European Witch Craze: A Hypothesis', *Journal of Social History* (Winter 1983), pp. 271–84.

Ewen, C. L'Estrange, 'A Noted Case of Witchcraft at North Moreton, Berks, in the Early 17th Century', *Berkshire Archaeological Journal* 40 (1936), pp. 207–13.

Fairchild, Letitia, 'The Supernatural in the Law Courts with Specific Reference to the Witchcraft Act, 1735', *Medical-Legal Journal* 14 (1946), pp. 27–38.

Forbes, Thomas, 'Midwifery and Witchcraft', *Journal of the History of Medicine and Allied Sciences* 17 (1962), pp. 417–29.

Foster, George M., 'Peasant Society and the Image of Limited Good', *American Anthropologist* 67 (1965), pp. 293–315.

Gallinek, Alfred, 'Psychogenic Disorders and the Civilization of the Middle Ages', *American Journal of Psychiatry* 99 (1942–3), pp. 42–54.

Garrett, Clarke, 'Witches, Werewolves and Henri Boguet', *Proceedings of the Western Society for History* 4, pp. 126–36.

—— 'Women and Witches: Patterns of Analysis', *Signs* 3 (Winter 1977), pp. 461–70.

—— 'Reply to Honegger and Moia', *Signs* 4 (1979), pp. 802–4.

Geertz, Hildred, 'An Anthropology of Religion and Magic 1', *Journal of Interdisciplinary History* VI (Summer 1975), pp. 71–89.

Geiss, G. 'Lord Hales, Witches and Rape', *British Journal of Law and Society* 5 (1978), pp. 26 ff.

Gluckman, M. 'Psychological, Sociological and Anthropological Explanations of Witchcraft and Gossip: A clarification', *Man* 4 (1968), pp. 20–35.

Guskin, Phyllis, J., 'The Context of Witchcraft: The Case of Jane Welham (1712)', *Eighteenth-Century Studies* 15 (Fall 1981), pp. 48–71.

Harper, Clive, 'The Witches Flying Ointment', *Folklore* 88 (1977), pp. 105–6.

Hemphill, R. E., 'Historical Witchcraft and Psychiatric Illness in Western Europe', *Proceedings of the Society of Medicine* 59 (1966), pp. 851–901.

Henningsen, Gustav, 'The Papers of Alonso de Salazar Frias', *Temenos* 5 (1969), pp. 85–106.

––––– 'Witchcraft in Denmark', *Folklore* 93 (1982), pp. 131–7.

Hoak, Dale, 'Witchhunting and Women in the Art of the Renaissance', *History Today* 31 (Feb. 1981), pp. 22–7.

Holdsworth, William K., 'Adultery or Witchcraft — A New Note on an Old Case in Connecticut', *New England Quarterly* 48 (1975), pp. 394–409.

Honegger, Claudia, 'Comment on Garrett's *Women and Witches*', *Signs* 4 (1979), pp. 792–8.

Hsu, Francis, 'A Neglected Aspect of Witchcraft Studies', *Journal of American Folklore* 73 (1964), pp. 35–8.

Jones, William R., 'Political Uses of Sorcery in Medieval Europe', *The Historian* 34 (1972), pp. 670–87.

Kaelbling, B., 'Comparative Psychopathology and Psychotherapy', *Psychotherapy and Psychosomatics* 9 (1961), pp. 10–28.

Karlen, Arno, 'The Homosexual Heresy', *The Chaucer Review* 6 (1971) pp. 44–63.

Katz, Jack, 'Deviance, Charisma, and Rule-Defined Behavior', *Social Problems* 20 (1972–3), pp. 186–201.

Kelly, Henry Ansgar, 'English Kings and the Fear of Sorcery', *Medieval Studies* 39 (1977), pp. 206–38.

Kennedy, John G., 'Psychological and Social Explanations of Witchcraft: A Comparison of Clyde Kluckman and E. E. Evans-Pritchard', *Man* 2(1967), pp. 216–25.

Kibbey, Ann, 'Mutations of the Supernatural: Witchcraft, Remarkable Providences and the Power of Puritan Men', *American Quarterly* 34 (Summer 1982), pp. 125–48.

Kirsch, Irvine, 'Demonology and the Rise of Science: An Example of the Misperception of Historical Data', *Journal of the History of the Behavioral Sciences* 14 (1978), pp. 149–57.

––––– 'Demonology and Science During the Scientific Revolution', *Journal of the History of the Behavioral Sciences* 16 (1980), pp. 359–68.

Kittredge, George, L., 'King James and *The Devil is an Ass*' *Modern Philology* 9 (1911–12), pp. 195–209.

Ladner, Gerhart B., 'Homo Viator: Medieval Ideas on Alienation and Order', *Speculum: A Journal of Medieval Studies* 42 (1967), pp. 233–59.

Larner, Christina, 'Is All Witchcraft Really Witchcraft?' *New Society* (10 October 1974), pp. 81–3.

––––– 'Witch Beliefs and Witchhunting in England and Scotland', *History Today* 31 (Feb. 1981), pp. 32–6.

Lauderdale, Pat, 'Deviance and Moral Boundaries', *American Sociological Review* 41 (1976), pp. 660–76.

Law, I. G., 'Devil Hunting in Elizabethan England', *Nineteenth Century* 35 (1894), pp. 397–411.

Leff, Gordon, 'Heresy and the Decline of the Medieval Church', *Past and Present* 20 (1961), pp. 36–51.

Lerner, Robert E., 'The Black Death and Western European Eschatological Mentalities', *American Historical Review* 86 (1981), pp. 533–52.

Levack, B. P., 'The Great Scottish Witch Hunt of 1661–1662', *Journal of*

British Studies 20 (1980), pp. 90-108.

Lewis, I. M., 'Spirit Possession and Deprivation Cults', Man I (1966), pp. 307-29.

McLachlan, Hugh V., 'Functionalism, Causation and Explanation', Philosophy, Sociology, Science 6 (1976), pp. 235-40.

—— 'Witchcraft Belief and Social Reality', Philosophical Journal 14 (1977), pp. 99-110.

—— and J. K. Swales, 'Lord Hale, Witches and Rape', British Journal of Law and Society 5 (Winter 1978), pp. 251-61.

—— 'Stereotypes and Scottish Witchcraft', Contemporary Review 234 (1979), pp. 88-94.

—— 'Witchcraft and Anti-Feminism', Scottish Journal of Sociology 4 (May 1980), pp. 141-66.

Mair, Lucy, 'Witchcraft, Spirit Possession and Heresy', Folklore 91 (1980), pp. 228-38.

Matossian, M. K., 'Ergot and the Salem Witchcraft Affair', American Scientist 70 (1982), pp.355-7.

Middleton, Paul, 'Seventeenth Century Witchcraft in Northumberland', Archaeologica Aeliana 45 (1967), pp. 161-6.

Midelfort, H. C. Erik, 'Recent Witch Hunting Research, or Where do We Go from Here?' Bibliographical Society of America: Papers 62 (1968), pp. 373-425.

—— 'Witchcraft and Religion in Sixteenth Century Germany: The Formation and Consequences of Orthodoxy', Archiv Fur Reformation Geschichte 62 (1971), pp. 266-78.

—— 'Heartland of the Witchcraze: Central and Northern Europe', History Today 31 (Feb. 1981), pp. 27-31.

—— 'Madness and the Problem of Psychological History in the Sixteenth Century', Sixteenth Century Journal 12 (1981), pp. 5-12.

Moia, Nelly, 'Comment on Garrett's Women and Witches', Signs 4 (1979), pp. 798-802.

Monter, E. William, 'Witchcraft in Geneva 1537-1662', Journal of Modern History 43 (1971), pp. 179-204.

—— 'The Historiography of European Witchcraft: Progress and Prospects', Journal of Interdisciplinary History 2 (1972), pp. 433-51.

—— 'French and Italian Witchcraft', History Today 30 (Nov. 1980), pp. 31-5.

—— 'Patterns of Witchcraft in the Jura', Journal of Social History 5 pp. 1-25.

Muchembled, Robert, 'L'Autre Côté Du Miroir: Mythes Sataniques et Réalités Culturelles Aux XVIe et XVIIe Siècles', Annales ESC 40-2 (mars-avril 1985), pp. 288-306.

Murray, Alexander, 'Medieval Origins of the Witch Hunt', The Cambridge Quarterly 7-1, pp. 63-74.

Neugebauer, Richard, 'Treatment of the Mentally Ill in Medieval and Early Modern England: A Reappraisal', Journal of the History of the Behavioral Sciences 14 (1978), pp. 158-69.

Newman, L. F., 'Some Notes on the History and Practice of Witchcraft in the Eastern Counties', Folklore (March 1946), pp. 12-33.

Nichols, David, 'The Devil in Renaissance France', History Today 30

(Nov. 1980), pp. 25 – 30.

Nugent, Donald, 'The Renaissance and/of Witchcraft', *Church History* 40 (1971), pp. 69 – 78.

—— 'Witchcraft Studies 1959 – 1971: A Bibliographical Survey', *Journal of Popular Culture* 5 (1971), pp. 710 – 25.

Parker, Geoffrey, 'The European Witchcraze Revisited: An Introduction', *History Today* 30 (Nov. 1980), pp. 23 – 4.

Patrides, C. A., 'The Salvation of Satan', *Journal of the History of Ideas* 28 (1967), pp. 467 – 79.

Peel, J. D. Y., 'Understanding Alien Belief Systems', *British Journal of Sociology* 20 (1969), pp. 69 – 83.

Radding, Charles M., 'Evolution of Medieval Mentalities: A Cognitive – Structural Approach', *American Historical Review* 83 (1978), pp. 577 – 97.

—— 'Superstition to Science: Nature, Fortune and the Passing of the Medieval Ordeal', *American Historical Review* 84 (1979), pp. 945 – 69.

Rattansi, Pyarali, 'Alchemy and Natural Magic in Raleigh's *History of the World*' *Ambix* 13 (1966), pp. 122 – 38.

Robbins, Rossell Hope, 'The Heresy of Witchcraft', *South Atlantic Quarterly* 65 (Autumn 1966), pp. 532 – 43.

—— 'Pandaemonium and the Sadducees', *Thought* 52 (1977), pp. 167 – 87.

Robson, H. N., 'Witchcraft and Wonder Drugs', *Proceedings of the Royal Institution of Great Britain* 42 (1969), pp. 345 – 55.

Rogers, Susan Carol, 'Female Forms of Power and the Myth of Male Dominance: A Model of Female/Male Interaction in Peasant Society', *American Ethnologist* 2 (1975), pp. 727 – 56.

—— 'Woman's Place: A Critical Review of Anthropological Theory', *Comparative Studies in Society and History* 20 (1978), pp. 123 – 73.

Rosen, George, 'Psychopathology in the Social Process: Dance Frenzies, Demonic Possession, Revival Movements and Similar So-called Psychic Epidemics: An Interpretation', *Bulletin of the History of Medicine* 36 (1962), pp. 13 – 44.

—— 'The Mentally Ill and the Community in Western and Central Europe during the Late Middle Ages and the Renaissance', *Journal of the History of Medicine and Allied Sciences* 19 (1964), pp. 377 – 88.

Ruether, Rosemary, 'The Persecution of Witches: A Case of Sexism and Agism', *Christianity and Crisis* 34 (December 1974), pp. 291 – 5.

Rushton, Peter, 'A Note on the Survival of Popular Christian Magic', *Folklore* 91 (1980), pp. 115 – 18.

—— 'Women, Witchcraft and Slander in Early Modern England: Cases from the Church Courts of Durham, 1560 – 1675', *Northern History* 18 (1982), pp. 116 – 32.

Schoeneman, Thomas, 'The Role of Mental Illness in the European Witch Hunts of the Sixteenth and Seventeenth Centuries: An Assessment', *Journal of the History of Behavioral Sciences* 13 (1977), pp. 337 – 51.

Soman, A., 'The Parlement of Paris and the Great Witch Hunt 1565 – 1640', *Sixteenth Century Journal* 9:2 (1978), pp. 31 – 44.

Spanos, N. P., 'Ergotism and the Salem Village Witch Trials', *Science*, 194 (24 Dec. 1976), pp. 1390 – 4.

―――― 'Witchcraft in Histories of Psychiatry: A Critical Analysis and an Alternative Conceptualisation', *Psychological Bulletin* 85 (1978), pp. 417–39.

―――― and Jack Gottlieb, 'Demonic Possession, Mesmerism and Hysteria: A Social Psychological Perspective on their Historical Inter-relations', *Journal of Abnormal Psychology* 88 (1979), pp. 527–46.

Spitz, Lewis, 'Occultism and Despair of Reason in Renaissance Thought', *Journal of the History of Ideas* 27 (July–Sept. 1966), pp. 464–9.

Sullivan, Jane, 'A New Look at Witchcraft', Review article from *Der Spiegel*; Melbourne, *Age* (26 Dec. 1984), p. 10.

Swales, J. K. and Hugh V. McLachlan, 'Witchcraft and the Status of Women: A Comment', *British Journal of Sociology* 30 (1979), pp. 349–58.

Tambiah, S. J., 'The Magical Power of Words', *Man* 3 (1968), pp. 175–208.

Teal, John L., 'Witchcraft and Calvinism in Elizabethan England: Divine Power and Human Agency', *Journal of the History of Ideas* 23 (1962), pp. 21–36.

Thomas, Keith, 'Witches', *Listener* 83 (12 March 1970), pp. 339–42.

―――― 'An Anthropology of Religion and Magic', *Journal of Interdisciplinary History* VI (Summer 1975), pp. 91–109.

Thompson, E. P., 'Anthropology and the Discipline of Historical Context', *Midland History* 1 (1972), pp. 41–55.

Thorndike, Lynn, 'Some Medieval Conceptions of Magic', *Monist* 25 (1915), pp. 107–39.

Tongue, R. L., 'Folk Song and Folklore', *Folklore* 78 (1967), pp. 293–303.

Trethowan, W. H., 'The Demonopathology of Impotence', *British Journal of Psychiatry* 109 (May 1963), pp. 341–7.

Truckell, A. E., 'Unpublished Witchcraft Trials', *Dumfriesshire and Galloway Natural History and Antiquarian Society Transactions* 51 (1975), pp. 45–58.

Wallace, D. D., 'George Gifford, Puritan Propaganda and Popular Religion in Elizabethan England', *Sixteenth Century Journal* 9 (1978), pp. 27–49.

Wax, Murray and Rosalie Wax, 'The Magical World View', *Journal for the Scientific Study of Religion* 1 (1962), pp. 179–88.

―――― 'The Notion of Magic', *Current Anthropology* 4 (1965), pp. 495–518.

Wilson, P. J., 'Status Ambiguity and Spirit Possession', *Man* 2 (1967), pp. 366–78.

―――― 'The Outcast and the Prisoner: Models for Witchcraft and Schizophrenia', *Man* 13 (1978), pp. 88–99.

Vries, Jan de, 'Magic and Religion', *History of Religions* 1 (1962), pp. 214–21.

Vukanovic, I. P., 'Obscene Objects in Balkan Religion and Magic', *Folklore* 92 (1981), 43–53.

Zguta, Russell, 'Witchcraft Trials in Seventeenth Century Russia', *American Historical Review* 82–5 (Dec. 1977), pp. 1187–1207.

Select Bibliography

Contributions to Collections

Anglo, Sydney, 'Reginald Scot's *Discoverie of Witchcraft*: Scepticism and Sadduceeism', in S. Anglo (ed.), *The Damned Art: Essays in the Literature of Witchcraft* pp. 106–39.

———— 'Evident Authority and Authoritative Evidence: The *Malleus Maleficarum*', in S. Anglo (ed.), *The Damned Art: Essays in the Literature of Witchcraft*, pp. 1–31.

Baxter, Christopher, 'Jean Bodin's *De la Demonomanie des Sorciers*: The Logic of Persecution' in S. Anglo (ed.), *The Damned Art: Essays in the Literature of Witchcraft* pp. 76–105.

———— 'Johann Weyer's *De Praestigiis Daemonum*: Unsystematic Psychopathology', in S. Anglo (ed.), *The Damned Art: Essays in the Literature of Witchcraft* pp. 53–75.

Brouette, E., 'The Sixteenth Century and Satanism' in C. Moeller (intr.), *Satan* pp. 310–40.

Brown, Peter, 'Sorcery, Demons and the Rise of Christianity from Late Antiquity into the Middle Ages' in M. Douglas (ed.), *Witchcraft Confessions and Accusations* pp. 17–46.

Burke, Peter, 'Witchcraft and Magic in Renaissance Italy: Gianfrancesco Pico and his *Strix*', in S. Anglo (ed.), *The Damned Art: Essays in the Literature of Witchcraft* pp. 32–52.

Chodorow, N., 'Family Structure and Feminine Personality', in M. Rosaldo and L. Lamphere (eds), *Women, Culture and Society* pp. 43–66.

Clark, Stuart, 'King James's *Daemonologie*: Witchcraft and Kingship' in S. Anglo (ed.), *The Damned Art: Essays in the Literature of Witchcraft* pp. 156–81.

Cohn, Norman, 'The Myth of Satan and his Human Servants', in Ch. 1 of M. Douglas (ed.), *Witchcraft Confessions and Accusations* pp. 3–16.

Currie, Elliott P., 'Crimes without Criminals: Witchcraft and its Control in Renaissance Europe', in E. A. Tiryakian (ed.), *On the Margin of the Visible* pp. 191–209.

Gregory, Anita, Introduction to T. K. Oesterreich, *Possession Demoniacal and Other Among Primitive Races in Antiquity, the Middle Ages and Modern Times* pp. v–xvi.

Harner, Michael J., 'The Role of Hallucinogenic Plants in European Witchcraft' Ch. 8 of Michael J. Harner (ed.), *Hallucinogens and Shamanism* pp. 124–50.

Herlihy, David, 'Life Expectancies for Women in Medieval Society' in R. T. Morewedge (ed.), *The Role of Women in the Middle Ages* pp. 1–22.

Hole, Christina, 'Some Instances of Image Magic in Great Britain', Ch. 5 of Venetia Newall (ed.), *The Witch Figure* pp. 80–94.

Kiev, Ari, 'The Study of Folk Psychiatry', in A. Kiev (ed.), *Magic, Faith and Healing: Studies in Primitive Psychiatry Today* pp. 3–35.

Larner, Christina, 'Crimen Exceptum? The Crime of Witchcraft in Europe', Ch. 2 in B. Lenman, G. Parker and V. Gatrell (eds), *Crime and the Law: The Social History of Crime in Western Europe since 1500* pp. 49–75.

Lhermite, Jean, 'Pseudo-Possession' in C. Moeller, *Satan* pp. 280–99.

Macfarlane, Alan D., 'A Tudor Anthropologist: George Gifford's

Select Bibliography

Discourse and Dialogue', in S. Anglo (ed.), *The Damned Art: Essays in the Literature of Witchcraft* pp. 140–55.

—— 'Witchcraft in Tudor and Stuart Essex', Ch. 4 of M. Douglas (ed.), *Witchcraft Confessions and Accusations* pp. 81–99.

McGowan, Margaret, 'Pierre de Lancre's *Tableau de l'Inconstance des Mauvais Anges et Demons*: The Sabbat Sensationalised' in S. Anglo (ed.), *The Damned Art: Essays in the Literature of Witchcraft* pp. 182–201.

Maquart, F. X., 'Exorcism and Diabolical Manifestation' in C. Moeller, *Satan* pp. 178–203.

Midelfort, H. C. Erik, 'Were There Really Witches?' in Robert M. Kingdom (ed.), *Transition and Revolution* pp. 189–205.

—— 'Witch Hunting and the Domino Theory', Ch. 7 of James Obelkevich (ed.), *Religion and the People 800–1700* pp. 277–88.

Muchembled, Robert, 'The Witches of Cambrèsis: The Acculturation of the Rural World in the Sixteenth Century', Ch. 6 of James Obelkevich (ed.), *Religion and the People 800–1700* pp. 221–76.

Nadel, S. F., 'Malinowski on Magic and Religion' in Raymond W. Firth (ed.), *Man and Culture* pp. 189–208.

Newall, Venetia, 'The Jew as a Witch Figure', Ch. 6 of Venetia Newall (ed.), *The Witch Figure* pp. 95–124.

Norman, H. J., 'Witch Ointments', Appendix to Montague Summers, *The Werewolf* pp. 291–2.

Ortner, Sherry B., 'Is Female to Male as Nature is to Culture?' in M. Z. Rosaldo and L. Lamphere (eds), *Women, Culture and Society* pp. 67–88.

Parrinder, Geoffrey, 'The Witch as Victim', Ch. 7 in Venetia Newall (ed.), *The Witch Figure* pp. 125–38.

Parsons, Anne, 'Expressive Symbolism in Witchcraft and Delusion: A Comparative Study', Ch. 17 of Robert A. Levine (ed.), *Culture and Personality* pp. 315–32.

Reville, Albert, 'History of the Devil' in St Elmo Nauman (ed.), *Exorcism Through the Ages* pp. 217–58.

Robbins, Rossell Hope, 'Exorcism', in St Elmo Nauman (ed.), *Exorcism Through the Ages* pp. 201–5.

Rosaldo, M. Z., 'Women, Culture and Society: A Theoretical Overview', in M. Z. Rosaldo and L. Lamphere (eds), *Women, Culture and Society* pp. 17–42.

Rosen, Barbara, 'Introduction' to B. Rosen (ed.), *Witchcraft* pp. 4–58.

Rubin, Gayle, 'Traffic in Women: Notes on the ''Political Economy'' of Sex', in Rayna R. Reiter (ed.), *Towards an Anthropology of Women* pp. 157–210.

Russell, Jeffrey Burton, 'Medieval Witchcraft and Medieval Heresy', in E. A. Tiryakian (ed.), *On the Margin of the Visible* pp. 179–89.

Thomas, Keith, 'The Relevance of Social Anthropology to the Historical Study of English Witchcraft', Ch. 3 of M. Douglas (ed.), *Witchcraft Confessions and Accusations* pp. 47–80.

Thurston, Herbert, 'The Church and Witchcraft', in C. Moeller, *Satan* pp. 300–9.

Tiryakian, E. A., 'Preliminary Considerations', Introduction to E. A. Tiryakian, *On the Margin of the Visible* pp. 1–15.

Webster, Paula, 'Matriarchy: A Vision of Power', in Rayna R. Reiter

(ed.), *Towards an Anthropology of Women* pp. 141–56.
Widdowson, John, 'The Witch as a Frightening and Threatening Figure',
Ch. 11 of Venetia Newall, *The Witch Figure* pp. 200–23.

Other

Baldwin, L. G., 'Witchcraft in East Lothian', Ph.D. thesis (work in progress), University of New England.
Hickey, Sally, 'An Alternative View of Witchcraft: Hallucinogens and the 16th and 17th Century English Witches', Litt.B. thesis (unpublished), University of New England.

Index